JOE SALSBERG

A Life of Commitment

This book follows the life and intellectual journey of Joseph Baruch Salsberg, a Polish-Jewish immigrant who became a major figure of the Ontario Left, a leading voice for human rights in the Ontario legislature, and an important journalist in the Jewish community. His life trajectory mirrored many of the most significant transformations in Canadian political and social life in the twentieth century.

Award-winning historian Gerald Tulchinsky traces Salsberg's personal and professional journey – from his entrance into Toronto's oppressive garment industry at age fourteen, which led to his becoming active in emerging trade unions, to his rise through the ranks of the Communist Party of Canada and the Workers' Unity League. Detailing Salsberg's time as an influential Toronto alderman and member of the Ontario legislature, the book also examines his dramatic break with communism and his embrace of a new career in journalism.

Tulchinsky employs historical sources not used before to explain how Salsberg's family life and surrounding religious and social milieu influenced his evolution as a Zionist, an important labour union leader, a member of the Communist Party of Canada, and a prominent member of Toronto's Jewish community.

GERALD TULCHINSKY is an emeritus professor in the Department of History at Queen's University. He is also the author of *Canada's Jews* and a winner of both the J.I. Segal Award and the Toronto Jewish Book Award.

Joe Salsberg

A Life of Commitment

GERALD TULCHINSKY

UNIVERSITY OF TORONTO PRESS
Toronto Buffalo London

ISBN 978-1-4426-4628-5 (cloth)
ISBN 978-1-4426-1432-1 (paper)

∞

Library and Archives Canada Cataloguing in Publication

Tulchinsky, Gerald, 1933–
Joe Salsberg : a life of commitment / Gerald Tulchinsky.

Includes bibliographical references and index.
ISBN 978-1-4426-4628-5 (bound).   ISBN 978-1-4426-1432-1 (pbk.)

1. Salsberg, J. B. (Joseph B.), ca. 1903–1998.   2. Communists – Ontario –
Biography.   3. Labor union members – Ontario – Biography.   4. Politicians –
Ontario – Biography.   5. Jews – Ontario – Toronto – Biography.
6. Toronto (Ont.) – Biography.   7. Ontario – Politics and government –
1943–1985.   8. Ontario – Social conditions – 20th century.   I. Title.

FC3075.1.S24T84 2013   971.3'04092   C2013-900267-7

University of Toronto Press acknowledges the financial assistance
to its publishing program of the Canada Council for the Arts and
the Ontario Arts Council.

Canada Council   Conseil des Arts
for the Arts   du Canada

ONTARIO ARTS COUNCIL
CONSEIL DES ARTS DE L'ONTARIO
50 YEARS OF ONTARIO GOVERNMENT SUPPORT OF THE ARTS
50 ANS DE SOUTIEN DU GOUVERNEMENT DE L'ONTARIO AUX ARTS

University of Toronto Press acknowledges the financial support of the Government of
Canada through the Canada Book Fund for its publishing activities.

This book has been published with the help of a grant from the Canadian Federation
for the Humanities and Social Sciences, through the Awards to Scholarly Publication Program, using funds provided by the Social Sciences and Humanities Research
Council of Canada.

In memory of
J.M.S. (Maurice) Careless,
distinguished historian of Canada,
and Ben Kayfetz,
dedicated Jewish public servant and historian

Contents

Illustrations follow page 76.

Preface: Spadina

Joe Salsberg, it was said, took anywhere from three to five hours to walk down both sides of Toronto's Spadina Avenue running north and south between College and Dundas Streets – probably with a detour through Kensington Market – a distance that usually could be covered at a normal pace in twenty-five or thirty minutes. And he would likely have taken just as long moving east and west to traverse College Street between McCaul and Grace Streets. But Salsberg did not just stroll along like others through the city's Jewish community. While in office as alderman of Ward 4, as member of the Ontario legislature for the riding of St Andrew, or as a leading labour organizer, Salsberg would inch his way down, stopping every few paces to greet *landsleit* (hometowners), family members, old friends, kibitzers, and comrades of the United Jewish People's Order or the Communist Party of Canada, conversing, or listening to petitions for information and help. He might ask: "How is your son doing at university?"; "How is business at your butcher shop [or fruit stand or delicatessen]?"; "How is the women's coat trade this year?" or dozens of other personal questions while fielding pleas for help in locating jobs, securing pensions, and navigating government bureaucracy. He loved Spadina, once proclaiming that while he supposed New York's Fifth Avenue, London's Piccadilly, and Paris's Champs-Élysées "have their place, none of them can compare with this broad, throbbing, full of life thoroughfare known as Spadina, the heart of my constituency."[1] He exuded empathy, told stories and jokes, and extended twinkly-eyed warmth and understanding to people in distress. He was instantly recognizable: a man of above-average height, with auburn hair and moustache, nattily dressed, presenting a jovial smile and open face, and an expansive manner, greeting in Yiddish – the language of the immigrant Jews who predominated in the area – and English the people of this bailiwick in the city's downtown core.

Often on a wintry day during the depression-ridden 1930s he would stand on a Spadina Avenue street corner in Toronto's "fashion district" addressing a noontime crowd of workers, manufacturers, and visiting retailers on the problems of capitalism. People still remember Salsberg, nicknamed 'J.B.' (in honour, it was said, of the legendary Cape Breton labour leader J.B. McLachlan) or, to his many Jewish friends, 'Yosele,' the Yiddish diminutive for Yosel, or (from the Hebrew) Yosef, his eyes aflame and arms spread wide as he held forth with unsurpassed eloquence as the passers- by stopped and listened. Salsberg was a *mensch* (a kind and decent human being), full of understanding. He was deeply respected for this quality and for his devotion to securing better lives for the workers, shopkeepers, women, and the many non-Jews inhabiting the quarter. And as he spoke to a growing crowd, he stretched out his arms while his voice extended into the spare noonday sunlight that filtered through the alleyways and streets between the clothing factories. He would be proclaiming: "There is a better way than this one, with its massive unemployment, seasonal work, low wages, oppressive bosses, and inhuman working conditions. Workers and their families shouldn't have to live in rat-infested rooms in dirty slums. Unemployed men shouldn't have to ride the rods on freight trains across the country looking for work while begging for bread along the way. Kids shouldn't have to go to school hungry or shoddily dressed. People should have adequate health care and decent housing and fair prospect of jobs. There is a better way."

In his walk down Spadina Joe would pass Ladovsky's dairy restaurant, several smoke shops and cigar stores, Sam the Hatter, The Labour Lyceum, Rotman's Men's Wear, Goldberg's and the Quality restaurants, Shopsy's and Switzer's delicatessens, Hyman's book store, and Goldman's and Naftuli's butcher shops. When, as Rosemary Donegan explains, "the seeds of Spadina's cultural traditions were sown, ... a time when life was more coherent," these were all informal communal nodes where in good weather groups of people foregathered, debated, clustered, dawdled, and quickly dispersed like sparrows briefly resting on a pine tree then flying off to another perch nearby.[2] News, wisecracks, and gossip were dispensed among housewives, neighbours, *landsmen*, union members, fellow workers, wise guys, and drifters. Joe greeted them all; he likely knew their names, their families, their shul (synagogue) affiliations, and their addresses. They accosted him with 'Yosele, vos hertzach?' (What's new?), 'Can you help me get a job, Joe?,' 'Why don't City ploughs come down my street, Joe?,' 'How come the scabs can get into the shops, Joe, and I get arrested for picketing?,' 'Speak up for us, Joe!,' 'Hey, Yosele, how's your family?,' 'Joe, how can I get my brother out of Poland to Canada?,' 'Listen, Joe, I have something to tell you – in confidence you understand,' 'Joe, let me shake your hand,' 'Yosele, Yosele.' Every few paces, Salsberg was stopped and buttonholed. Some, however much they admired or liked him personally, despised his communist politics and could well have heckled or hurled profane epithets at him.

He listened, laughed, joked, consoled, and explained while smiling, embracing, shaking hands along the street. He might even have taken time out for a brief stop at his parents' home just paces off the Avenue at 59 Cecil Street for hugs and a cup of tea. Then back to his beat, down past Dundas to Queen Street. Along the way he would stop and hold court at various eating places: the Homestead, Eppes Essen, Shapiro's, Goldenberg's, and, later, at Abella's Lunch to meet constituents who knew of his closeness to power and sought his help. Tales abounded about Salsberg. Is it true that people came out of their houses during his electioneering to actually touch him? Did he really carry bags of coal up flights of stairs to the homes of the impoverished, including a rabbi? Did his photograph hang in the homes of hundreds of Jewish constituents – even the religious ones, where he was positioned next to that of the revered, world-famous rabbi named the *Hafetz Chaim*? These and many other legends about his *menschlichkeit* (loving kindness) and popularity could well have been true and many people believed them. In October 2008, many hundreds of admirers, mostly elderly Toronto Jews who knew Yosele from the old days and for whom his memory was a blessing, packed a large hall to honour Salsberg's memory on the tenth anniversary of his death and traded stories of his good deeds. One of his contemporaries, Norman Penner, speculating on his electoral success in St Andrew perhaps put it best: "For [the *Jewish* voters of St Andrew] he wasn't a Communist, he was J.B. Salsberg."[3]

Going down Spadina Salsberg would often stride further south to Richmond Street, past the multi-storied Balfour, Fashion, and Darling buildings and numerous lesser structures all the way down to Welling-ton and King streets, where clothing factories and showrooms of manu-facturers, wholesalers, jobbers, and contractors abounded. Here, and along back streets, more marginal shops proliferated in the Toronto needle industry whose fragility, especially in the dress trade (referred to jocularly as the *shmatta* [rag] business), was legendary: factories that were no more than basement, back alley, or attic work spaces of penny-capitalist contractors and subcontractors performing piece work for large manufacturers. Many such firms existed precariously for only a year or two; then they disappeared, driven out of business by bad luck, unwise style choices, credit crunches, labour disputes, predatory chain stores, or poor management, their owners often forced back to work on the shop floor, where some stayed while plucky ones tried again. Re-emerging entrepreneurially, perhaps partnered up with others willing to risk their all in this "trade for nervous men," these jumped-up former tailors, cutters, and salesmen were bellwethers of an industry in flux. Salsberg was well acquainted with its secrets, its tropes, and its rhythms; from boyhood he had worked here and knew many of its actors. He could empathize with both bosses and workers. And as he proceeded down the street over the years he became the heart of Spadina, its rebbe (revered rabbi and teacher), some would even say its godfather.

Salsberg's message resonated with many listeners. By 1933, Canada was in the midst of the worst depression in living memory. Hundreds of thousands of Canadians lived marginally on relief; men ate at soup kitchens, slept in crowded hostels, and hitched rides on freight trains. People despaired and grew bitter as their lives were put on hold. Marriages were postponed, education interrupted, homes sold off, savings depleted, crops failed and farms were abandoned. Dignity blew away like topsoil off a Saskatchewan wheat field. Many Canadians stared poverty and humiliation in the face, and that ugliness was reflected in their attitudes to others, such as the immigrants who had come after them.

Generally poor, unskilled, and speaking imperfect English, Jews and other non-Anglo-Saxons in the Toronto of those times were located on the margins of mainstream society. Discrimination against them was manifested in many ways. They worked, when work was available, usually in the dirtiest and lowest of jobs, in abattoirs, tunnels, sweatshops, and in heavy construction. Many of them lived in inner-city slums in shack-like housing adjacent to railway yards, giant factories, and busy streets. By the 1930s many of them lived on the streets east and west of Spadina between Dundas and Bloor, where they shopped, ate, and congregated for religious, social, and political activities.

Beyond Canada – where for Jews and others a general atmosphere of peace, freedom, and opportunity (though severely curtailed by the Depression) prevailed – the outlook in the 1930s was bleak. Fascism was growing menacingly throughout Europe and by March 1933 the violently anti-Semitic Nazis ruled Germany. In Palestine, the Jewish settlement, the Yishuv, faced mounting opposition from Arab nationalists.

To Salsberg, who had joined the Communist Party of Canada in 1926, the solution to the "Jewish problem" – as he explained in interviews he gave in the 1970s – lay in the benefits promised by the advancement of socialism through world revolution. In the Soviet Union Jews, he claimed, were an integral part of the new national fabric, equal in every respect to other nationalities and free to participate in all social, cultural, and political endeavours. Jewish culture flourished and there was even a new Jewish republic in Birobidjan. But Joe knew that no solution was possible, for Jews or others, without the improvement, revolutionary if necessary, of the general material conditions of life for all, all of human-ity, all of the people. Everywhere! It was a dream, an illusion perhaps, which Salsberg shared with so many others on the radical Left. Though a loyal communist, Salsberg never seemed to take more than passing interest in Marxist ideological disputation or shifts in Moscow's policy, except insofar as they affected what he regarded as nuts-and-bolts issues of labour mobilization or human welfare legislation.

People reached out to Salsberg. They knew he would try to help. He would hear them out – Jew and non-Jew alike – at length, offering the guidance they needed. He was one of them, born like many of his listen-ers in a Polish *shtetl* (small town), an immigrant boy who grew up on a nearby street, whose father struggled for a living as a junk peddler, who belonged to the Lagover Society, one of the city's many *landsmanshaftn* (hometown associations), and who, as a child, had attended the local schools and played in the local parks and streets. Since age fourteen Joe was a worker, a cutter in a cap and hat factory, and a union organizer in the city's tumultuous needle industries. He was like *mishpocha* (family) and people admired him for his attitude towards them, and his com-mitment to making the world and their environment better. Because of these qualities and an "easy, joking manner," people were drawn to him "like flies to honey."[4]

Salsberg was one of the most important communist labour figures of his generation. His work in the trade unions, in the Workers' Unity League, and as one of the Communist Party's leading labour activists was legendary. And his work in the Ontario legislature as MPP for St Andrew, advancing progressive labour and human rights legislation, was nothing short of monumental, earning him enormous respect. He led a life of total commitment to the advancement of the welfare of working people. And with his later journalistic and organizational activities, he was a major advocate for the rethinking and retrenchment of values and priorities in the Ontario Jewish community.

Being Jewish did not impede his work in party affairs or in the Ontario legislature. In his private life he rejoiced with his extended family on Jewish festivals, especially on Hanukah, when he and his wife, Dora Wilensky, would host an annual family *latke* (potato pancake) party, where they distributed gifts and fussed over their many devoted nieces and nephews. It was as if the Communist Party was his synagogue, and his comrades the quorum for prayer. Far from suppressing this Jewish identity, Salsberg actually emphasized it as an important element in his union organizing, which started in the needle trades, then dominated by Jewish workers and union officials. As well, he participated in activities of the United Jewish People's Order, a left-leaning cultural and social organization. He spoke their language, Yiddish, with eloquence and passion and he shared their yearnings for a better life than previously endured in Poland, Romania, Ukraine, or Galicia. He always emphasized that he was one of them. They knew that he was, and they loved him.

Joe Salsberg could not have been anything else, for he came from Toronto's *Yiddishn gass* (Jewish street) and reflected its idioms, tempo, and values. He grew up in the Toronto Jewish immigrant community. Like many youth of his generation, Salsberg was imbued with the Zionist dream of a Jewish homeland in Palestine and for several years served as a key figure in the youth wing of the Labour Zionist movement. But by his mid-twenties he had embraced the emancipation of all mankind and joined the Communist Party of Canada. This set him on a thirty-year career of labour and political activities that ended when, in growing disgust over the refusal of party leaders in the Soviet Union to acknowledge the existence of anti-Semitism there, he quit in early 1957. From then until his death in February 1998, Salsberg immersed himself in the Toronto Jewish community as a journalist, Yiddishist, and 'rebbe' to his many friends and admirers.

I never met Joe Salsberg, though as a student at the University of Toronto in the early 1950s I had friends who would rush over to Queen's Park to hear him speak when the legislature was in session, so famous was he for his social passion, his eloquence, and his humour. As a student of Canadian Jewish history I am interested in examining Salsberg's career in the social and economic context in which he lived and, like so many others, pursued aspirations for that 'better world in birth' as an expression of his Jewish identity. When this biography was suggested to me I could not resist the opportunity to try to understand and explain the public career of this most important, interesting, and appealing Toronto

Jew. My research revealed to me the story of an immigrant's commitment to ideals and his espousal of communism as a vehicle for social and
economic reform in Canada and the emancipation of the Jewish people.
I hope that this book will illuminate the most important features of Joe
Salsberg's public career and contribute to an understanding of the social
and political world in which he spent his life. It is a Canadian story of immigration, idealism, labour, politics, and the Toronto Jewish communal
experience in the transformative decades of the twentieth century.

November 2012
Gerald Tulchinsky

Acknowledgments

This book would not have been possible without the foresight and dedication of Professor Adam Fuerstenberg, who diligently gathered and preserved Joe Salsberg's records, and of Sharyn Salsberg Ezrin, who offered this collection to the Queen's University Archives. My research was generously supported by the Social Sciences and Humanities Research Council of Canada, the Office of Research Services and Department of History of Queen's University, and the Toronto Jewish Foundation. I acknowledge, with special thanks, the permission of the family of the late Paul Kligman, the assistance of Lillian Petroff of the Multicultural History Society of Ontario, Rosemary Donegan, and Rick Stow to consult taped interviews with Joe. Irving Abella allowed me to quote from his eulogy at Joe's funeral.

Research assistance was provided by Rebecca Efrat, Robbyn Gulka, Carley Dunster, Kate Shaughnessy, Todd McCallum, Gordon Dueck, Eiron Harris, Melissa White, Lara Campbell, Jessie Stephenson, Matt Towery, and Rebecca Stelter. Myron Momryk, now retired from Library and Archives Canada, has been a pillar of research strength for me at LAC over many years; he has kindly answered my many requests for information with speed and enthusiasm. Translations from Yiddish sources were done by Larry Gamulka and Ala Gamulka, and from Polish by Ewa Dutkewicz.

Jack Granatstein served frequently as a generous source of information, warm encouragement, and critical comment. (Who could ignore his frequent admonitions: "I hope that you are writing!!" and "Press on!!") William Kaplan supplied help on Salsberg's role in the Canadian Seaman's Union and Esther Reiter gave me the benefit of her insights on the United Jewish People's Order and the broad theme of secular

Judaism. Larry Black supplied some otherwise unobtainable material and the late Dr Stephen Speisman, former director of the Ontario Jewish Archives and distinguished historian of the Toronto Jewish community, gave me much encouragement, as have his successors, Dr Ellen Schein- berg and Donna Bernardo-Ceriz, and their staff, especially George Wharton, who often went well out of his way to be of help. Ira Robinson kindly allowed me access to the manuscript of his book "A Kabbalist in Montreal: The Life and Times of Rabbi Yudel Rosenberg," and Dr Jack Lipinsky permitted me to consult the manuscript of his book on the To- ronto Jewish Community between the world wars, "Imposing Our Will." The late Ruth Borchiver generously supplied copies of her notes on early Toronto Jewish radicals, and Stephen Endicott sent me the manuscript of his most helpful recent book on the Workers' Unity League, *Rais- ing the Workers' Flag*. Ron Biderman and Erick Wredenhagen provided very helpful legal advice. Readers for the University of Toronto Press and the Aid to Scholarly Publications Program supplied very helpful ideas which enlarged my thinking on the context in which Salsberg worked. I drew heavily on information from interviews kindly given by Morris Biderman, Ron Biderman, Hesh Troper, Thelma Pritzker, Ben Shek, and Nat Salsberg. My friends and colleagues Hilary and Peter Neary, Ian McKay, Bryan Palmer, Ron Biderman, Jim Pritchard, Peter Campbell, Ted (my brother) Tulchinsky, and Jack Granatstein made many helpful comments on earlier drafts of this book.

I warmly thank also the helpful staffs at Queen's University Archives, Library and Archives Canada, the Canadian Jewish Congress Charities Committee Archives, the Public Archives of Ontario, the University of Toronto Archives, the Thomas Fisher Rare Book Room, York Univer- sity Archives, the Jewish Public Library of Montreal, the City of Toronto Archives, the Ontario Jewish Archives, and Sylvia Szymanska at the Pol- ish State Archives (Warsaw). Dasha Laforeva did productive work at the State Archives (Moscow). I acknowledge with thanks permission from the Canadian Committee on Labour History to republish here my article in *Labour/le Travail* 2005 as chapter 4. Len Husband, Frances Mundy, and John St James at the University of Toronto Press have been strongly supportive throughout. Harvey Spiegel supplied the photograph of early Lagow and Barry Kaplan expertly sharpened the image.

Ian McKay and Bryan Palmer have helped me enormously through- out to understand the world of Joe Salsberg and other Toronto Jew- ish communists, as well as the wider ideological and political context in which they lived. We conferred frequently. I consider Ian and Bryan as my rebbes, my teachers, in this field, and I hope that they and other students of the radical Left in our national story will find something of value in this presentation of Salsberg's life and times. Because this work is very much a Toronto story, it was in part inspired by two devotees of that city's past, Ben Kayfetz, one of Ontario Jewry's earliest historians and a dedicated public servant of the Canadian Jewish Congress, and J.M.S. (Maurice) Careless, a distinguished long-time professor in the Department of History at the University of Toronto and eminent historian of Canada. It is to their memory that I dedicate this book.

Finally, I warmly thank the dedicated and compassionate doctors and nurses at the Kingston Regional Cancer Centre and the Kingston General Hospital for their superb care. My numerous friends have been of great help, among them Mel Wiebe, who authors many hilarious bons mots. My loving family has provided me with endless blessings.

November 2012

JOE SALSBERG

A Life of Commitment

Chapter One

From Lagow to Toronto

When Sarah-Gitel Salsberg, her son, Yosef Baruch, and baby daughters, Pearl and Lillian, reached Toronto's old Union Station on a summer's day in 1913 to join Abraham, husband and father, in their new Canadian home, they were at the end of a long and harrowing journey.[1]

Their old home in Lagow, a shtetl in the Opatow district of Radom Gubernia, then part of Congress Poland ruled by Russia, lay thousands of miles behind them. Lagow's Jews numbered about 1200, roughly half the town's population, and lived by buying and selling at local markets and fairs, and from crafts and trades, like tailoring, shoemaking, carpentry, masonry, tin- and blacksmithing, and the like. It was generally a meagre living in an impoverished area, where the majority of the Polish population were small farmers eking out a poor existence on tiny properties. With the rapid rise of population and a lack of capital in the countryside, much of rural Poland was in crisis. Contemporary studies showed that unemployment and poverty levels were high, and education levels low, problems that were only partially alleviated by emigration to North and South America and Western Europe. While generally no better off than the local peasantry, nevertheless, the town's Jews possessed the rudiments of traditional communal life, including a cemetery, *mikveh* (ritual bath), and a new synagogue built in the early 1900s, when Rabbi Tsvi Dov Rosen was appointed by the government as the community's Crown rabbi.[2]

Poor though it was, Lagow lived on in memory. In one of his columns for the *Canadian Jewish News*, Salsberg, then eighty years old, waxed nostalgic about the old home town, noting that it was in his day "still steeped in superstitions," such as belief in the existence of *sheydim* (imps) that would emerge from the attics at night to create mischief in the town.

Potions were mixed and administered while rabbis were consulted to ward off the little invaders.[3] There was also a widespread belief that "sharply at midnight the dead arose from their graves ... [to] find their way (covered in white shrouds, of course) to the synagogue for prayers." But the town was also influenced by far-reaching cultural transformations from the outside world emanating from the Jewish enlightenment. This *Haskalah* movement stressed an emerging modernism, a rational approach to religion, the popularization of the new Yiddish and Hebrew literature, an emphasis on the critical teaching of the Prophets rather than just traditional texts like Talmud, and an openness to other cultures. The nearby town of Opatow had been a local centre of the *Haskalah* since the late eighteenth century and, through traders and other contacts, its influence on the region was strong. Some of Lagow's Jews, Salsberg remembered, spoke Polish and French, while others subscribed to the St Petersburg Yiddish daily *Der Fraynd*.[4]

Many changes were then under way throughout the western reaches of the vast Russian empire, and Yosele must have heard of the pogroms, the failed revolution of 1905, the Russo-Japanese War, the establishment of the Duma and its troubled evolution, and the rise of the Polish National Democratic Party with its virulently anti-Semitic overtones. He was certainly aware of dangerous anti-Semitism right in Lagow. "There were certain places you just didn't go," he recalled, "because they didn't want you. Or it'll be bad." The effects of ongoing economic changes also filtered into town, as rising industrialization, improved transportation and communications, and modern commerce were undermining the traditional Jewish economy that relied on crafts, small-scale shops, and peddling. Heated discussion in the marketplace, synagogues, and homes on these developments centred on the question "Is this good or bad for the Jews?" and its corollary "What is to be done?" Anarchism, Marxism, and Zionism among other ideologies presented possible answers for many who were unsettled by these uncertainties. Many Jews thought of emigration to America. Continuing bloody pogroms and allegations of Jewish ritual murder, such as the 1911 case in Kiev of Mendel Beilis, who was accused of this crime, reminded most Jews that their future in Eastern Europe was uncertain.

Meanwhile, intimations of deliverance, escape, and renewal were in the air. Zionism in various ideological shadings advocated national Jewish revival in the ancient homeland. Those with Marxist and collectivist ideals in the powerful *Poalei Zion* movement stressed "going up to the land [of Israel]" "to build and to be rebuilt upon it." In opposition to

Zionism stood the even more influential Bund (Polish Jewish Workers Bund, or General Jewish Workers' Alliance), which, since its formation in 1897, promised relief through Jewish political action in concert with socialist parties and Jewish cultural autonomism.[5] Jews were also active in revolutionary movements, while a tiny number even joined terrorist groups.

But for all these and other advances – railways, yeshivas, and emigration connecting the shtetl to the outside world (Salsberg remembered the town's two ice cream parlours!) – Lagow was far from the vibrant urban culture of major industrial and commercial centres like Lodz and Warsaw. Nevertheless, it was more than just a rural backwater, belying its outward appearance shown in a photograph of the period portraying simple country houses scattered around lanes leading towards the church located on a rise near the town centre.

Thursday was market day, when the "Jewish tailors, carpenters, and shoemakers from out of town would come in on wagons loaded with their merchandise and set up stalls."[6] Huge flocks of geese were driven from Lagow's market for miles down country roads to the nearest railway line and shipped off to Germany; in town horses were traded while bake shops and dry goods stores thrived on the business of country folk who came in for those special days. Interestingly, Salsberg's memoir includes little mention of the Poles with whom Lagow's Jews were in frequent contact in business transactions, except that "there was a reasonably good relationship" in Lagow but not elsewhere, probably reflecting the general atmosphere of tension and conflict between Jews and Poles, especially within the rising middle class. The Holocaust swept all of this away. In June 1942, occupying German forces herded Lagow's Jews, including the Klein-Salsberg extended family, into a ghetto, and in October marched them to Kielce, where they were forced onto trains which took them to the gas chambers at Treblinka.[7]

Introduced to each other by a traditional matchmaker, Sarah-Gitel, the daughter of Shimon and Miriam Klein, at age sixteen had wed Abraham Salsberg, a baker from the nearby town of Rakow, in 1899. This being an unusually young age for female marriage in the czarist empire, when some 65 per cent of all Jewish women at marriage were over twenty-one years of age, it would seem that Lagow and Sarah-Gitel were as yet uninfluenced by the modern ideas of romantic and companionate marriages.[8] Yosef Baruch, their first child, was born in 1902 and named after his mother's grandfather. Sarah-Gitel came from a prosperous family of horse dealers, while Abraham's family for generations were bakers, and were less well off and of a lower social status than their in-laws. Abraham, who had been born in Rakow, had in all likelihood received his elementary studies in a local *heder*, a school that provided a basic Jewish education with an emphasis on Hebrew prayers, the first five books of the Bible, and, at about age ten, study of Mishna and Talmud. He was the eldest in a family of seven sons and one daughter. After his marriage he tried to work at his trade in Lagow, but was unsuccessful. Using his wife's dowry, he then set himself up in the grain business; it eventually failed, and he was at loose ends.

The new world beckoned and, in 1910, intending to work for a year or two and save enough to make a new start back home in Lagow, he took ship for Canada, perhaps responding to encouraging news from neighbours or relatives who had previously moved there. Typical of many emigrants, Abraham arrived alone in Toronto, then partnered up with a few friends and rented a house on Centre Street in the Ward, a poor centrally located slum composed mainly of Italians, Jews, and Blacks.[9] He scrounged around for work, even the most menial. But after two years he returned to Lagow, uncertain that he could establish a Jewish future in an environment which he regarded as godless and profane.

Abraham, affectionately known to some by the Yiddish diminutive *Avromeleh* (little Abraham), like many Jews in this region of Poland had been deeply influenced by Hasidism, a revolutionary mystical movement that had swept through Eastern Europe in the eighteenth century and became, in the words of Antony Polonsky, "a major force" in Jewish life; it drew many thousands of adherents to its message of strict religious services, ethics, prayer, and meditation along with joy and messianic hope in the midst of poverty and persecution.[10] Thus, when he returned to Canada on a visit almost two years later, he was still ambivalent about uprooting his family and moving them to a place where adhering to traditional observances might be difficult; but he suppressed his doubts and stayed on. Working at odd jobs – even carrying bricks on building sites – he decided to remain and save enough money to send *shifskarten* (steamship tickets) to bring his family over, using the services of Sandle Pyman, one of several Toronto Jewish *shifskantorn* (steamship ticket agencies).[11] Meanwhile, he had joined the *Tomchai Shabbos* (observers of Sabbath), a small and short-lived congregation on Chestnut Street formed in 1907 of some one hundred strictly religious families.[12] When this community later dissolved, Abraham probably joined one of the other Toronto Polish *shuls* (synagogues), possibly the Kielcer at the corner of Huron and Dundas Streets, then headed by the venerable Hasidic *ilui* (enlightened one)Yehuda Leib Rosenberg.[13] Abraham would have met Rabbi Joseph Weinreb, known as the "Galitzianer" rabbi, one of the earliest Toronto teachers of Talmud and other holy texts.

Meanwhile, Abraham corresponded regularly with his wife, who was still in Lagow, urging her to join him in Toronto, fully realizing that she would find it extremely difficult to leave her loving family and the familiar townscapes. "There's no future in Poland for a Jew," he pleaded, asking her to visit the "court" of a renowned Hasidic rabbi in Opatow for advice on the matter.[14] Deeply attached to her parents and extended family, and uncertain of the future for her children, while especially anxious not to interrupt Yosele's rapidly advancing studies in Mishna and Talmud – whose humanistic principles she had him put into practice by collecting money around the town on Fridays to buy food for the poor – she accepted Abraham's advice and journeyed with Yosele to consult the rabbi. She was ushered into a room crowded with people waiting anxiously to seek the great rabbi's wisdom – and waited. "We were called in," Salsberg recalled, "and I remember the face of the rabbi, very impressive, old, spiritual man, and she told him [the situation]. And he looked at me and he said if your husband ... says you should go, then you should go. And she says, but he [Yosele] is a good boy, he studies well, what will happen to him in [Canada]? And the rabbi called me over, he beckoned and I walked over in trepidation and he pinched my cheek like this and he said [to her], 'You can go with him, he will be all right, don't worry.' And that settled the question ... And the preparations started."

Sarah-Gitel's father, Shimon, however, was in deep agony over his beloved daughter's impending move to Toronto, a place on the other side of the world from which she and her children would likely never return and which he would probably never visit. The day of departure in mid-summer 1913 approached and at the final Friday evening meal to usher in the Sabbath, with the entire family in attendance at the Klein festive table, Shimon started to recite the blessing, the *Kiddush*, over the wine ... but collapsed in tears halfway through, sending everybody there off into floods of grief, crying long into the night. Amidst such sadness the departure took place after the end of Sabbath the next night, according to tradition only after three stars could be clearly discerned in the darkened sky. A large wagon drawn by two horses was loaded up with the little band of Sarah-Gitel, Yosele, and the baby daughters. Their luggage included kosher food for the trip: herring, *vorshtn* (dried sausages), onions, garlic, dried fruit, and many varieties of baked cookies.[15] More tears were shed as the horses pulled away. "I remember the scene very,

very vividly," Salsberg recalled. "It was almost like a funeral with half the town escorting us out, with tears and wailing, and crying, and promises on both sides that we will still see each other." Salsberg described the scene: "Day began to break, the sky turned blue ... and my grandfather walking beside the wagon, literally like a bereaved person, crying, crying, crying, following the wagon." Shimon, at one point could go no further and turned back, wailing all the way home. The emigrants nevertheless continued – but soon were called back: Shimon Klein was reported to be "severely ill" and desperately needed his daughter's immediate attendance.[16]

Determined to carry through with her commitment to join her husband, Sarah-Gitel and her three children set out again for Toronto two months later, this time for good, with railway and steamship tickets sent by Abraham safely in her portmanteau. They were to travel from the German border by rail to England via Channel ports and on to Quebec City by Cunard liner from Liverpool – in tourist, not steerage, class! (Abraham, who had probably put himself deeply in hock to friends, Toronto's new Hebrew Free Loan society, or his steamship agent, wanted his family to travel in comfort.) But because Sarah-Gitel had delayed her departure by the few weeks needed to console her father, their ship had already sailed and their tickets were effectively invalid; consequently, no Cunard representative was on hand at the German border to shepherd them forward.

Sarah-Gitel was flummoxed, and the children were frightened, while confusion prevailed. Taking advice from total strangers, they unwisely boarded a train to Vienna! Here they were met by a Cunard representative, who told them that since their ship had already sailed, they would need new bookings, and would have to pay extra, much more money than Sarah-Gitel had with her. What to do? She wired Abraham for more funds, which arrived quickly. She and the children then boarded a train to Antwerp and from there proceeded by boat and train to Liverpool. Here they learned that they would have to wait a week for their ship to sail – unless they were willing to leave that very afternoon on another liner going to Quebec. She took that option and the little band of emigrants boarded ship and set out at last for Canada. Though Sarah-Gitel was seasick the whole way over, Yosele enjoyed the shipboard experience, which lasted ten days to two weeks, no doubt making friends with fellow passengers. They landed at Quebec – it was July 1913 – hoping to get to Toronto within hours.

That was not to be so easy. A frenzied search for lost luggage delayed their departure on the train for which they had tickets and, in utter confusion, they boarded another train, for which their tickets were invalid. Despite Sarah-Gitel's pleas, in Yiddish or Polish, a hard-hearted conductor stopped the train and put her and the children off at a railside shed just outside Quebec. Here the Salsbergs sat desolate by Canada's great St Lawrence River, Sarah-Gitel in distress and the baby girls no doubt confused and cranky. Yosele remembered that it was a beautiful day, a Sabbath in fact, and he enjoyed watching the ships plying the river as he and his family awaited a train that would take them back to Quebec, where they would have to await the right connection to Montreal and Toronto.

"So we returned to Quebec City in the middle of the night," Salsberg recalled. There would be no train until morning so they were allowed to bed down in the station master's office – a generous concession under the circumstances – and were just nodding off when a loud knock on the door interrupted them "and a voice in Yiddish came back, it was like the voice of an angel, a woman" offering to take them to her home. She did so, and the next day they boarded the right train, reached Montreal, where a representative of a local Jewish immigrant aid group, the Baron de Hirsch Society, met them and took them to Bonaventure station and put them aboard an overnight train to Toronto.

But when they arrived at the old Union Station the next morning, expecting Abraham to greet them, he was not there! He had been informed that they would arrive the previous day and had waited for hours and hours, despairing by the minute. With no one to meet her, probably not surprised given all the confusion she had just experienced, Sarah-Gitel simply hailed a horse cab, showed the driver Abraham's address, got herself, the children, and their baggage conveyed to 73 Cecil Street, knocked on the door, and was greeted by her husband, who was probably praying for his "lost" family, now found and embraced in his loving arms.

The four new additions to the Salsberg household constituted just one tiny segment of the estimated 11,624 Jews who arrived in Canada that year (1912–13).[17] The Toronto Jewish community was in the midst of remarkable expansion in a booming city that, in the words of Maurice Careless, "neared the rank of a national metropolis ... second only to Montreal in national scope and influence." The city's Jewish population grew by nearly 600 per cent between 1900 and 1911 to 18,300 persons and about doubled again in the next decade; by 1921 Jews constituted 8.6 per cent of the city's population, up from 1.4 per cent a decade earlier.[18] Most of this growth is attributable to immigration from the western reaches of the Russian empire known as the Pale of Settlement (to which Jews were largely confined), Poland, and the Austro-Hungarian provinces of Galicia and Bukovina. Like the Salsbergs, these Jews brought their multi-faceted Yiddish culture and an enthusiasm – indeed passion – for creating a new life for themselves and their children in what before long they regarded as a land of peace, freedom, and opportunity – though one, nevertheless, beset by anti-Semitism.

And while the community grew, it began to fill up and overflow the area of first settlement in Toronto's "Ward," the down-at-the-heels quarter located east of University Avenue, north of city hall, into newer areas west along Dundas and adjoining streets and north along Beverly and Spadina towards College Street, in the heart of what is now Chinatown.[19] This area was roughly within the municipal boundaries of Ward 4, the provincial riding of St Andrew and the federal constituency of Spadina. Jewish geographical transformation in this quarter was marked also by distinct new cultural landmarks, including synagogues (like the Ostrovster, Kiever, and Hebrew Men of England) housed in former churches, or in new structures occupied by comparatively well-to-do congregations like Holy Blossom in a toney uptown location, Goel Tzedec on University Avenue, and the Beth Hamedresh Hagadol on McCaul Street. Some of the smaller congregations, usually composed of immigrants from the same town or district in Poland, met in converted houses, empty stores, or rented rooms. This transforming Jewish quarter teemed with activity. Kosher butchers abounded, restaurants and delicatessens flourished, storefront synagogues sprang up, while other establishments catered to their clienteles.[20]

The vast majority of Jewish immigrants, many of them newly proletarianized as workers in the clothing shops, lived in circumstances as modest as the Salsbergs'. Or worse. Allan Grossman, later an Ontario government cabinet minister, who grew up in the Jewish quarter, remembered a home "where the struggle for existence engaged our attention so much that we missed a great deal."[21] Others were raised amidst serious social problems – some of them resulting in brushes with criminality and unemployment. Toronto's booming economy, amidst escalating national economic expansion in these years, held out few dividends to most of its working class, especially those employed in manufacturing. Michael Piva pointed out that while capital investment in this sector grew over fourfold between 1900 and 1914, real annual earnings during the same period in the needle trades, the largest employer and the industry to which thousands of Jewish workers gravitated, actually fell by about 15 per cent, and further still during the First World War.[22] So low had those incomes dropped that only if two persons per family had full-time jobs, or if they took in boarders, could families get above poverty levels and afford the bare minimum expenses for food, fuel, lighting, and rent (but not clothing, furniture, or entertainment).

The number of women in the Toronto workforce in the 1910s increased five times more rapidly than males, and this trend was especially pronounced in the clothing factories, many of them contractors' sweat-shops – despite royal commission revelations and factory inspections – featuring abominable working conditions, a "virtual second serfdom," in Ian McKay's words.[23] Of nearly 14,000 clothing workers in the city, 58.6 per cent were women, most in low-paid unskilled jobs at wages half, or less than half, of those paid to adult men. The rising trade unions tried, with very limited success, to alleviate some of the worst abuses, but the uncertainties of the industry – the rapid rise and fall of firms, layoffs due to seasonality of production, predatory purchasing by the major retailers, and market volatility – created precarious conditions unequalled in other industrial sectors. Unemployment wreaked havoc and misery widely among the working class, particularly the city's immigrants, as Piva has pointed out; many thousands were out of work in the winter of 1914 for about fifteen weeks, putting severe strains on relief agencies, including those serving the Jewish community.

Eking out a living in this economic environment, the Salsberg family lived at 73 Cecil Street, a small house Abraham bought for a $300 down payment in one of the newer areas of Jewish settlement. Later they moved down the street to a more commodious home at 59 Cecil. But the economic challenge was ever present. Many Jews were associated with self-help organizations like the Lagover Society, one of the numerous *landsmanshaftn* (hometown associations) that served social and welfare needs of the immigrants living down in the ever-transforming Jewish quarter of the city; meanwhile, Sarah-Gitel busied herself with charitable works such as the *Malbush Arumim* (clothing the poor) society that she founded to provide new garments for the community's poor children.[24] All the while, the humble and devout Abraham – he attended synagogue daily – strained to make a living; first he plied his trade as a baker, but refused to work on the Sabbath, and took up what was euphemistically called "junk peddling," later developing other business interests.[25] The struggle to make a living and raise numerous children precluded the possibility of a return visit to family in Lagow. Neither Abraham nor

Sarah-Gitel saw their parents again. Letters and photographs had to sub-
stitute for hugs, kisses, and endless talk. But the yearning to be with them
again would never cease.

Having begun life in Toronto as a casual labourer, moving briefly back
to his former trade, then to penny-capitalist entrepreneurship as a junk
peddler, Abraham exemplified what Daniel Soyer terms "the ambiguity
of class among East European Jewish immigrants."[26] A form of business
though it was, junk peddling was not for the timid or physically weak.[27]
The business necessitated much lifting of heavy materials onto and off
wagons and trucks as well as rough exchange with suppliers, weigh-scale
attendants, and customers. A junkman like Abraham would typically
begin his day with a predawn trip to his barn or stable, which could be
some distance away, to attend to his horse. Feeding, watering, and har-
nessing the animal to his wagon might take up to an hour. Abraham
would then proceed atop his wagon out onto the streets of Toronto, as it
was awakening to the day's traffic and noise, to look for his wares. Boxes
of bottles were his special targets as were old clothes, tin cans, bundles
of paper or books, and broken things made of metal no longer of use to
householders or businesses, who left this detritus by the curb or tossed
it into back alleyways, where they knew the junkman would come –
perhaps on certain days – to haul them away.[28]

Atop his perch, perhaps with Yosele sitting wide-eyed by his side, Abraham would cry out with loud shouts or noise from a handbell he carried in the wagon: "Hallo, boddles, rags, iron. Hallo, boddles, rags, iron.
Hallo." Slowly up the streets and down the alleyways the wagon, horse,
and two-person crew proceeded, Abraham perhaps reflecting aloud to
his son on a passage from the Bible, Mishna, or Talmud, perhaps asking Yosele to report on his studies with Rabbi Weinreb, who was Yosele's
teacher of Talmud.[29] Often Abraham would jump down to load up the
cast-offs, sometimes even paying a small price for certain especially interesting items, while the little boy would peruse any books that might have
been collected.

These junkmen did not get a good press. Toronto writer Margaret Bell
in 1913 described "a much bewhiskered father [who] comes in from
his rounds in the lanes and alleyways," surveying a yard which is "the
receptacle for the thousands of bottles … gathered on the streets, every
day. Beer bottles, whisky bottles, medicine bottles of all descriptions have
hurtled out of the itinerant collector's sack. The much-whiskered man
smiles grimly as he fingers each one. In one barrel, he puts the beer bottles, in another the whisky bottles, and so on." Another observer wrote of

"the 'sheeny' you see frequenting the lanes, and uttering raucous cries of rags, bones, and bottles. Any rags today, lady? ... They continue to toil many hours after the union Canadian workman has gone home for the night ... At this work he can make probably a dollar a day from the start." The "respectable" Jews were also embarrassed, and worried that the sight of these junkmen would lessen their precarious status. The *Canadian Jewish Times*, a Montreal publication, nervously urged the Toronto Jewish elite to try to stop this occupation, which it described as "unfortunate" and "a real nuisance bringing the Toronto Jewish name into bad repute."[30]

Meanwhile, the horse, to which a name had undoubtedly been attached, had to be fed its ration of oats and chaff, which was carried already prepared in nosebags, and watered from the municipally supplied troughs situated along the city streets. Lunch or snacks would be eaten en route or at a shaded stopover in a city park. Finally, the day ended, Abraham would head back to his barn, probably for several more hours of work, first unharnessing the horse, feeding and grooming her, then spreading fresh hay in the stall. Then began more heavy labour to unload his "merchandise" and sort it into piles or bins inside the barn, or in the adjoining yard. Large metal objects might have to be knocked apart with a sledge hammer, or cut with hacksaws (later an acetylene torch), in preparation for the next visit from brokers driving up in big trucks to buy metals for sale in bulk to the Hamilton steel makers who required this scrap for their furnaces; other brokers came by to take away his rags, bottles, and other reprocessable junk. In this way, Abraham Salsberg and hundreds of other Jewish peddlers throughout Toronto, along with many located in outlying cities and towns, gathered the cast-offs of modern civilization for recycling into newer goods, while eking out a hardscrabble living.[31]

Amidst heavy competition from hundreds of others who followed this occupation Abraham made a modest living and, as four more children – Bob, Nathan, Thelma, and Betty – came along, the family of nine struggled to keep up. The Salsbergs had entered the Toronto Jewish scene as "greener," the somewhat contemptuous epithet employed by those who had arrived earlier, and into a life of hard work, shared housing (with male boarders or newly arrived relatives), and poverty.[32] While many were religiously observant, memoirist Leah Rosenberg recalled that "there existed deep division between Jews from Poland and Jews from Russia," the Poles mostly Hasidic and the Russians mainly opposed to that mystical movement's "strange" practices. Abraham's Hasidic faith was deep. He was what Ben Kayfetz called a "*t'hillim Yid*" (a pious Jew given to reciting from the Book of Psalms); praying fervently in his little shul and whenever possible after a day out on his wagon, he would "open a book," the expression that describes a person who thought it sinful not to use spare time for studying the holy texts.[33] Joe also studied "a page or two of the Talmud" every morning (before school) and every evening with Rabbi Weinreb.

The economic struggle was intensified by religious laws which forbade working on Sabbath or on the many other holy days throughout the year. Still, Abraham's business was increasing and in the larger house he accommodated not only his own growing family but also, briefly, his newly arrived brothers Petel, Moishe, and Yidl, as well as three of Sarah-Gitel's brothers and one sister. With subsequent marriages and the birth of children, the extended Salsberg family constituted a widening network of which Abraham and Sarah-Gitel were the centre, where kinsmen, neighbours, friends, suitors, drifters, landsmen, kibitzers, and business and religious associates congregated from morning till night. Sarah-Gitel presided over the kitchen and the children. Abraham was known as "tatte" and Sarah-Gitel as "mamme" to the children, who spoke Yiddish at home. It had a traditional religious atmosphere where *kashrut* (kosher meat and separation of dairy from meat dishes and utensils) and *Shabbat* rules were strictly observed, even though Yosele, despite his rigorous religious instruction, was beginning to have reservations about strict orthodoxy as "the influence," he recalled, "of Isaiah and Amos turned the direction of my development in the area of social justice."[34] This transformation was facilitated by tough debates at his parents' Friday evening Sabbath table, which was "a forum for religious, social, and political discussion" often attended by the learned rabbi Abraham Disenhaus.

Yosele's secular schooling began in the fall of 1913 at Lansdowne School, a two-and-a-half-storey Victorian structure with a substantial Jewish enrolment situated on Spadina Avenue on the west side of the circle embracing Knox College. Here he took to his studies, learning English with enthusiasm. A little more than two years later, he showed his penchant for protest and reform, as well as a talent for organization, when, as a mere bar mitzvah boy, he led a strike of Jewish pupils at the school against the required singing of Christmas carols. "The news spread like wildfire in the Jewish community ... I was referred to as the ringleader," Salsberg recalled.[35]

To help his struggling family, in 1916 Salsberg quit school, even before he had reached the legal age of fourteen, to work full time in a leather-goods factory on Wellington Street producing items for the army, then undergoing massive wartime expansion. He was paid three dollars for a forty-nine-hour week, but he gave his wages to his mother, who cried at having to accept the money. From labourer, Salsberg quickly graduated to cutter, a skilled job, which earned him ten dollars a week, well above the average wage for child workers. He moved on to a cap and hat shop on Adelaide Street and then to the largest firm in the business, Cooper Cap Company on Spadina Avenue, by which time he had joined the United Hatters, Cap, and Millinery Workers International Union, an affiliate of the American Federation of Labor, and was earning up to thirty-five dollars a week, a huge wage for those days[36] in an industry undergoing far-reaching changes in production methods, styling, and fabrics. As a cutter he was responsible for designing and laying out patterns on multiple layers of fabric and then, using an electric knife, cutting the pieces that sewing machine operators then stitched together to produce the finished output. The layout was all-important because more pieces cut from the fabric meant a higher profit margin. In the rising mass-produced ready-to-wear hat production industry men performed the heavy machine work of pressing, blocking, and finishing, while women sewed in bands and linings.[37]

Stung by deplorable working conditions in the industry, Salsberg joined the union's battle against home work, which vulnerable workers felt compelled to complete after hours at piece-work rates. When he joined the union in the early 1920s, the United Hatters, Cap, and Millinery Worker International Union was experiencing the stressful process of amalgamation into one North America–wide formation. Toronto workers in these trades in the early 1920s, like many locals across North America, were also undergoing stresses created by conflicts between communists and non-communists in the union; the communist-led Trade Union Educational League was alleged to be trying to discredit the union's existing leadership.[38] The situation in Boston and Chicago was especially volatile, for as the union's historian, Charles Green, described it, "their object was to rule or ruin."[39] By 1925, Salsberg had achieved a strong position as the Canadian organizer, with an office in Toronto.[40] He spent much of his time organizing the industry's French-Canadian women in Montreal – an even larger clothing centre than Toronto[41] – with whom he established strong credibility as well as with the Jews in the shops.[42] Perhaps under Salsberg's influence, the Toronto locals supported the left-leaning Labour Representation Political Association and, in Montreal, the Canadian Labour Party.[43]

With his minimal public school education, Salsberg felt handicapped and he enrolled in a few high school courses, but apparently never finished any of them, probably for lack of sufficient time for serious study. His early schooling had been in Jewish sacred texts in preparation for the rabbinical career that his father had mapped out for him. Later on, in his twenties, and purely for personal fulfilment, he took evening courses at McMaster University, City College of New York, and the University of Chicago, mainly in English literature. But he was essentially an autodidact who schooled himself in the fundamentals of economics, some of the socialist classics, and general literature. His library included a number of these works, reflecting his interest in the argumentation of leftist and other social thinkers.[44] As well, it is not difficult to see in him the continuation of his father's Hasidic influences. Hasidism, Eli Lederhendler points out, "while not an anticipation of Marx," nevertheless "displayed an alternative, even provocative egalitarianism."[45] The movement emphasized the fellowship of all believers, rich and poor, in "the mystical communion effected through the agency of the zaddick or rebbe." The ideal was a *gemeinschaft*, where traditional Jewish values would be "subordinated … to eschatological and charismatic communitarianism." These ideas, combined with influences from the Prophets, run through Salsberg's later writings and speeches, reflecting the roots of his powerful commitment to social justice that was the foundation of his career in public life.

Notwithstanding the deeply religious atmosphere at home, then, Salsberg obviously was developing ideas of his own as a teenager, causing serious tension between him and his parents. "There was a lot of faith in the house I come from," he later mused, "[but] I am not guided by faith. I want to be guided by reason and reason tells me – I want to know." In an interview he gave in the 1970s for the Multicultural History Society of Ontario, he recounted with some emotion how his parents reacted to his momentous announcement. The year was 1918 and Salsberg, then only sixteen, told them he had decided to abandon Talmudic studies and embrace Zionist socialism. "*Gevalt! Gott zoll uphitin!* (Disaster. May G-d protect us!)" His father Abraham, who, like many religious Jews, regarded Zionism as anathema, had worried about Yosele's growing left-wing *apikorsus* (heresy) for some time, desperately consulting cronies and rabbis while Sarah-Gitel, to use Joe's words, "started in fainting."[46] Various relations and neighbours probably commiserated with both sides of this dispute over a wilful son's decision on his life's path, and a well-known Spadina district luminary known as "Kalman the Judge" was sought out for his opinion on the matter. But Joe stuck to his guns, saying, "This is my conviction," and realizing his ideological incompatibility with the family's traditional ways – his father was furious – threatened to move out of the house. Abraham then quickly relented, although Sarah-Gitel was still in distress; relatives and neighbours continued to be vocal, and rabbis were consulted yet again – and Joe remained in the bosom of his family on Cecil Street.

But there is no evidence in his meagre correspondence, or in his voluminous journalistic writings and political speeches, that he lamented his choice or felt guilty about leaving the world of Torah Judaism for a life on the Left. The angst that comes through in the 1970s interview is probably an elderly man's reflections on the phantom pain of the event that had happened more than fifty years earlier, but he was not – as far as the evidence indicates – in torment about his decision in 1918. Political independence, however, did not seriously mar family relationships for long. Joe agreed not to try to recruit his siblings, who remained loving admirers of their elder brother throughout. Even Abraham and Sarah-Gitel adjusted to the new reality. Abiding love and, no doubt, quiet pride in their Yosele's pursuit of social justice overcame disappointment that he would not become a rabbi.

In his parents' house Joe adhered to tradition and out of respect for their beliefs he would have worn a skullcap. On Sabbath eve he would have watched his mother light her candles and, following custom, with closed eyes move her arms in circles beside them – symbolically embracing the whole world – while reciting the blessing thanking the Lord for the Sabbath day. Joe would have observed and, given his love of singing, probably joined Abraham in chanting the melodious blessing over the wine and challah, and belting out the tuneful hymns after the meal. Boyhood memories of Lagow, love of family, and reflections on his early learning wove together on these occasions as spiritual and emotional reinforcement, even though he did not believe a word of the hymns, such as the familiar "*Ya ribboin olam* ..." Its universalistic and humanistic subtext, however, he well understood. "My comrades," it begins, "bless the Lord whose food we ate! We ate and have some left ..."[47]

These were momentous times of world war and revolution. Less than a year earlier, both the October Revolution of 1917 exploded and the Balfour Declaration was proclaimed, the one marking the Bolshevik takeover of Russia, promising 'peace, bread, and land,' and the second announcing the British commitment to fostering a Jewish national home in Palestine. Salsberg, like many young Jews of those times, felt profoundly moved by both epochal events, and was initially drawn to left-wing Zionism. "Because of my new reading and associations with other young people," he later reflected, "I was very much attracted to … the theory of labor Zionism, or Zionist socialism, a synthesis of what really mattered to me already then, namely that socialism offered justice and fairness and equality … All the great ideas of the Prophets and the new Zionism offered an opportunity for an escape from age-old persecution and isolation and discrimination and pogroms."[48] This outlook, which was inspired by Marxist Zionist intellectuals like Ber Borochov, envisioned a Jewish state in Palestine built on cooperative and socialist principles as the means for the emancipation and redemption of the Jewish people and the ultimate establishment of a just social order for all mankind. This belief, which, Mark Raider asserts, "placed a premium on Palestine as a progressive Jewish society in the making,"[49] conflicted with the contemporary Jewish Orthodox outlook, which held that God, not man, would end the Exile and bring Jews back to the Holy Land. Salsberg, therefore, had had to adopt all kinds of ruses to keep his parents in the dark about his new outlook and attendance at meetings of the organizations he joined. Among these was the *Yunge Poalei Zion* (the Young Workers of Zion), a North American–wide offshoot of the Poalei Zion, the left-wing political party affiliated with labour groups in Palestine.[50]

Like Salsberg, most members of Toronto's Yunge Poalei Zion were idealistic Yiddish-speaking young workers – some of them Marxists – who felt alienated "in this new world in which they were cast" and whose cultural activities at the Peretz Schul were intensely directed to their class interests and social outlook, including political economy, socialism and trade unionism, and the publication of a monthly journal, *Yunger Yiddisher Kemfer* (Young Jewish Fighter).[51] World labour Zionist leaders on tour in North America would usually visit Toronto, and it is likely that Salsberg met movement luminaries like Nachum Syrkin, Ber Borochov, David Ben-Gurion, and Yitzchak Ben-Zvi seeking funds and recruits for their settlements in Palestine. Salsberg immersed himself in the movement's intense cultural and political life and was soon recognized as one of its major leaders. As his commitment grew, he argued for the inclusion of a more Marxist platform in the movement. Still involved in labour organizing, he rose rapidly in its conclaves, where his eloquence, command of issues, and personal charm won wide admiration.

In 1921, then only nineteen, Salsberg moved to the organization's New York headquarters to become national secretary and editor of the *Kemfer*. He even got involved briefly in local Jewish politics, campaigning for the re-election of the socialist candidate Meyer London for the United States House of Representatives. His main concern, however, was that the labour Zionist movement by this time was splitting into two factions: the "right," which favoured moderate policies, and the "Left," which inclined towards a Marxist orientation and affiliation with the Communist International, the Comintern. Increasingly concerned over this split, Salsberg suddenly abandoned his New York commitments in the spring of 1923, leaving behind him a number of unsolved administrative problems. These were the subject of a testy correspondence between him and comrades who tried earnestly to bring him back to New York, to his organizational responsibilities, and to the ideological conformity of the movement. "Greatly surprised at [not] having heard from you," chaver (friend) Hamlin wired Salsberg on 29 May 1923. "Great deal of correspondence ... preparations necessary for third [convention] ... youth activities for party organ must start soon wire immediately when you are coming."[52] Another chaver wired Salsberg angrily: "Your failure to return creates very dangerous situation in our movements ... you must return immediately to settle junior affairs and arrange July convention where comrades will become acquainted with situation."[53]

Salsberg, however, was adamant despite more appeals and reprimands; he decided to stay in Toronto and let New York decide what to do about these matters; he had broken with labour Zionism and moved to the radical Left. He had been unable to resolve the internal disputes within this movement over whether or not it would associate itself with the Third International, "Lenin's rigid authoritarian international," as Salsberg later described it, or the "more radical, internationally minded ... second and a half international," a reference to the International Working Union of Socialist Parties, also known as the Two and a Half International, which favoured a less dogmatic approach to distinctive national contexts, and was described by theorist Karl Radek as "the scum of history."[54] Salsberg, nevertheless, inclined to the latter and, tiring of the endless petty administrative responsibilities and factional disputation in New York, he walked out, hoping to take university courses while pursuing his leftist ideals through union and political activities in Canada. During the ensuing three years, he resumed his work with the union, vigorously debating policy at the Sunday evening forums at the Church Street Labour Temple and meetings at Alhambra Hall on Spadina, "the revolutionary centre of the Jewish workers in Toronto," while shifting ever leftward in his outlook until, outraged by the British government's suppression of the 1926 general strike, he joined the Communist Party of Canada.[55]

This was more than a significant shift to the left. It was a radical break with the past and a momentous adoption of communism and all that it implied at the time. It meant acceptance of the Communist International's goal of proletarian revolution, which in the early 1920s Canadian context was muted, Ian Angus writes, by "a struggle to escape from this type of 'leftism' and adopt policies which corresponded to the realities of Canadian life."[56] The Communist Party of Canada, which had been formed in May 1921, was led from 1923 by national secretary Jack Mac-Donald, a militant Ontario trade unionist who "brought dozens of radical trade unionists with him" into the movement.[57] Salsberg cannot have been unaware of this trend, nor of powerful influences from Canadian communism's leading intellectual of the time, Maurice Spector, editor of the party's publications, *The Worker* and the *Canadian Labor Monthly*.[58]

In his early union work in the clothing trades, Salsberg already would have met Jewish party members like Michael Buhay and Joshua Gershman. Why he waited until 1926 to sign on is not entirely clear, though the 1970s interviews indicate that his thinking was moving ever leftward. He explained that he was searching, in Ian McKay's felicitous phrase,[59] "reasoning otherwise": "I looked for answers to the disturbing problems of those days both at home and abroad. The Soviet Union and the theories and practices which brought it into being seemed to provide the answers [I] looked for. Communism in Russia spoke of equality, of liberation, of opportunity for work and study, of national cultural freedom for all nations and nationalities who had been oppressed by the Czars and it proclaimed its dedication to the creation of a new society in which man will not oppress man nor will one exploit the other ... My joining the Communist movement constituted a dedication to a great cause and an involvement in a crusade for the fulfillment of the idealistic dreams of my generation as well as those of the age of the prophets of old."[60]

For Salsberg and many other Jews, there were even more compelling reasons for becoming communists: the realization of Jewish emancipation in the Soviet Union, where Jews were equal with all other citizens and anti-Semitism was made illegal, condemned even by Lenin himself. "Many of us," Salsberg later reflected, "certainly in my case, saw in [communism] a new opportunity for Jewish survival because Russia gave so much promise for Jews." These convictions were shared by other Jewish contemporaries. "In the first years of the revolution," Joe's close friend Morris Biderman recalled, "Jews were given every opportunity to live freely and develop their distinct culture and way of life."[61] Many Jewish writers and artists immigrated to the new socialist paradise to be a part of this "Jewish renewal." "It was the dream of a just society," Biderman continued, "with Jews participating as equals that motivated J.B. and young radicals of the time."

In the meantime, Joe had fallen in love with Dora Wilensky, a clever, charming, and witty undergraduate at McMaster University.[62] She was born in Russia in July 1901, and named Deborah, D'voreh (or the diminutive D'voireleh), the daughter of Hyman and Mary Wilensky, who had migrated to Toronto in 1905. Hyman was a capmaker supporting his wife and four daughters and probably got to know Salsberg as a rising star in the union. The Wilenskys were members of the *Arbeter Ring* (Workmen's Circle), a left-wing workers' organization that was linked to the Bundist ideology of creating an autonomous Jewish socialist subculture in the diaspora and "virulent anti-Zionism." (Zionists sometimes jokingly referred to Bundists as "Zionists with seasickness.") As Stephen Speisman points out, the Arbeter Ring's Toronto branch was riven by ideological disputation between communist and social-democratic factions, though it is not known which side the Wilenskys favoured.[63]

Dora, whose family lived in the small Jewish enclave east of the main community, could well have met Joe informally at Queen's Park, where many Jewish youth congregated, or through one of the city's Jewish youth groups, possibly across ideological barriers in the Culture Club, organized by Joe's friend Itche Goldberg in 1922, or in the Young Poalei Zion. She attended the Workmen's Circle's Peretz Schul and graduated from Jarvis Collegiate in 1919 with a scholarship to McMaster University (then situated in Toronto).[64] She graduated in 1924 with a BA in English and History. Though on entry to the university she had indicated a preference for journalism as her future occupation, by the time she graduated, Dora evinced an interest in child welfare and spoke on this subject at the graduation celebration put on by the Peretz Schul to honour her and two others.[65] She went on to a distinguished career in social work with Toronto's Jewish Family and Child Services. Meanwhile she and Joe courted – he used to take the old Belt Line streetcar that connected their two neighbourhoods out to see her – and they were married in 1927. Throughout their lives together she was a powerful influence on Joe, as evidenced by his social orientation and speeches on welfare issues in the Ontario legislature.

Joe was set on the path he was to follow for the rest of his political life, a communist labour and political activist. He had rejected the Torah Judaism of his parents, he had abandoned the Zionism he had embraced as a youth, and he had despaired of moderate trade unionism. He was already a well-experienced political organizer, first with the Young Poalei Zion and now with the United Hatters, Cap, and Millinery Workers International Union and the Communist Party of Canada. With his associations through the immigrant Jewish community of Toronto, the personal qualities which endeared him to many of those who met him, his experience in the Yiddish-speaking labour movement in the clothing trades, and his commitment to communism, and bolstered by his gifted and adoring partner, Dora, Salsberg was well prepared for the tasks ahead.

Chapter Two

Party Maverick

Even though he was no longer affiliated with Zionist organizations, Joe Salsberg remained a Jewish cultural nationalist while adhering to Moscow's rejection of the Zionist enterprise aimed at creating a Jewish national home in Palestine under the British Mandate. The Communist Party of Canada's (CPC) position followed that line,[1] which, Jonathan Frankel points out, "condemn[ed] Zionism as a colonialist enterprise ... [and] as an integral part of British imperial policy," and urged the Arabs "to wage the war for national liberation."[2] The position taken by the CPC was that the Zionist movement was the expression of "the Jewish bourgeoisie and the national socialist reformers [to solve] the 'Jewish question,'" thus playing into the designs of British imperialists. The reality, however, was otherwise, *The Worker* stated: the "so-called 'Jewish question' has already been solved in the Soviet Union by the unfettered equality that the Jewish workers possess" and the encouragement of "declassed Jews" to become productive workers and colonists. Salsberg was fully in line with this policy, but he remained, like many other Jewish communists, a cultural nationalist, however inconsistent this might have been with Moscow's directives.

Salsberg joined the radical Left movement in which there already was a substantial Jewish presence, although, unlike in the United States, Jews were not the largest ethnic group, being heavily outnumbered by Finns and Ukrainians.[3] Many Jews brought working-class and socialist ideals with them from Europe along with a detestation of czarism and the harrowing experiences of ghetto and shtetl life. Sophie Mushkat, a native of Warsaw and an immigrant to Canada in the early 1900s, Linda Kealey points out, became such an active union and socialist organizer among striking coal miners in Springhill, Nova Scotia, that she earned the title of "Mother Jones of the Canadian Socialist movement."[4] She and many other Jews were among the earliest members of the Socialist Party and the Social Democratic Party of Canada before the First World War. Jews were believed to be some of the leaders of the Russian Workers' Party that operated in Montreal and Vancouver in 1918 and 1919; during the Winnipeg General Strike of May/June 1919, according to the Royal North West Mounted Police, the Russian Workers' Party and the Bolshevik-oriented Jewish Social Democratic Party were "very much behind the scenes."[5]

In the strike's bitter aftermath, Prime Minister Robert Borden was urged to take action "to combat the growth of Bolshevism in Montreal," which the Mounties' informant attributed to "the conditions among the Jewish workers in the garment trades."[6] The RCMP was keeping close watch on individuals and organizations suspected of radical left-wing activities. In August 1920 they reported that Toronto's Jewish Socialist Party had broken into two groups, "some forming the 'Jewish Socialist Democratic Party of Canada' (which seems identical with the 'Anarchist Communist Party') and others joining the 'Third International.'"[7] "Both are canvassing hard for recruits," the report continued, "and both meet in the same house on Beverly Street, one society on Wednesdays and the other on Fridays." A week later, the Mounties reported that "Morris Spektor [Maurice Spector] has attracted attention as a Communist in Toronto. He is a student at the University," they wrote, stating that the Jewish Socialist Revolutionary Party, as well as the Poalei Zion, were affiliated with the communist Third International.[8] In numerous reports thereafter, Jewish persons and organizations, not all of them necessarily radical, are mentioned in the Mounties' systematic scrutiny, which also included coverage of Finnish and Ukrainian groups. Some names persist, the Jewish Socialist League in particular, while many others simply faded out of existence.

In 1920 the Jewish radicals Becky Buhay and Annie Buller helped organize Montreal's Labor College, which offered night courses on economics, current events, and history and provided a debating forum and an intellectual seedbed for the Workers' Party. All three remained active in radical Left causes for many years.[9] Maurice Spector, while still a student at the University of Toronto, was a founding member of the party, soon emerging as its leading intellectual.[10] Until his expulsion from the party in 1928, he was at the centre of Canadian Marxism's ideological transformations, a veritable intellectual powerhouse of the radical Left.[11] But he was only one of several Jews in the forefront of its activities, mainly in union and political organizing, like Harvey Murphy and Sam and Bill Walsh, who emerged later.[12]

In joining the party, unlike others, Joe never abandoned his Jewish identity. On the contrary, with other Jewish comrades he saw the party as a vehicle for celebrating secular Judaism and cultural nationalism expressed through the medium of Yiddish. Like so many other Canadian Jews on the Left, he fostered and eagerly participated in the cultural and social activities of left-wing organizations like the Labour League, founded in 1927 and headquartered in the heart of Jewish Toronto at College and Brunswick streets, and, after it came into being in 1944, the United Jewish People's Order (UJPO) which, as Ester Reiter explains, was "a social world outside the increasingly commodified life."[13] In the minds of its members there was no conflict between Jewish identity and belief in the communist cause, although most of them, as Henry Srebrnik writes about Jewish communists in Britain, "concentrated on different aspects of Soviet socialism from other Communists, being most interested in what they saw as the solution to the 'Jewish question' and the elimination of anti-Semitism; in the regeneration of the Jewish working class; and in the construction of a Jewish socialist republic in Birobidjan, in the Soviet Far East."[14] Many shared the beliefs of the Jewish secular idealists of the early years of the Russian Revolution who strove, Kenneth Moss explains, to achieve a "Hebrew- or Yiddish-language culture characterized by universality of theme and individuality of expression," while others "obediently began to remake their [Yiddish] culture – and themselves – in accordance with the Revolution's ideological imperatives."[15] This early Jewish radical Left of diaspora nationalists, therefore, was based on more than just political persuasion. It was a people's movement that expressed itself in a rich cultural and social life. UJPO, which had branches in several Canadian cities, embraced many Jews, not all of them necessarily committed communists, who in varying degrees supported collectivist ideals and tried in interesting ways to emulate some of those values in their personal lives. Camp *Naivelt* (New World) in Brampton, Ontario, which also stressed collectivist values and a spirit of internationalism, drew thousands of children over its seventy-eight-year existence – it is still going – while many UJPO members rented or owned modest cottages in a colony at Eldorado Park north of Toronto, where they lived for a few weeks each year a modified communal existence and socialized long into the summer evenings.[16]

The Jewish Folk Choir since 1927 held concerts – in several of which the celebrated Paul Robeson participated – mainly of Hebrew and

Yiddish music, drawing packed houses and even selling records of its renditions. There were cultural evenings at the UJPO building with poetry and literature readings and lengthy discussions. Such evenings sometimes included dance and dramatic presentations as well as many speakers (Joe Salsberg was a favourite!) on a wide range of topics. In florid Yiddish, occasionally in other languages, and, later, often in English, speakers held forth on the issues of the day: the progress of socialism in the Soviet Union, the imminent decline of capitalism in the West, the horrors of colonialism in Africa, the dire plight of the working class everywhere, and, of course, "the Jewish question." And always with the kind of commitment and passion that is inherent in people whose lives were driven by the eternal question of "what is to be done?"

Canadian Jewish communists saw themselves as Jews, Canadians, and internationalists, though members of a distinctive community which included the celebration and enhancement of Yiddish culture and Jewish national continuity. This was the cultural environment of Joe Salsberg and the Toronto Jewish rank and file who fervently believed that "a better world's in birth." Even though his labour union and legislative commitments kept him busy, he frequently attended events, where he was generally seen as a celebrity. And he was always in the forefront of the communist throng that gathered with other Jewish left organizations on Spadina each May Day before marching with flags and banners aloft to a nearby park to hear speeches proclaiming the rights of labour. These events were more than just celebrations or street rituals, they were public proclamations of the Jewish radical presence in Toronto, a claim for notice in public places – a statement, almost, of defiance in a city where Jews and radicals were not made welcome, and the equivalent of other ethnic marches like those on St Patrick's Day and the Orangemen's parade.

By the time Salsberg signed on, the Comintern, David Priestland asserts, at Stalin's direction, was insisting that "member parties had to become Bolshevik parties ... In practise this meant that Communist parties were increasingly transformed into tools of Soviet foreign policy."[17] Under direction from Moscow, the CPC operated to a large extent under the umbrella of its US counterpart, the Communist Party of America. Indeed, after 1922, one of its affiliates, the Trade Union Educational League, which was formed two years earlier to advance the cause of industrial unionism in both Canada and the United States, boasted of its success "in practically all the important industrial centres" in both countries.[18] From Moscow, Canada was administered by a Comintern Anglo-American sub-secretariat that included all English-speaking countries;

in the 1920s Canadians regularly attended the plenary of the American party.[19] Salsberg and many others did not seem to understand the full implications of this control and, later, the nature of Stalinism's insistence on even more rigid centralization of power.

Despite these overarching directives, the Canadian Communist Party at this early stage was not monolithic, but rather an association of regional and ethnic elements. Like other groups, many Jewish comrades such as Salsberg were still, as Ian McKay points out, "often isolated from broader debates and insulated in their own cultural communities," asserting their distinctive cultural personality in Yiddish under the communist umbrella. This was not unusual. Ukrainians in Winnipeg, Jim Mochoruk demonstrates, stoutly defended themselves and their north end Ukrainian Farmer Labour Temple Association's People's Co-op against micromanagement from party headquarters in Toronto, while insisting that the movement, "in their understanding, had much room for cultural, linguistic, and even national differentiation. In short, they saw themselves as *Ukrainian communists*, the two words being inseparable in their minds." Meanwhile, disparaging treatment, like an early marked preference for English-only delegates, bald references to some senior comrades as "old Ukes" by Toronto officials, open discussion at the party's 1925 convention of the "'liquidation' of the language federations," and attempts by Party officials to block the election of Ukrainians to Comintern congresses were deeply resented.[20] Directives from Moscow, which, Bryan Palmer points out, insisted "that Communist work must be based on class rather than language," resulted in Tim Buck, then CPC leader, "earn[ing] little respect among the party's Ukrainians, Finns, and Jews."[21]

Certainly, relations between the party and Jewish comrades anxious to uphold their cultural autonomy were, on occasion, less than harmonious. Party stalwart, and close friend of Salsberg, Morris Biderman recalled instances of open anti-Semitism. Nor did the party's universalistic message dispel old prejudices among many of its members. While much inter-ethnic toleration was present in party conclaves, on occasion the past intervened; Donald Avery points out that Ukrainians and Finns "had, on occasion, been quite contemptuous of other ethnic groups, especially Jews and Blacks."[22]

Salsberg joined the movement at a time when communists in Canada were being subjected to intense government scrutiny, heavy condemnation, and severe repression.[23] Continuing a practice begun in the early 1920s, Toronto's chief constable from 1928, Denis Draper, acted

as special watchdog over suspected communist activities. The city's East
European immigrants (whose meetings were conducted in Finnish, Polish, Ukrainian, Yiddish, or other languages, as the case might be) were
harassed by mounted constables – sometimes referred to as "Draper's
Cossacks" or "Draper's dragoons" – who rode their horses up onto the
sidewalk directly into the crowds at gatherings, using the horses' flanks
to push people aside as if to provoke a fight – and sometimes got one.[24]
Chief Draper, who preferred the title "general" because of his service
during the Great War as brigade commander of the Canadian Mounted
Rifles, strictly enforced a municipal ban on the use of "foreign languages" at public halls; infractions were deemed "disorderly conduct."[25]
Draper, who reputedly enjoyed the favour of the city's elite including the
Eaton's, regarded all Jews as "Commies" and directed special attention to
them. His infamous "Red Squad," which consisted of Detective William
Nursey and two other "tall, husky, well-fed and well-dressed [officers] …
would be the uninvited guests at every meeting, every concert, every
public gathering," activist Minerva Davis remembered. They were there
to intimidate people, most of whom were mostly innocent of politics of
any shade. For "foreigners" and suspected radicals, police jostling, stick-
swinging, arrests (Salsberg had his share of these), and punch-ups were
fairly common occurrences in Toronto during the late twenties. One
such incident at Queen's Park in August 1929 was so egregious that the
Toronto Star printed a full page of letters protesting Chief Draper's penchant for violence and complete disregard for the British constitutional
right to free speech.[26]

The Communist Party of Canada, which had been founded in May
1921 in Guelph, was experiencing wrenching internal debate over its
orientation: whether to adhere rigidly to Marxian doctrine and the abolition of capitalism or to a less extreme expression of the movement's
aims.[27] Tim Buck later admitted that the party "made the mistake of
catering to leftist sentiment and the demand for very agitational and
inflammatory ideas." At the same time, the party was attempting to attract supporters of Ukrainian, Polish, Russian, Finnish, and Jewish social-democratic organizations. Salsberg, it seems, was among those who
were becoming increasingly aware of the implications of Stalinist insistence upon "socialism in one country," focusing instead on the Soviet
Union. As Bryan Palmer explains, this impeded the Canadian ability
"to devise tactics and strategy that would implant communism within
the consciousness and activities of Canadian workers."[28] Salsberg soon
became embroiled in party controversy, accused, perhaps wrongly, of

being a Lovestonite, that is, a believer in American Communist leader Jay Lovestone's ideas of forming a broadly based class labour party and the doctrine of "American exceptionalism." By the late 1920s this group was out of favour and factional struggles in the Soviet Union and among Canadian adherents like Maurice Spector and Jack MacDonald lessened its standing still further.

At this time, Salsberg kept his communist affiliation secret, unwilling to risk splitting his union over political differences.[29] There was good reason for this restraint. From November 1927 to April 1928 he served as a union organizer in Chicago, a city where faction fights and violence among members of the United Hatters, Cap, and Millinery Workers International Union drew mobsters – "gunmen and sluggers" – into the fray and threatened to seriously undermine communist strength in the needle trades.[30] He was told that a local of the Teamsters and Milk Drivers union had been taken over by Al Capone's mob, which dominated the local labour scene with targeted extreme violence. Salsberg's attempted interventions led to death threats and the possibility of deportation (back to Canada or, possibly and much more frighteningly, to his native Poland) by the Federal Bureau of Investigation, who knew of his communist affiliations. Salsberg told this story with enormous relish in his later years, but he was not so amused at the time: he wisely got the hell out of town!![31]

But not alone. His sweetheart, Dora, had joined him during these months and shared his union travails while working in a social service agency. They were married in a modest ceremony in a rabbi's study only moments before Joe was forced to rush off to a crucial meeting that lasted most of the night. Negotiations failed and a bloody strike broke out, causing him to delay for hours more joining his bride. Meanwhile, Dora waited and waited until Joe finally arrived half a day late – and dog-tired.

Back in Canada, ready to take up his union activities, he was regarded by some party members as "one of the principal leaders of the Right-wing now coming to a head in the [Cap Makers]."[32] On his return to Canada in April 1928, he was appointed by the party as the national organizer of the Industrial Union of Needle Trades Workers (IUNTW),[33] launched that year, which was intended to include all workers in one industrial union; its provisional executive included activists Annie Buller, Max Dolgoy, Joshua Gershman, and Max Shur.

The clothing industry was always highly volatile, and in the early 1930s, as Stuart Jamieson points out, it had the second highest incidence of

strikes of any industry in the country, even though the International Ladies Garment Workers' Union (ILGWU) and the Amalgamated Clothing Workers' Union of America (the Amalgamated) had negotiated a
degree of industrial peace in Toronto in the late 1920s, including a forty-
four-hour week and time-and-a-half for overtime.[34] One of the burning
issues was the workers' strong preference for weekly wages in place of
the detested piecework system, which they regarded as a throwback to
the sweatshops, homework, and exploitation of family labour. Moreover,
agreements with employers often lasted only months, as firms – many
of them under-capitalized and poorly managed – rose and fell more
frequently than in any other industrial sector, often resulting in serious unrest. Besides, most dressmakers, almost all of them women, were
completely unorganized.[35] Jewish clothing workers, overall the industry's
largest ethnic component and the dominant element in the unions, took
inspiration from the knowledge gleaned from local and New York Yiddish newspapers that they were a part of a rising worldwide Jewish labour
movement. It stretched across North America and had sunk deep roots
in Palestine, where militants had organized the powerful Histadruth
labour federation. Meanwhile, in Poland, all-Jewish trade unions were
increasingly popular among a proletariat suffering from rapidly rising
pauperization and exclusions. Press reports that the Jewish Garment
Workers Union there had mobilized thousands of members in strikes,
protests, and demonstrations inspired Canada's Jewish proletarians in
North America in their own struggles, recognition of what Daniel Soyer
calls "the intertwining of the histories of American [and Canadian] and
European Jews."[36]

Because of his experience with the Capmakers, the needle industry
was Joe's turf and he was well aware that conditions were tumultuous
and unstable. Starting off aggressively in his new job in early September
1928, he and Joshua Gershman, assisted by Jeanne Corbin, campaigned
to organize cloak-makers and dressmakers, first in Montreal, and then
Toronto and Winnipeg. They hoped to recruit all workers to the IUNTW
in the women's apparel sector, where, in his view, the Internationals,
the ILGWU in particular, had utterly failed to establish strong unions.[37]
Some unions had expelled communists from their ranks. What Salsberg
called these "citadels of reaction and clique leadership" had left the unskilled masses to fend for themselves while arranging "sweetheart contracts" with manufacturers.[38] To replace them, the IUNTW promised "a
militant union not only for one craft, not just for a few centres, but for all
needle trades throughout the country from the Atlantic to the Pacific,"

in all some 30,000 workers. This was a bold new tactic which marked the CPC's abandonment of its Comintern-directed policy of the early 1920s of trying to infiltrate existing unions and inserting in them "revolutionary leadership."[39] The emphasis after 1928 in a new radical phase called the "Third Period" mandated the creation of a new labour strategy, the formation of industrial unions in opposition to the international trade unions. Paralleling a similar drive in the United States by the American Communist Party, the Canadian initiative built momentum in 1929, with Salsberg very much in the lead, headquartered in Montreal, the main centre of the needle trades.

At the IUNTW's organizing conference in May 1928, Salsberg spoke animatedly about the situation across the needle industry and the inadequacy of the internationals, whose "corrupt ... officials" in the United States had led to "open revolt."[40] He stressed that in Canada, where only a tenth of the 30,000 workers were organized, the internationals had failed miserably. By late December, however, the situation was reported by party official Sam Carr to be still "chaotic"; and, though membership was growing, "no apparatus [was] being developed."[41] "When Salsberg was in Winnipeg," Carr continued, "things [were] at a stand still in Montreal ... The [union] National Exec does not function," implying that Salsberg obviously needed help in co-ordinating the unionization drive across the country and in keeping abreast of a similar campaign by the Communist Party of the United States. These suggestions had no basis in fact: Salsberg was a seasoned organizer and enjoyed considerable stature south of the border, having recently been invited to address a convention in New York to amalgamate cloak-makers and furriers there. Carr might well also have been objecting to what he and others in the party leadership regarded as Salsberg's "bureaucratic, rightist tendencies and penchant for one-man leadership."[42]

But Salsberg was fully into the fight. In early January 1929, he reported to the party's National Trade Union Department that the IUNTW faced serious difficulties such as weak leadership and inadequate finances. While prospects were promising, "fractional [sic] differences" in Montreal party circles had caused a breakdown. Later that month, he returned to Toronto to spearhead a bitter strike already under way by raincoat makers against the Durable Waterproof Company, which had hired goons to intimidate workers, and "scabs" to keep production going.[43] Within a week, he had been arrested and the contest turned uglier; the strike was finally lost, mainly due to organizational inexperience and the fact that the trade was in a slack season.[44] But Salsberg got his own back. Returning to Montreal, by mid-February he had recruited all the workers at Taffert and Son, one of the city's largest cloak shops, and was making progress organizing pressers and cutters in the city's huge dress industry.[45] In a short few weeks, he had formed three separate locals, for dressmakers, cloak-makers, and pressers.[46]

The drive continued. In June, out in Winnipeg, long a major centre of labour radicalism and a dynamic scene of Jewish social politics, the IUNTW brought its members out in sympathy with glove workers striking against the imposition of piecework.[47] A month later, the union called a strike at the Freed and Freed Company, one of the city's biggest men's clothing producers, over the introduction of a piecework system that would result in pay cuts; within two weeks management concessions ended the dispute.[48] Capitalizing on this victory, Salsberg returned to Winnipeg to head yet another organizing drive. By the end of August 1929, he reported that several locals were active and a joint board had been established; a celebratory union picnic in Kildonan Park drew over three hundred workers, whom Salsberg praised for their militancy.[49]

Summing up the first nine months of activity on the eve of the IUNTW's first convention in May 1929, Salsberg reported that the union was now firmly established, especially in Winnipeg.[50] With twelve locals already in hand, he planned a nationwide campaign to recruit the rest of the unorganized workers, particularly those in the non-metropolitan centres, where manufacturers, fearing unions, were increasingly relocating their production facilities in what were called "runaway shops." When he rose to speak at the convention's closing, *The Worker* reported that Joe "was greeted with round after round of applause" as he extolled the grassroots strength of the new union and mapped out its future.[51]

Salsberg's report was triumphant, lengthy, and comprehensive. He stressed that the craft unions had failed the workers by confining themselves to Montreal and Toronto, neglecting the thousands toiling elsewhere. Moreover, these were corrupt unions that betrayed workers through fake strikes, "class-peace" policies, and toleration of open-shop hiring. Organizers wasted workers' dues by paying themselves fat salaries while living high off the hog in expensive hotels. The IUNTW, by contrast, had moved ahead impressively, even though financed by mere nickels and dimes.

Looking to the future, Salsberg stressed that more funds must be raised, organizers hired, and special attention given to recruiting French Canadians, women, and the young. Fraternal connections needed to be established with industrial unions in the United States and the International

Needle Workers' Committee of Propaganda and Action. He urged the funding of scholarships for students at working-class schools and libraries "for the purpose of the study of books in trade unionism and the labour movement in general."[52]

Not everything was rosy, however. Salsberg emphasized in May 1929 that despite his presence in Montreal, rampant party factionalism was affecting fund-raising.[53] In a candid mid-July review of IUNTW affairs to the party's central executive, he repeated his complaints about finances: "Our income is insufficient to finance expansion, and our debts already total [a huge sum] ... [There is] a lack of leadership due to factional differences ... For my own part, I cannot carry on in this way for much longer."[54] Urged by the political bureau to redouble his fund-raising efforts and give an accounting in early September, by the end of the summer of 1929, after intense activity in Montreal, Salsberg lost patience and resigned his post as national organizer.[55] In a letter to A. Lozovsky, secretary of the Red International Labour Union in Moscow, Canadian officials blamed Salsberg for the union's organizational problems, chiefly his failure to organize a general strike among Montreal's cloak-makers. This "finally resulted in the resignation of Comrade Salsberg and his expulsion from the Party."[56] But this was probably counterproductive, because the IUNTW drive had been chalking up some gains. Encouraged by these, in October 1930 the IUNTW brought out a new organ, *The Needle Worker*, to continue its organizing drive and combat the "social fascists" in the internationals, especially the ILGWU and the Amalgamated Clothing Workers' Union of America, both of them "yellow unions [affiliates of the American Federation of Labor] ... who have betrayed the workers and were always ready to defend the interests of the manufacturers and the bosses."[57]

In 1929 Salsberg had left the IUNTW along with others, like Joshua Gershman as national organizer, with Max Dolgoy working in Winnipeg, Myer Klig in Toronto, and Annie Buller in Montreal. He was not, therefore, directly involved in the major IUNTW strikes of the 1930s, although as Ontario organizer for the Workers' Unity League (WUL), he was likely consulted. Indeed, he was a featured speaker at the second national convention of the IUNTW in May 1931 in Toronto, where he asserted that while he was one of the IUNTW's founders, "I have disappeared from the picture" for reasons of party discipline.[58] "I do not want, however, to leave any room for any enemy of the Industrial Union," he continued, "to utilize this silence of mine as opposed to the revolutionary union ... I am, and I always will be, with both feet in with the

Revolutionary Trade Union." While Salsberg's name does not appear in articles in *The Worker* concerning the IUNTW, even during its bitter confrontations with the ILGWU, his interest never waned and he was deeply respected by its members. In January 1934, he exhorted striking Toronto dressmakers gathered for a rally at Toronto's Standard Theatre: "You are now a power which can insure shops [stay] closed until your demands are met" and promised WUL financial and picketing support.[59] In February 1935, he again endorsed Toronto's dressmakers' struggle for wage improvements.[60] And a few years later, needle workers were passing the hat to support Salsberg's radio broadcasts.

While Salsberg, in later life interviews, mused that organizing the IUNTW was a "mistake" because it split the clothing workers and thus made life easier for the employers, who lost no time in exploiting the differences, in the heat of battle in the late 1920s and early 1930s he had had no such reservations. With their dedication to revolutionary goals and working-class solidarity, Salsberg and his associates then had high expectations for the IUNTW. The vast majority of the industry's dressmakers, virtually all of them women, agreed, because, though other unions were successful, none of them could match the strength of the IUNTW throughout the women's wear sector, especially in the burgeoning and chaotic dress trade. The ILGWU scored its biggest successes in 1937, only after the WUL and its affiliate IUNTW had folded up.

Historians have differing views. Ruth Frager stresses that while the IUNTW's positive contributions to the garment workers' well-being "include the organization of the Toronto dressmakers, the vast majority of them women, in the larger context" the effect was harmful – for the reasons given by Salsberg and others.[61] Mercedes Steedman, however, is far more positive and argues that the "interunion struggles of the early 1920s served as a catalyst for organizing women workers in the dress sector in 1937," when the ILGWU achieved outstanding success.[62] She sees the IUNTW as a necessary force "having a crucial role to play" in the industry, given that neither the ILGWU nor the Amalgamated had much bothered to organize the working masses. Thus, she points out, "the Communist union's militancy paid off. Its members were able to articulate the issues and to mobilize the workers in the dress sector."[63]

In the meantime, as noted above, Salsberg had been expelled (he later called it a "suspension") from the party, in December 1929. He was found to be a Lovestonite, part of what he called the "resistance to [the] bolshevization process" then under way.[64] Following the Comintern's declaration in 1928 that "a new period [the famous 'Third Period'] of revolutionary politics had begun," in historian David Priestland's words, sharp divisions now had to be drawn between revolutionaries and reformists, now labelled "social fascists." Tim Buck, at that critical juncture secretary of the Party's political committee and in charge of implementing the Comintern line, issued a lengthy public statement justifying the expulsion on the grounds that Salsberg was party to "the dangerous and already provocative opposition currents within our party that have to be combatted."[65]

Why was Salsberg in trouble? In mid-October 1929 the party's political bureau, then led by Stewart Smith – who had only recently returned from the International Lenin School for Western Communists in Moscow – reacted strongly to Salsberg's resignation from the IUNTW because the "situation was very unsatisfactory" in Montreal, where the international unions were "showing considerable activity" in their efforts to regain primacy.[66] As well, "the situation was aggravated in the Jewish field by the recent happenings in Palestine," a reflection of the bitter debate between socialists and communists in the United States over the validity of the whole Zionist enterprise in the wake of the August 1929 Arab riots.[67] Perhaps worst of all was Salsberg's sudden resignation, which had impacted strongly on Jewish comrades and was responsible for the "general feeling of helplessness." Montreal needed immediate attention and, at Smith's insistence, Salsberg was ordered to go back there – or else. Jack MacDonald tried to head off a confrontation by moving that since "it cannot be expected that Salsberg maintaining his present position ... can render the necessary service to the Party in the NT [IUNTW] work, ... sending him to Montreal is only [a] makeshift [solution] which can bring no satisfactory results."[68] But the forces aligned against Salsberg were insistent. "Failing to abide with [the party's] decision," the relentless Smith moved, "Salsberg [was] to be expelled from the Party" and four days later, at Buck's insistence in a special meeting of the political committee, Salsberg was ejected for this "and the opposition to [party] political platform."[69] In a lengthy justification Buck explained that "because this decision marks a new stage in the fight for the line of the 6th World Congress of the Communist International and against the Right danger in our Party, the Political Committee issues this statement for the information and guidance of all ranks of the Party, as to the dangerous and already provocative opposition currents within our Party that have to be combated."[70]

Buck and Smith, angered by Salsberg's outright refusal to follow party orders, had been enraged five months earlier, in May 1929, when

Salsberg had challenged Buck's leadership at the party's sixth convention in Toronto. According to Buck, Salsberg had issued "slanderous accusations ... hoping to confuse many comrades as to the real issues involved" and on the basis of his "theoretical differences," openly opposed the Comintern's battle against "Right Oppositionists." His expulsion, Buck insisted – given the fact that Salsberg was no novice to party affairs – would serve as a warning to the faithful of the seriousness of the crisis. "Smash the Right Oppositionists," Buck demanded, "Defend the Party against the Liquidators."[71] Interviewed many years later on this contretemps, Salsberg stated that he was motivated by an apprehension of a leadership cult with Stalinist tendencies emerging in the party,[72] but that he refrained from attacking Buck openly, for fear of undermining party discipline. Clearly, Salsberg was becoming aware of the dangers of Stalinism and was ready to stand up to them.

He had indeed fully participated in the conflict that led to his expulsion.[73] No doubt fully aware of the internecine party strife in the United States resulting from Stalin's "proclaiming a rightist danger the most threatening to the health of the Communist International," and cognizant also of the risks involved, he decided to resist Moscow.[74] Several months before the convention, he openly aligned himself with "old guard" figures like Jack MacDonald, Florence Constance, Mike Buhay, and Maurice Spector, among others who opposed Tim Buck, and other supporters of the Comintern's attack on the "Right danger." Salsberg was prepared to challenge them, and with some backing from his base in the needle trades he had also mobilized support from leaders of the party's Jewish, Ukrainian, and Finnish sections. He was being a little coy, therefore, when he stated that he had "come to the convention determined to decide questions on their merits, and not to become involved in the factional infighting," but that Tim Buck and Stewart Smith "are most factional in their every utterance and stand."[75]

Now that the issue was out on the convention floor, Salsberg vehemently denied the Buck and Smith allegations that he was an "unprincipled factionalist." Up on his feet, his auburn moustache bristling and his arms waving as if to orchestrate support, Salsberg reminded the assembly that he had worked in factories since age thirteen and that, as a previous member of the left wing of the Poale Zion youth, he had rejected bourgeois nationalism and joined the Communist Party of Canada, fully convinced of its cause.[76] He stressed that he had accepted party discipline while occupying important positions in his union in Canada and Chicago, where he had tried to quell rampant factionalism. Since returning home in 1928 – at the request of Tim Buck, he emphasized – he had helped organize the IUNTW, even though the American party had wanted him to return to Chicago. He reminded the assembly that, once back in Toronto, he had made no secret of his dissatisfaction with Canadian affairs. In conversation with leading comrades, at party meetings, and in letters to the Pol Com (the party's trade union department) he had made fully public his belief that "our party is full of weakness," lacks clarity, and "fails to marshal its forces in the great tasks which now face the party." "Let there be no mistake about [my] real intentions," he declared. They were to achieve a "real bolshevization of the party," to make it "a real fighting section of the COMINTERN capable ... of fighting against the social reformists."

Turning on his adversaries in full oratorical flight, Salsberg charged that it was the Buck-Smith group who were the real factionalists at this convention. They held secret meetings and snobbishly jeered and ridiculed working-class Ukrainian comrades who rose to speak their minds with perhaps less than perfect command of the King's English. Instead, he admonished, the sneerers "should bow in reverence to those miners, to whose height they will never rise."

Salsberg reserved his sharpest barbs for Stewart Smith, the radical Protestant minister Reverend A.E. Smith's son, whom he obviously regarded as an insufferable young snot: "Since his return from the Lenin School [in Moscow], ... has assumed the air of a pompous professor who shows great impatience and irritation at anyone who may fail to completely swallow everything he says ... [He] will have to learn to become ... a leader and teacher of workers who are not all accustomed to class room manners." But he did not spare others for their "Snobbish attitude, the uninterrupted jeering and ridiculing of the healthiest proletarian elements in the party by such unproletarian elements at the Buck-Smith table as [Charles Arthur] Marriott and Becky Buhay. [This] was the most provoking and intolerable behaviour at this convention."[77]

The Buck-Smith charges were hogwash, Salsberg continued, now in unrestrained oratorical combat. He was no factionalist, he asserted, but was in full accord with the goals of the Comintern. "My past record and activity will ... speak louder than the factional declarations of those who excel themselves in little more than talk," he declared as he took his seat. But despite his spirited counterattack and his dramatic oratory, in Lita-Rose Betcherman's words, "in the manner of Maurice Schwartz playing on the Yiddish stage," before the political committee, he was expelled. Even though submitting an abject and lengthy plea for reinstatement and promising "to work for a united communist party, for a party with a true proletarian leadership and for a genuinely bolshevized Canadian section of the COMINTERN," he was now a political orphan.[78]

Despite Salsberg's willingness to compromise, once out in the open, this battle created long-lasting acrimony in party ranks.[79] The"Right danger," with which Salsberg and the vast majority of the CPC were alleged to be associated was aligned with what Buck and Smith called "American exceptionalism, and a variety of other serious ideological failings," and with "failing to understand that social democrats had now become 'social fascists'" (a Stalinist term slamming the social democratic tendencies of Nicolai Bukharin, head of the Communist International).[80] The Stalinists, led by Tim Buck, though a small minority of the party, within a few months, in the view of some, had fully intimidated the rank and file, and forced the democratically elected leader, Jack MacDonald, along with Mike Buhay, Mathew Popovich, and Bill Moriarty, to resign. Even though, as noted above, "Buck's leadership hung on a shaky nail through the first half of 1930 because of the dogged, passive resistance of the Finnish and Ukrainian sections" of the party, he held it in his control and kept it firmly in his grasp, following directives from Moscow.[81]

Nine months later, Salsberg petitioned for reinstatement, admitting his breach of party discipline.[82] But because he "has not acknowledged his political right wing errors ... in relation to the Union etc. has not condemned these, and has not departed from the right wing statement," he was required in the columns of *The Worker* to openly acknowledge and condemn his former political mistakes, and depart from all right-wing errors and groups and explain whether he wished to unconditionally submit to the Comintern and the CPC.[83] If Salsberg accepted these terms, then the Pol Com's decision would not be "published," in other words, his ejection would be null and void. The minutes of subsequent meetings contain no reply and Salsberg published no statement in *The Worker*.

Why not? It is likely that the political committee was privately persuaded, by Salsberg or others, that he would henceforth behave himself and publicly confess whenever possible to his egregious ideological errors, never again to let his thoughts stray into the dangerous field of right-wingism, or dip into the poisoned well of Lovestonean deviationism. His statement in 1931 at the IUNTW convention, a carefully worded admission of differences, was deemed acceptable, even though he was not formally readmitted to the party until 1932. Besides, even officially out of the party, Salsberg was entirely willing to be used, especially for union organizing.

While on the shelf, Salsberg, in a later "confession" (penned in 1935 or 1936), entered what he later self-abasingly called the "dark period of my active [political] life[,] ... a period of cleansing the Communist parties and a period during which were formed the renegade groups and factions of the anti-par[ty] elements in many countries including Canada."[84] To an IUNTW gathering in May 1931, he attributed his disappearance from party activities on his need "to develop in the Revolutionary movement."[85] "I, like other comrades, have inherited a past ... I have inherited quite a past, Labour Zionism, and this disqualified me for the time being." Salsberg, somewhat mysteriously, added that "a leading comrade of the Revolutionary Movement should be prepared to overlook his own interest." "I found," he continued, "that I could not get along with certain people ... in the Movement ... It was a question of discipline, and, for the moment, I was stronger in my personal interests than in my conviction."

Besides ideological and personal differences, Salsberg's statement could also have meant that he had developed certain personal interests that conflicted with, or drew him away from, party activities. He was the publisher of the 1931 edition of the *Toronto Jewish Directory*, a private enterprise that would absorb much time and energy.[86] This publication, which had begun in 1924, providing an important window on the economy and demographics of Toronto Jewry, was issued in 1925 and 1926, but then lapsed until taken up again in 1931 by Salsberg, possibly as an attempt to supplement his income. The project was discontinued the following year.

Although officially expelled, he was nevertheless still vaguely in the party's orbit and was trying hard to be readmitted; to vindicate his loyalty he served, as he later put it, "under instructions of the Party,"[87] in some of its mass organizations and became national secretary of the Canadian Friends of the Soviet Union. He supported some of the party's subgroups, such as ICOR *Yiddishe Kolonisatsye Organisatsye in Rusland*, an ill-fated scheme to set up a Jewish homeland in Birobidjan, the Soviet Union's easternmost territory.[88]

Salsberg was formally readmitted to party ranks in 1932, only, as he wrote in his abject confession to party bigwigs, "after I had outlived and overcome the last remnants of my anti-party positions and had accepted the correct (proven by life itself) policies and leadership."[89] Now contritely back in the fold, he was again deployed as a labour organizer, and because of his experience in the United Hatters, Cap, and Millinery Workers Union, he was assigned to spearhead the party's drive to orga- nize industrial unions, starting with clothing, under the umbrella of the Workers' Unity League (WUL).This was his forte, after all, and he seems to have lost whatever interest he might have had otherwise in internal party politics and its chief actors. His relationship with the new lead- ers, like Tim Buck, was apparently "correct," though clearly not warm. Many years after this contretemps, Salsberg praised Buck as "Canada's best union leader," forecasting that "as for the historian – the honest, objective historian – of Canada's trade union movement, he will place Tim's leadership position in the unions of his time on the highest pedes- tal, while those who seem high at the moment will hardly earn mention … For Tim is Canada's leading Marxist."[90] Without warmth, this asser- tion suggests that Salsberg was really calling attention to his own widely regarded prominence as the party's leading union strategist, and faintly damning an old adversary.

Chapter Three

Labour Stalwart and Political Novice

Joe Salsberg now became a key figure in the Workers' Unity League (WUL), a revolutionary labour front intended to replace the Trade Union Educational League, which had existed since 1920. The WUL was a product of the "Third Period" of the communist movement, which, between 1928 and 1935, in Bryan Palmer's words, "stressed ... the radicalization of the masses and that the task before workers was to foment revolution."[1] The WUL was formed by the Communist Party of Canada (CPC) in December 1929 as the umbrella under which it would "organize the unorganized" in all industrial sectors that traditional unions had not penetrated. It was also intended to infiltrate those "reformist" and craft unions, many of them affiliated to the Trades and Labour Congress (TLC), which was associated with the American Federation of Labor (AFL), to pursue socialist revolution, and to mobilize previously excluded ethnic groups and the unemployed.[2] As Stephen Endicott explains, the "WUL was proud of the fact that it was linked to militant workers all around the world by virtue of being the Canadian section of the Red International of Labour Unions, headquartered in Moscow." The CPC followed the Kremlin's new line and sponsored the WUL, which announced its commitment to a "revolutionary struggle for the complete overthrow of capitalism and its institutions of exploitation, and the setting up of the State power of the workers and poor farmers through a workers and farmers government." Since 1927, Canadian communists had collaborated with various labour circles to establish the All Canadian Congress of Labour and made efforts to form industrial unions, most of which had failed.[3]

Now, in the wake of economic uncertainty and mounting unemployment, many workers became radicalized, as Judy Fudge and Eric Tucker explain, "making them responsive to campaigns for jobs that paid a liv-ing wage or adequate relief."[4] Though not an official arm of the party, the WUL was led by its members like Salsberg and was seen as a vehicle for building a mass revolutionary movement through its national Unem-ployed Workers Association. While the WUL-affiliated unions grew from 7000 members in 1931 to 30,000 by 1934, the league had much greater impact on the labour movement than these numbers suggest because it organized the majority of strikes in Canada between 1932 and 1934 in many industrial sectors, thus educating workers in mass industrial action and, in Joshua Gershman's words, "conducting a bitter struggle inside AFL unions against the collaborationist policies of their leaders."[5] As WUL district organizer in a wide variety of industries in southern On-tario, Salsberg, who argued for labour unity "not ten years from now, not bye and bye – but as speedily as humanly possible," was fully occupied during the thirties.[6] He was part of the strategy of what John Manley argues was an emphasis on "operat[ing] as 'good trade unionists' rather than 'good bolsheviks,' using every opportunity to modify and adapt to local realities," placing "flexibility above revolutionary purity." Salsberg favoured merging with AFL craft unions whenever possible; for example, in March 1934 he set up the Building Trades Workers' Industrial Union, after recruiting a lapsed AFL Jewish local of the International Painters' and Paperhangers' Union.[7]

At Ontario WUL headquarters in Toronto, Salsberg worked with a team that included Myer Klig, local organizer for the IUNTW, and Jack Scott, a recently arrived Irish immigrant, who organized in the industrial heartland of Kitchener, Brantford, Sarnia, and London, mostly in tex-tile and shoe factories.[8] Some of the leading WUL activists were women, including Lillian Himmelfarb, known as "Red Lilly," remembered by Scott as "a real rabble-rouser. Little Jewish girl. She was just fantastic. She would battle with police until they had her in jail. Really out there."[9] Off in the field, Izzy Minster, whom Scott described as "a little, short, Jewish guy with glasses, very thick glasses," led a partially successful furniture workers' strike in Stratford in September 1933.[10] The Army was briefly called in to "maintain order"; nevertheless, workers won significant wage increases, the forty-four to fifty-four hour week, and shop committees (rather than union recognition), a victory which, in John Manley's view, "more than any other single event established the WUL as a national presence [and] an increasingly confident local working class."

As co-ordinator of Ontario's WUL activity, Salsberg monitored every-thing, travelling throughout the province as needed and coaching local leaders on strategy and tactics, especially where strikes were in progress. Because of his background in the needle trades, his connections in the Jewish working class, and "his outstanding ability ... [and] very likeable personality," as his fellow WUL organizer, Tom Ewen, described Salsberg, he was well-suited for this work: "'J.B.'" did an excellent job of building and consolidating the WUL, not only in Toronto itself, but throughout the key industrial centres of southern Ontario."[11] "The strike," Salsberg asserted in *The Worker*, the WUL's principal organ, "is an important weapon in the hands of the workers. It is the most powerful weapon at the disposal of our class in the struggle for immediate improvements, for political rights, etc."[12] Even unsuccessful strikes provided valuable experience: they "help us to win future struggles." Thus, "the cause of every defeat must ... be fearlessly analyzed," like the "long and bitter battles" in Stratford and at Colonial Shoe and Haliman and Sable in Toronto. Defeats, he reflected, are caused by poor strike preparations, insufficient mass action, and perhaps worst of all, the organized opposition of "the bosses, the banks, the government and their police forces, the press and the misleaders of labor."

The strike was not just an instrument for "immediate improvements," but as Salsberg explained in *The Worker*, it was a vehicle for working-class mass action in which all workers in an industry should – but often did not – support their comrades out on strike with mass picketing. Failure to do so resulted not only in defeats but also the undermining of the league's overall goal of raising working-class revolutionary consciousness.[13] One way of achieving this was by getting to the grass roots. "We cannot merely appoint an organizer and send him out," Salsberg instructed the league's executive in December 1934. Among the bitter lessons learned from the defeats to date, he stressed, was the fact that the league must focus on mobilizing working-class organizations such as fraternal and political formations involving thousands of workers and adopt effective industry-wide strategies to create cadres of leadership from within these groups. "Unless we are able to consolidate [them]," he warned, "we will fail to develop" and losses to the AFL unions will continue.

While critical collegially within the movement, Salsberg took no guff from hostile outsiders, presenting them with tough talk. When Ontario's attorney general, William H. Price, sanctioned the wide distribution of pamphlets attacking the WUL as "agents of revolution" in February 1934, Salsberg called a special mass meeting of supporters at Massey Hall, where he addressed a crowd of 3500 persons. "We have no apologies to make to Price and [Prime Minister] Bennett," he announced, "nor will we make any." "We make no defence," he continued. "We are proud of our record. We face [their] attacks with an accusation. We charge them with sending workers to slave camps, clubbing and intimidating workers. We say Price and his kind are those actually accused, not the Workers Unity League."[14]

Famously effective behind his desk in Toronto and in closed-door party meetings, Salsberg was even more powerful when he was on his feet addressing a crowd out on the street or at a mass meeting of workers and sympathizers, often in his florid and dramatic Yiddish in the Alhambra Hall or the Victory Theatre on Spadina. And he was equally eloquent in his slightly accented English. He opened the enormous gathering at Maple Leaf Gardens in early December 1934 to welcome home Tim Buck on his release from prison. He addressed crowds at Queen's Park and other venues to protest against weaknesses in legislation governing labour conflicts, low relief rates, and evictions; he orated at rallies to celebrate May Day, Lenin Day, and the October Revolution. Salsberg gave speeches at election rallies, union gatherings, strikes and lockouts; he proclaimed the need for tax reform, lower gas-meter charges, and help for the unemployed. He lambasted General Draper's police harassment, red-baiting, and links to the rising fascism in Toronto; he attacked dominion, Ontario, and Toronto politicians. He wrote articles for the party's publications – *Kamf, The Worker,* the *Daily Clarion,* and the *Canadian Tribune* – on all these topics as well as the WUL's drive to organize workers in industries like textiles, clothing, shoes, trucking, coal handling, furniture, laundry, and public services.

The league under Salsberg's guidance did not eschew the use of violence, because "violence and other illegal acts [were useful]," as Marcus Klee argues, "in not only winning sweatshop struggles, but building a vibrant union movement."[15] While strikes shut down production for the duration and might – they often did – force owners to make concessions, they could also benefit employers: when orders were slack, warehouses full of unsold merchandise, and workers redundant. Some employers, who were concerned about union drives, might use strikes as a form of lockout to intimidate workers, or force monetary concessions.

There were even more aggressive tactics in the employers' arsenal: injunctions, criminal prosecution, scab employees, and, ultimately, goon squads (sometimes also used in the clothing industry) to rough up strikers and their leaders. Klee points out that after mounting an all-out drive to organize footwear workers through the WUL-affiliated Shoe and Leather Workers Industrial Union in September 1933, most

Jewish-owned plants signed on, perhaps because they were newer, smaller, and less well capitalized than others and because of Salsberg's connections in the Jewish community.[16] The 'gentile' factories, however, were a much tougher nut and the union was subjected to injunctions against mass picketing, scabs, and violence. Salsberg was personally subjected to some of these methods. During the strike at the Colonial Footwear Company in Toronto in May 1934, he and several others faced contempt of court charges for unlawful picketing,[17] just before he was to head up strikes in Brampton, Kitchener, and Galt and to lead a province-wide anti-injunction drive.[18] Meanwhile, Salsberg was arrested in New Toronto while picketing the Tilley-Williams factory in late August,[19] precipitating a massive sympathy strike at plants across Toronto, which finally resulted in a victory with an industry-wide contract.[20] By early 1935, the WUL was also organizing shoe workers in Quebec, despite competition from the Catholic union and the AFL.[21] While concerned principally with the lot of workers in mass-production industries, Salsberg was aware of poor conditions elsewhere, a sensitivity he expressed many times during his later career in the Ontario legislature. In March 1935, he spoke up for domestics, demanding that the government legislate a minimum wage of thirty dollars a month, an eight-hour day, the right "to entertain friends in congenial surroundings," amendments to the Workman's Compensation Act to cover household injuries, and the abolition of private employment agencies. He urged office and retail employees to "organize, join hands with other workers and rise to higher standards ... Alone you are unable to gain one penny on the hour. Only when you are united are you capable of demanding better wages and improvements."[22]

Salsberg dutifully reflected the WUL's loyalty to Moscow's philosophy of "the class struggle," arguing in August 1935 for the destruction of the "class collaboration ideology which is so skilfully spread by the bourgeoisie and their labor bureaucracy." Instead, he proclaimed, "We inject the class interests and raise high the banner of class struggle in the midst of [the] poisonous propaganda of the bosses and their labor agents."[23] From this perspective he announced that WUL affiliates and their members would join in September 1st Labour Day observances while not forgetting that it was "on May Day [that] the workers of all countries hold high the banner of struggle for immediate conditions and for ultimate emancipation." The purpose of participating in Labour Day was for the WUL, "the militants in the labor movement ...[,] [to] inject the class issues into the parades, mass meetings and literature which is issued to the workers, ... and call upon [them] to fight for their interests as against

the profit interests of the bosses ... and raise before the workers the
aim of a Socialist society." Fraternization on Labour Day with the wider
labour movement, he continued, would thus help to "win them over to
our program and policies ... and ... turn Labor Day into a day of struggle
and unity of all workers in this country ... and win them for the international day of working class solidarity – May Day." Following Moscow
directives and the WUL's decision in November 1935 to foster one union
in each industry, thus abandoning its previous insistence on revolutionary unions like the IUNTW, Salsberg obediently sang a different tune.
The Third Period's "class war" was over, to be replaced by the Popular
Front, and Salsberg issued its battle cry: "We unite the trade unions."[24]
The WUL had served its purpose and a new policy was in place. "Unity
at any price," Manley stresses, was the new motif and Salsberg was on
guard against the "uncontrolled return of the international [unions]"
by strengthening "the Party's hold on unions in which WUL forces had
merged, even though he was shelving the industrial union principle."[25]

Meanwhile, now as the party's major labour activist in Ontario, Salsberg was a key figure in organizing seamen on the lakes and canals,
where, William Kaplan writes, sailors were denied the amenities of a civi-
lized existence, like proper living conditions, decent food, and reasonable hours. Authoritarian control by captains and mates (and sanctioned
by maritime law) left sailors open to exploitation and abuse,[26] in some
respects not unlike the conditions their eighteenth-century forbearers
had to endure.[27] The initiative for change came from Pat Sullivan, a
ship's cook, who rebelled against the Canadian Seaman's Union (CSU),
which had been organized in the early 1930s and was headed by Captain
Hubert N. McMaster, a close associate of the shipping companies.[28] Sullivan organized his own union, the National Seaman's Union (NSU),
which affiliated with the All-Canadian Congress of Labour.[29] When, in
1935, Sullivan's NSU members' wildcat strike protesting low wages and
poor conditions seemed to be failing, Salsberg intervened. "Recent developments among the Seamen and Longshoremen (SL) on the Great
Lakes and the failure of the [wildcat] Seaman's strikes, which have been
demoralized by the leadership of the National Seaman's Union, place
before us very sharply the question of work among these workers," he
informed sympathizers.[30]

Besides the CSU and the NSU, Salsberg pointed out, in Montreal
there was a Catholic Seamen's Union and an independent longshoremen's union. Meanwhile, in Toronto, Windsor, and the Lakehead,
independent formations of longshoremen existed, as well as various

other unions scattered around Great Lakes ports. So, although sea-men and longshoremen were willing to battle "against the deplorable conditions," leadership was weak, while Captain McMaster's CSU was guilty of "a shameless 'give-away.'" Salsberg called for a convention to form an all-inclusive union for maritime workers and the formation of "special forces" to recruit members; he also asked for feedback and names of contacts. Although taking the lead, Salsberg stepped back to let others – actual workers – do the negotiating with Canada Steam-ship Lines, the largest shipping company on the St Lawrence–Great Lakes system.[31] Out of this experience, a new formation, the Maritime Workers Union of the Great Lakes, arose and was later merged with the NSU, and called the Canadian Seamen's Union – a much different for-mation than the 1930s union of the same name – under Pat Sullivan's leadership.

Salsberg continued to be involved in CSU affairs for several years and kept abreast of developments there.[32] When the union won a landmark strike in April 1938, he hailed the victory as "an event of outstanding significance," praising "the admirable militancy and consciousness of the importance of their fight."[33] In place of working twelve-hour shifts seven days a week while sailing, receiving abysmal pay, and being under the control of brutal first mates, under the CSU sailors got an eight-hour day, decent minimum wages, and the right to dignified treatment.[34] Always pressing for "organizing the unorganized," Salsberg warned against the possible encouragement of company unionism implicit in the Industrial Standards Act enacted in Ontario in 1935.[35]

Following Moscow's August 1935 directive to Communist parties ev-erywhere to abandon the attempts to set up revolutionary unions and, in John Manley's words, "the privileged status of the industrial struggle," the CPC dutifully terminated the WUL a few months later.[36] In this new phase, labelled the "Popular Front" or "People's Front," Salsberg contin-ued as the party's leading labour spokesman in Ontario.[37] And he took no prisoners, "direct[ing] the unity drive without undue concern about trade union democracy ... [and] provok[ing] considerable rancour at the grass roots." He intervened at the 1936 convention of the Trades and Labour Congress of Canada (TLCC) to oppose a left-wing resolution, leaving observers, Manley continues, "gasping for breath." He champi-oned the TLCC as the home of the CIO unions and he muffled criticism at every turn. Like others in this new formation, Salsberg "ruled from above," leading the party's "retreat from the class struggle" and blocking incipient revolt from the angry left wing.

He was now, in fact, a labour bureaucrat. Only a year after he had almost single-handedly organized Toronto's coal handlers and independent truckers into a militant WUL union, in keeping with the November order from Moscow, he urged the union to join the Trades and Labour Congress, which had always opposed the industrial union philosophy.[38] This action troubled many party members, notably the venerable Cape Breton radical J.B. McLachlan, who was not persuaded by Salsberg's argument that disaffiliation would advance workers' interests. In line with the new policy, however, in November 1935 Salsberg wrote to the Upholsterers' Industrial Union,[39] a WUL affiliate, announcing, "We are orienting ourselves toward joining the AFL through your union." Salsberg inquired about financial terms as well as "the relative strength of the progressive forces in your union and the attitude of the International leadership towards them."[40] Reflecting many years later on this transformation, Salsberg stated: "It seemed to me so sensible and so politically essential that everything else was secondary, and the unification of the forces of labour on a global scale to combat the threat of war and fascism was overriding."

By the time the WUL was dissolved, Salsberg had contributed enormously to developing, in Irving Abella's words, "a faithful and militant nucleus of experienced party members who knew how to chair meetings, make motions, give speeches, print pamphlets, mimeograph handbills, and organize picket lines."[41] "During its brief but stormy life," Leo Roback observes, the WUL "did develop, train and 'blood' a surprising number of rank-and-file militants and professional organizers" who were active in the CIO."[42]

Now known widely as "J.B.," Salsberg was working for the party to set up ever more CIO-affiliated unions, even travelling to New York and Washington to plead with CIO leaders there to get more active in Canada. All the while he was continuing to serve as the party's chief labour expert.[43] For years thereafter he contributed columns regularly to *The Worker* on the labour scene, on specific conflicts, and on broad themes and trends.[44] His articles on strikes at Toronto restaurants and laundries, as well as a weekly column on the broad union scene were featured in the *Daily Clarion* week after week. The metal workers soon became another target of Salsberg's organizing efforts. By June 1936 he was advocating the formation of an industrial union for the Canadian steel and metal workers in the Amalgamated Association of Iron, Steel, and Tin Workers. A similar union had already been formed in the United States and he urged all industrial unions in the CIO to sponsor the campaign.[45]

Like others in the labour movement, Salsberg was alert to the short-comings of labour laws and their dangers to the interests of workers. In January 1935, while still a WUL organizer, he sounded a loud alarm in *The Worker* concerning the threat that the Hepburn Liberal government would introduce a version of Quebec labour law in Ontario, the infamous "Arcand law," which effectively reduced wages, deprived workers of the right to join a union of their choice, and set limits on strikes and picketing.[46] "The WUL," he proclaimed, "will therefore utilize every opportunity to rally the masses of the workers in Ontario against this reactionary and anti-working class legislation." Salsberg called for a united WUL labour front with the AFL and ACCL unions to combat the trend. He headed a delegation to interview Arthur Roebuck, Hepburn's minister of labour, to find out if the threat was indeed real and imminent. Salsberg proposed four additional clauses: allowing workers to join a union of their own choosing, abolition of industrial zoning (which would permit employers to move production to open shops and unorganized areas of the province, thereby encouraging the already existing pattern of "runaway shops"), non-recognition of company unions, and the right to strike and picket.[47] To the readers of the *Daily Clarion*, he summed up the legislation: "The capitalist governments seek to carry through all of their attack upon the workers under the guise of 'progressive legislation' and screened by 'radical' phrases."[48] Salsberg's labour journalism of the late 1930s covered a variety of issues: the unfairness of injunctions stopping strikes,[49] the shortcomings of the Trades and Labour Congress of Canada, where, he pointed out in one of his frequent *Daily Clarion* columns, "the Congress and its leaders do not participate in the struggles of the workers ... [and] come before the masses of unorganized as their organizer and leader." "The real problems," he continued, "are not forced to the forefront."[50] On a variety of issues Salsberg continued his fight. In early January 1937, together with the Toronto District Trades and Labour Council representatives, he led a delegation pressing the city's hospitals for union recognition, better pay, and shorter hours; the effort failed.[51]

Salsberg's personal life during these years embraced much happiness. He and Dora were an adoring couple; photos showed them close together, she blushing and he slightly moonstruck. But their attempts to have children ended in disappointment and then, in 1933, tragedy and lasting heartbreak when twin boys died soon after delivery, Joe tearfully holding them in his arms. While Joe continued his union labours, Dora became head of Toronto's Jewish Family and Child Services, the community's leading welfare agency, where she pioneered in the modernization of its services to women and children. She won significant recognition from colleagues in the field and, in April 1936, joined two other Toronto social workers on a ten-week study tour of facilities for mothers and children in Britain, Scandinavian countries, and the Soviet Union. She and her colleagues were thrilled with the advances they observed in the Soviet Union and presented reports which were featured in the *Toronto Star*.[52]

Salsberg had a major role in the famous strike at the Oshawa General Motors plant in April 1937. For at least a year before that time, he had kept himself informed about the emergence of the United Auto Workers (UAW) in the United States, in particular the bloody sit-down strikes at General Motors plants in February of that year. He acted as a party consultant to GM workers, trying clandestinely to form a union in Canada and distributing bundles of UAW newspapers to sympathizers in plants in Oshawa, St Catharines, and Windsor.[53] "I would go to Oshawa once a week, sometimes twice a week," he recalled. "The meetings [of] five, six [people] took place in the unfinished basement of a General Motors Ukrainian worker." He was their "outside person, guiding, developing, [and] giving directions." Once scheduled to speak at a workers' mass rally in Lakeview Park, Salsberg was threatened by GM's thugs bearing baseball bats, but managed to escape a beating.

He was thus continuing the communist's "primary orientation towards the industrial struggle" and, as John Manley explains, slowly encouraging the workers to learn "that their collective future lay with industrial unionism ... and buil[ing] an organizing cadre."[54] A widely supported strike at GM in 1927 had been unsuccessful. But for a decade unrest simmered. Then, in mid-February 1937, when GM ordered a speed-up on its assembly line (with little additional pay), some workers decided to strike.[55] But, first, the strikers sent a delegation to Salsberg, who had already appealed to the newly formed Committee of Industrial Organizations for help, in the middle of the night to solicit his assistance.

"And I'll never forget," he recalled. "I was awakened in the wee hours of the morning. I lived on Spadina Crescent, and there was a carload of auto workers from Oshawa with whom I had been working underground and they said, 'Joe, you must pack up and get dressed and come with us to Oshawa!' At that hour of the morning! 'She's a-busting to-day! The boys are walking out to-day!' I dressed, I went into one of their cars; they had a private room for me [in Oshawa] so that I could be incognito there because there would be a charge that we Communists are running the new unions."[56]

Although publicly denying any CIO-communist link-up, Salsberg was operating with party approval behind the scene as the militant strike began; he persuaded the strikers "to utilize the strike as a means of organizing all Canadian auto workers in the United Auto Workers of America."[57] He asked Homer Martin at the UAW's United States headquarters to send a representative to Oshawa, where, after a brief but tumultuous interval, the decision to call a strike was taken and a union formed, the first major one in the entire Canadian automobile industry[58] and a momentous victory for the party in its long struggle for industrial unions. Salsberg kept a particularly keen watching brief on auto union developments. In November 1938 he wrote a lengthy letter to Joe Spence, his contact at the Ford Windsor plants, commenting on developments there. They were "symptomatic of the dangerous undercurrents now prevailing in the Union." Advising that we "must do all in our power to halt ... divisions within the leadership [and] divert the dissatisfaction which may be fully justified, from dissipating itself into reckless personal squabbles," he urged Spence to undertake a "revived organizational drive, the strengthening of the Union within the plants, and the firm establishment of a united collective leadership."[59] "Organizing the unorganized" in mass production industries, Joe helped to achieve what Irving Abella describes as "a landmark in the history of the Canadian labour movement ... next only to the [1919] Winnipeg General Strike."[60]

As a party stalwart, Salsberg was quick to denounce what he called the "disruptive tactics" of Trotskyists in the union movement.[61] In March 1937 he accused one Potts of being a Trotskyist agent who had nefarious designs on the Toronto Coal Handlers' Union. Other agents of the "Prophet Outcast" had infiltrated themselves into the Toronto local of the Canadian Shoe Workers and Allied Trades with a view to blocking the election of a progressive-minded business agent, while yet another Trotskyist was allegedly obstructing progress in the dressmakers' union.[62]

Files on his work during 1938 as permanent chairman of the CPC's National Trade Union Commission (TUC) reveal that Salsberg was in regular correspondence with party members or sympathizers in industries across the dominion and kept a weather eye out for promising young organizers like C.S. Jackson of the United Electrical Workers.[63] Be it the organizational status or problems of workers on buttons and shirts in Kitchener; needle trades in Montreal, Toronto, Winnipeg, or Edmonton;

hard-rock mining in Val D'Or, Sudbury, and Timmins; automobiles in Oshawa, St Catharines, Windsor, and Regina; ships on the Great Lakes; boilers and canning in Vancouver; textiles in Cornwall; forestry at the Lakehead and in British Columbia; or steel, rubber, furniture, printing, railways, confectionery, retail stores, stationary engines from Glace Bay and Dalhousie to London and Edmonton, Salsberg was in the know, on the alert for RCMP spies and informants, and aggressively advancing the formation of industrial unions. To Tom Ewen out in the field and to sympathizers everywhere Salsberg wrote detailed, frequent letters passing on information, advising on tactics, and, sometimes, ordering action, while receiving from these quarters frequent intelligence and appeals for guidance. He had no patience for incompetents or Trotskyites.[64]

Few details escaped his attention. He ordered Jack Scott to hustle out to Sarnia because "all hell has broken loose" at a foundry workers' strike there. To a correspondent in Port Arthur he wrote in April 1938 of the urgent need "to broaden the campaign to eliminate the medical racket [a contract system of medical fees] now forced upon the lumber workers of Ontario."[65] He tried to rally support for strikes from unionists everywhere. "We must do all in our power," he wrote in July 1938 in a letter intended for broad distribution to "Dear Comrades" "to help the union win the strike" of the United Hatters, Cap, and Millinery Workers International against the Fashion Hat Company of Toronto.[66] He summoned "Comrades" to meetings of the TUC with the mandate "You must attend!" and demanded an explanation if they did not show up. Rival unions got short shrift; during the bitter conflict, well described by Ruth Frager, between the communist-controlled International Fur Workers Union (affiliated to the CIO) and an AFL union controlled by Max Federman in the fur industry in 1938, Salsberg confided to a correspondent in New York that while the "abominable 'boss rule' which the Federman machine maintained in the union was liquidated ... the struggle for honest, broad, collective leadership was not prosecuted in an aggressive fashion."[67] He saw the party members as shock troops in the battle for labour's interests.

In the wake of the CSU victory in 1938, he demanded that "feverish activity must be developed in every port along the Canadian side of the Great Lakes ... Our Party must lend every assistance to the Seamen's Union."[68] Party men must get jobs on the boats, he urged, cautioning that "this should be handled carefully and those who will secure employment should be properly prepared for their union and Party tasks aboard ship." In the summer of 1938 he conducted a voluminous correspondence with

"Dear Comrades" across the nation about the forthcoming convention of the Trades and Labour Congress, urging them to "take the necessary steps to guarantee the broadest mass campaign for trade union unity" by "stress[ing] the importance of the unity of the International Trade Unions in Canada to the workers and the people at large" and the necessity of keeping the AFL and CIO united.[69] After the convention, Salsberg exulted over the defeat of "the splitting forces" and urged comrades to continue their vigilance, noting that the struggle for peace in the trade union movement should be extended to national and international affairs, where fascism threatened peace abroad and Quebec's Padlock Law menaced civil rights at home.[70]

In pursuit of labour unity, in 1938 and 1939 Salsberg opposed the expulsion of CIO-affiliated unions from the TLC, at whose annual convention he was "working behind the scenes and directing the communist party machine," arguing that division and discord would weaken the labour movement.[71] In 1940 he challenged CPC policy on trying to prevent the CIO from uniting with the All-Canadian Congress of Labour and, believing that the communists would be able to influence this larger formation, argued strenuously for the merger.[72] With Toronto lawyer Jacob L. Cohen, Salsberg drafted the constitution of the new body,[73] and he remained key party liaison to CIO unions emerging in the Ontario auto, mine-mill, rubber, steel, electrical, lake shipping, textile, and clothing sectors as the party's "commissar of the trade unions."[74] "It was the Communists under the able guidance of J.B. Salsberg," Irving Abella states, "who helped organize most of the CIO unions in Canada in the 1930s" and helped to keep them under communist control. Through the early 1940s he was active in shifting the affiliations of several unions to radical formations and in fostering the growth of the TLC. At the same time, he was still closely attentive to the needs of his own community. Approached by representatives of Toronto ritual slaughterers (*shochtim*) who felt exploited by the city's kosher butchers and packing houses, he helped them form a union. These men, who were by definition Orthodox Jews, felt completely at home working with Salsberg, the "antichrist," as he jocularly referred to himself. So he arranged to meet them well outside the Jewish community, in an east end location, to explain to them the steps to follow. He also used his influence in May 1939 to successfully mediate between the Hebrew Master Painters and a union.[75]

Salsberg's philosophy of labour was simple and direct: communists must "organize the unorganized," and though the slogan might not have originated with him, he became associated with it throughout his life, and not just during his years in the Workers' Unity League. But he was not a one-note Charlie; he thought about these issues deeply and his library of well-thumbed books indicates that his ideas emerged from his familiarity with the classical literature in the field, from frequent discussions with his colleagues in Canada and the United States, and from reading the party press. (He had read some of Marx's and Lenin's works, A. Lozovsky's *Marx and the Trade Unions*, and W.Z. Foster's *American Trade Unionism*.) By the early 1930s he emerged, as Manley states, as the party's "leading labour theoretician and tactician."[76] With his experience, person-on-person skills, connections, and outstanding qualities as an orator, Salsberg accumulated some enormously important achievements, and it is clear that he had earned deep respect, and a minor if accidental "cult of personality" in the ranks of the radical Left. Moreover, as Ian McKay observes, Salsberg's "relative independence of the 'party line' is very interesting and important – it essentially contradicts the 'traditionalist' emphasis on Party people as minions of Moscow, and the issues on which Salsberg is exerting his independence are not minor ones ... but go to the heart of its 'industrial strategy.'"[77]

Salsberg's theoretical background is suggested in his lecture notes for a course he taught at the Labour College in 1938 on the history of trade unions in Canada. He began with Karl Marx's dictum that "without being aware of it, (trade unions) become the focal points for the organization of the working class, just as the medieval municipalities and communities bec[a]me such for the bourgeoisie."[78] He stressed that the development of the proletariat, however, could not rest with trade unions, which, as Marx wrote, are a "lever in the hands of this class for the struggle against the political power of its exploiters" (citing Marx's 1866 article on trade unions for the IWA congress in Geneva). Referring to what he understood as the opposition to workers and unions in the writings of Proudhon, Bakunin, and Lasalle, Salsberg emphasized that the modern business unionism of Samuel Gompers, Percy Bengough, and others was opposed to unions taking independent political action. But Salsberg emphasized that "under different circumstances and in different periods lenin, stalin and all communists carried on [the] struggle with social reformism and with bourgeois idealogies as to the true role and tasks of trade unions."

His point was that trade unions alone would not win state power for the proletariat. "Only a Marxist-Leninist party ... a party of a special kind ... the highest form of class organization [is] capable of doing that." A Marxist party, nevertheless, seeks "to win labor and unions for [the] struggle for socialism not by replacing, competing with, dictating to, or capturing unions, but by helping them to organize and participating in all their struggles, by saving them from puerile opportunism, ... [and the] opportunist swamp." Communists must educate the trade union movement "to understand [the] class character of its problems and struggles, ... to raise [their] political consciousness," and to strive to "politicize [the] movement to recognize [the] primacy of [its] political tasks." Union members must be helped to see the "overall national and international problems which affect [their] industry and local affairs." This was the path to victory, "the winning of labour and unions for [the] struggle for socialism."[79]

Alongside other party luminaries like Stanley Ryerson, Tim Buck, Leslie Morris, Stewart Smith, William Kashtan, and Paul Phillips, Salsberg gave lectures on the history of the labour movement in Canada at various schools or seminars for party organizers, such as the one held at a Finnish camp near Sudbury in the summer of 1946.[80] His notes indicate that he opened with a discourse on the One Big Union and the Trade Union Educational League and stressed the need for trade union unity and industrial labour organization. He argued that the "Bourgeois Offensive" against the labour movement in the 1920s, the growing belief in "American exceptionalism," along with production-line speed-up and industrial rationalization, which put additional pressures on workers, all stymied the move towards unity. The 1929 stock market crash and the ensuing depression further weakened this cause. It was this situation that the Workers' Unity League was intended to improve. Its successes, achieved in "years of struggle" between 1929 and 1935, were significant. But the world situation, Salsberg lectured, including the rise of Hitler and the emergence of powerful fascist forces throughout the world in the mid-1930s, led labour progressives to believe that the Congress of Industrial Organizations in 1936 and 1937 offered a better hope for labour unity in Canada, especially in basic industries like steel, automobiles, and rubber.

The fight both for labour's rights and against fascism was, in Salsberg's mind, part of the same process before and during the Second World War, at least after June 1941. Following the war, he stressed that the economic expansion in Canada was accompanied by strong pressures from the United States to dominate the world economy.

After reviewing in detail the achievement of the 1930s, Salsberg stressed that four "cardinal points" characterized the Canadian labour scene: the Left had taken the lead in (1) organizing the unorganized, (2) achieving economic and social gains for the Canadian working class, (3) the struggle for trade union unity, and (4) the struggle against United

States domination of the Canadian union movement, the Canadian Sea-man's Union being "the most glaring example."[81]

While in the mid-1930s Salsberg began shifting his principal focus to politics and contests for political office under the party banner, he re-tained a strong interest in labour matters. Besides his lectures, he wrote regularly on these topics well into the 1950s for the *Canadian Tribune* and other party publications, always stressing that the goal of fair employ-ment practices and the pursuit of decent wages and working conditions for the working class were at the very core of what the communist move-ment stood for. Labour unity was just as important to Salsberg in the climate of the fascist and Nazi menace of the 1930s, and especially after the German attack on the Soviet Union in June of 1941, and he was one of the party's most outspoken activists against fascism. After June 1941, when "the war became kosher," as he put it in a late-in-life interview, and "all the attention of the Communists immediately overnight turned for pro-war," he attempted to quash an incipient shipbuilders' strike as far away as British Columbia.[82] "I got on the phone," he recalled, and said: "You can't do that! This war is a war we are for and you're not going to upset ... What the hell do you think this is? ... [Do] not stop the pro-duction of ships." Salsberg also played a major role in the formation of the International Union of Mine, Mill and Smelter Workers in northern Ontario.

In his pamphlet *A Wartime Labour Policy for United All Out War Effort* he wrote that fascism "has ... led toward the unification of all labor and progressive forces ... [and] forged a universal determination to wipe out the beastly menace from the face of the globe."[83] Labour unity and a democratic wartime labour policy were integral parts of the effort to achieve national unity and an all-out war effort ... all component parts of the one all-embracing aim – the destruction of the Nazi-Fascist power, ... the freeing of mankind from this gangrenous disease and the ... causes which brought that scourge into being."[84] Salsberg continued to present his views on labour issues to the CPC's national committee, urging in his May 1947 report a far-reaching seven-point program to mobilize the la-bour movement for the coming battle against "monopoly capitalism['s]" attacks in the context of economic crisis and the threat of war. His spirited weekly columns in the *Canadian Tribune* during the late 1940s advocated union militancy and solidarity in the face of ever-rapacious capitalism. And he was scathing in his coverage of union leaders Aaron Mosher and Charles Millard, whom he accused of raiding and splitting established unions and of virulent red-baiting.[85]

In the meantime, following the party's decision to enter electoral politics, Salsberg ran for one of the two aldermanic seats in Ward 4, the provincial riding of St Andrew, and the federal constituency of Spadina, all of them seats that Jews had previously held.[86] Toronto's Jewish community was still adjusting to the wave of immigrants from Poland, many from the Kielce region in the southwest of the country (judging from the names of the city's hometown associations, the *landmanshaftn*), in the 1920s experiencing severe economic depression. As well, modernization of the Polish economy led, in B. Garncaska-Kadry's words, to "severe displacement inside Jewish society." The immigrants and their children were on the whole making their accommodation, in many cases successfully. Their occupational profile in these years showed interesting diversity, most importantly, the emergence of a significant class of professionals and small-business owners.[87] While many earned their living exclusively within its confines as rabbis, ritual slaughterers, and suppliers of foods – butchers, bakers, delicatessen operators, grocers, poultry dealers, and fishmongers – by 1931 a rising professional cadre of accountants, insurance and real estate agents, doctors, dentists, lawyers, opticians, and pharmacists had emerged, many of them university graduates. Tradesmen abounded, including barbers, blacksmiths, building contractors, carpenters, electricians, machinists, painters and decorators, plasterers, plumbers, printers, shoe repairers, and tinsmiths. Many operated penny-capitalist enterprises as grocers, cleaners and dyers, confectioners, tobacconists and small-shop owners selling dry goods, furniture, crockery, and men's and ladies retail. At the same time, a substantial Jewish working class persisted. In the clothing factories and contractors' sweatshops in the lower Spadina Avenue area, thousands of Jewish operators and pressers toiled amid difficult conditions in crowded, unsanitary, and potentially dangerous shops. They were dogged by seasonal unemployment, broken union agreements, strikes, lockouts, and violence. This was Salsberg's turf, which also included other ethnic groups: blacks, Ukrainians, Poles, and others who shared the uncertainties of the immigrant poor in the 1930s.

Salsberg stood for Ward 4 in 1934 and for Spadina in 1935, both times unsuccessfully. In the contest for Spadina in 1935 Salsberg pleaded for a united front with the CCF, arguing that "only united working class action and … the election of tried … leaders will stave off the coming attacks and accelerate the movement for a socialist Canada" and prevent wage cuts to the riding's 10,000 needle workers and 3000 railroad employees.[88] This appeal failed and Salsberg was defeated soundly. He

stood for a Ward 4 aldermanic seat in 1936, appealing for unemployment assistance, slum clearance for better housing, higher taxes, and
cheaper coal prices, but was defeated again.[89] Nevertheless, he kept up
his campaigning for the underdog, appealing for higher rent allowances
for those on relief, better housing, and joining picket lines to stop evictions. "We [communists] were all as green as grass in electioneering of
that kind," he later revealed, explaining that "the language used in ap-
proaching large numbers of people had to be learned. The sectarianism
of the movement at that time was such that one consciously had to make
an effort to speak somewhat differently to the uninitiated that one encountered at [an] election meeting than one used at Party meetings ...
or meetings organized by the left-wing for a special purpose."[90]

Despite mounting a very vigorous campaign for the St Andrew provincial riding in 1937, Salsberg was defeated again, but by a mere 151
votes. The contest had been a bitter and hotly contested effort to unseat
Liberal John Glass, a prominent uptown Jewish lawyer.[91] The CCF's insistence on running its own candidate (despite contrary advice from David
Lewis, CCF national secretary) contributed to Joe's defeat, while alleged
electoral fraud might also have been a factor. With Salsberg's defeat, "the
Jewish people of Ontario heaved a sigh of relief," one source claimed,
"for whether it is openly admitted or not, the election of Salsberg ... in
St Andrew, which is predominantly Jewish, would have been interpreted
by all anti-Jewish forces as proof positive that all Jews are Communists,
and his defeat has saved the Jews of Canada not only from serious embarrassment but perhaps from serious consequences. For such reasons the
battle of St Andrew will go down in the history of Canadian Jews as one
of considerable consequence to their future happiness in this country."[92]
Salsberg had spared no effort in this campaign, supported by a party machine that distributed leaflets and other materials across the riding once
or sometimes twice daily. But Salsberg was elected to city council in 1938
(and again in 1943) just as his communist confreres were successfully
contesting political office elsewhere in Canada; the party had elected
one member to the Manitoba legislature in 1936 and two Winnipeg city
councillors in 1938.[93]

Salsberg's 1938 victory did not come easily. The prominent uptown
lawyer Samuel Factor, Member of Parliament for Spadina (who had
bested Salsberg in this riding in 1935) and a former alderman for Ward
4, weighed in during the campaign, advising Jewish voters to cast their
ballots against Salsberg and "the subversive doctrine of communism."
The *Globe and Mail* endorsed these admonitions, saying that "Jewish

electors have a special responsibility in this respect, because the Communist Party is frequently described as a Jewish organization," and adding the universally espoused lie that "indications are that a large percentage, and probably a majority, of Communists are Jews."[94] Meanwhile, Factor declared that it was the duty of Jewish electors to "block ballot support to Communists like Salsberg, and the strongly anti-communist *Telegram* noted that the Toronto Zionist Council urged Jews not to vote for any communist candidate "because the Communist Party is an avowed enemy of our great aspirations in Palestine ... [and] because Communism in its present form, with its terrorism, violence and dictatorship is a calamity to mankind in general."[95] The Orange Order, which, legendarily, exercised powerful, but indirect influence in municipal politics, cannot have been sympathetic to the candidacy of a Jewish communist.

Winning, nevertheless, at the hustings, on New Year's Day 1938 Salsberg took his seat and immediately was on the qui vive, often working closely with Stewart Smith, an alderman for Ward 5, on a number of social-welfare issues before council such as opposition to hikes in gas rates, threatened hospital closures, and TTC drivers' safety. Not only did he serve actively on several committees, but he tried also – often with a dash of humour – to defend the weak and dispel ignorance, especially in those who ought to have known better. Responding to an allegation, in February 1938, by mayor Ralph Day that the city was home to twenty-one communist schools, Salsberg quipped: "He shouldn't let Inspector Marshall [of the City of Toronto Police] be his spiritual guide."[96] While acknowledging that a number of part-time Jewish schools did indeed exist, (including one run by the Labour League, a leftist forerunner to the United Jewish People's Order), Salsberg pointed out that "even the Scottish people have a small class at which children are taught Gaelic [and] ... the Germans, Italians, Russians, Ukrainians and other nationalities have their own institutions." Salsberg stood for re-election in December 1938, with strong support from the *Toronto Star*, which hailed him and fellow communist Stewart Smith for the "excellence of their work in council," while arguing that "their interest in the underprivileged classes ... is not communism but humanitarianism," perhaps in recognition of their efforts to get jobs and resist evictions in their wards. He was defeated, a victory celebrated by the *Globe and Mail* as helping to "stamp out the Communist menace."[97]

Salsberg – and, no doubt, other communists on Toronto City Council – was certainly being watched and his activities fully recorded. Besides constant RCMP surveillance, the Ontario Provincial Police (OPP) were on guard. A report in June 1940 by Alex S. Wilson, a top official in the OPP's Criminal Investigation, on Salsberg and other so-called "definite" communists reveals a high level of police scrutiny. Wilson warned that "in these days and times, with the situation in Europe such as it is, we can ill afford to take any chance of harbouring any members or sympathizers of any subversive group."[98] And, as noted above, the Toronto City Police, whose chief constable, Dennis Draper (1928–46), had been harassing "Reds," for years kept its eyes on Salsberg and other communists, whom they deemed "a constant threat to public order and constitutional authority." In June 1938, Draper presented a report to Mayor Day, entitled ominously "the Red Shadow,"[99] on communist activity throughout Canada, especially in Toronto. "Red Squad" detectives reported that there were no fewer than 20,000 communists in the city and some twenty party branches! Salsberg poured ridicule on these charges while pointing out that Draper had not carried out a similar investigation of fascist occurrences in the city; Draper, Salsberg thundered, had even written to fascist leader Ross Taylor expressing "the fullest satisfaction with that organization." While "the Red Shadow" died a sudden death, the Red Squad was undeterred. In a lengthy report the following year, Detective William Nursey warned his superiors that alderman Salsberg "had access to valuable City records."[100] (Like what, one wonders, applications for dog licences?)

Joining Salsberg in defeat in the annual municipal elections of January 1939 were six out of seven communists, according to the watchful RCMP, because of "stiff opposition on the part of the people and organizations pledged to fight Communism ... the United League of Canada, the Board of Trade and the Canadian Corps Association."[101] He was strongly opposed by members of the Jewish establishment, notably Rabbi Samuel Sachs, who held the pulpit of the tony Goel Tzedec synagogue. One party observer of the scene, Beatrice Fernyhough, commented: "There is one sure thing, the club of anti-semitism has been held over the Jewish people's heads and they were afraid to vote for Communist Candidates." Though defeated, Salsberg had increased his share of the popular vote by about 25 per cent. He would fight again for Ward 4 the following year, although it was to be a disaster.

On 23 August, news that Soviet Russia and Nazi Germany had signed a nonaggression pact created confusion among the radical Left. The RCMP, hardly an unbiased source, likened the news to "the effect of a bomb exploding in the midst of the Communist Party, leaving ... dark consternation and bewilderment ... Profound confusion and embarrassment was manifest in every language section of the ... Party ... most[ly] by the Jewish and Polish sections ... On the day news reached Canada, groups of Jewish Communists [and, no doubt Jews of other political persuasions] could be seen on the streets everywhere talking, unable to determine the magnitude of the stunning blow ... At a complete loss to understand the significance of the situation, they added to the confusion by indulging in disruptive arguments."[102] The report noted that "Jewish supporters of the Communist Party rose to loud denunciation and withdrew their support for the time being. They were not able to understand the reason for this betrayal, or for Stalin's joining hands with their most hated foe, Hitler. The foundation for their support of the Communist policies had suddenly caved in."

Within a month many Jewish members had quit the party. The Mounties harboured the belief that it had fully 3500 Jewish members and that 70 per cent of them had decamped.[103] Although the CPC's central committee supported the Soviet Union's action, after 3 September, labelling the war an imperialist war, Salsberg, along with Fred Rose of Montreal, took an independent position, declaring that "Canadian labor is, more than any other section of the population, anxious to achieve a decisive victory over fascism [and] desires a complete defeat of the [Nazi] regime." While repeating the line that Britain and France "are not unfriendly to the fascist forms of government and ... hoped to direct the arsenal and strengthened the Nazi monster towards the Soviet Union," Salsberg proclaimed that "labour stands for the fullest support of Poland [and] seeks the restoration of full national independence" for Czechoslovakia and Austria.

But he soon knuckled under to party discipline.[104] On the eve of the election, which was to take place on New Year's Day 1940, Rabbi Samuel Sachs, in an obvious attempt to scupper Salsberg, appealed to Toronto Jews "not to allow themselves to be deceived by the sheep's clothing of righteousness these Communists don at election time ... It is the type of audacity that has no match anywhere except in Nazi Germany."[105] While the good rabbi's plea may not have had much influence on the Jewish working class, his appeal nevertheless reflected the wider community's fear and revulsion. Meanwhile, Jack Lipinsky points out, the Joint Public Relations Committee of the Canadian Jewish Congress and B'nai Brith, "terrified" by the prospect of Salsberg returning to city council, were distributing statements to the press opposing communism.[106] Lipinsky states that Congress also sent "volunteers" to visit Jewish homes and businesses asking for the removal of Salsberg's and other communist candidates' campaign signs, distributed anti-communist "educational packages," and recruited Holy Blossom's Rabbi Maurice Eisendrath to make a radio appeal to Jewish voters. These assaults were successful and Salsberg was resoundingly defeated, garnering less than half of the votes he had won only a year earlier.[107]

When the round-up of communists began under the Defence of Canada Regulations in 1939, Salsberg was in hiding, somewhere in the Toronto area presumably, although, as Ian McKay states, "this was part of an orchestrated tactic involving many other CPC militants." He turned himself in to the police in July 1942 and was incarcerated in the Don Jail.[108] He was charged with being a member of the Communist Party of Canada, which had been declared illegal, and with failing to register under the National Registration Regulations. With the aid of his lawyer, Jacob L. Cohen, and the campaign to free him on the grounds that "his services in aiding the war effort would be extremely effective at this time, for he [has] the support of workers throughout Canada," he was released the following October,[109] like most jailed party members, after only a few months in custody.[110] And he lost no time getting back into politics.

Salsberg was re-elected as alderman in January 1943, besting Nathan Phillips, who had represented Ward 4 for nineteen years and continued as alderman – this was a two-seat ward – alongside Salsberg, and defeating incumbent David Balfour.[111] Balfour was such a doughty foe of communism that he demanded that both Salsberg's and Stewart Smith's successful election in Ward 5 be set aside until the legality of their candidacies – as members of a banned party[112] – be determined; his objection went nowhere. Salsberg was appointed to several committees and, again collaborating with Stewart Smith, took spirited part in current welfare issues such as the sudden jump in the price of coal, the conditions of work at the municipal abattoir, and the unavailability of ice during the summer.[113] He objected to the statement by Red Squad veteran Detective William Nursey, now an inspector and warden of the Toronto Civilian Defence Committee, that the CDC would be necessary postwar to "suppress labour disturbances and things of that sort."[114] Salsberg did not contest Ward 4 again because, as of 4 August 1943, he was the newly elected member of the Ontario legislature for St Andrew. But, by this time, he had other matters on his mind – disturbing rumours from the Soviet Union of a re-emergence of anti-Semitism.

While virulent and violent anti-Semitism was an old story in tsarist Russia, this poison was supposed to be eliminated in the new revolutionary system. Old habits and attitudes did not die, however, and as

readers of Isaac Babel's graphic "Red Cavalry" stories know, army units
loyal to the communists perpetrated some horrific pogroms against Jews
during the Civil War.[115] With the massive social and economic transformations under way in the USSR during the late 1920s, when significant
numbers of Jews moved to new areas and into the industrial workforce,
anti-Semitism took a sharp upturn,[116] despite the fact that the criminal
code made it an offence. Mikhail Kolinin, the president of the Soviet
Republic, noted in 1926 that "the Russian intelligentsia is perhaps more
anti-Semitic today than it was under Tsarism."[117] Articles about anti-Semitic incidents appeared in *Komsomolskaya pravda*, the young communist newspaper, while leading writers, including Maxim Gorky, publicly
denounced anti-Semitism as it spread among Soviet workers in factories
and collectives, where violent, sometimes deadly, attacks were not un-
common. Even Leon Trotsky, before the 1917 Revolution perhaps the
quintessential "non-Jewish Jew,"[118] Bryan Palmer observes, "could not
escape the 'fact' of his Jewishness"[119] and, when Lenin offered him the
pivotally important post of commissar of the interior, turned it down because his acceptance might stimulate Russian anti-Semitism.[120] Because
so many Jews supported Trotsky, latent anti-Semitism coincided with
"ideological hostilities."[121]

Salsberg's concerns about the Soviet regime's attitude towards Jewish
cultural life had grown since the 1930s, when the Jewish section of the
Communist Party of the Soviet Union [CPSU], *Yevsektsiya*, was suddenly
terminated, Jewish schools were closed, and cultural life restricted.[122] In
the words of David Shneer: "The project to create a secular Yiddish culture and a people who identified with that culture" had not succeeded
because of the lack of Jewish support and government policies. At the
same time, all expressions of Jewish national identity were targeted for
suppression, while anti-Semitism, which had been severely suppressed
by Lenin, re-emerged as Stalin consolidated his political control. Jews
who were prominent in politics – especially Trotsky and others of Jewish origin who opposed Stalin's policies – were singled out, tried, and
imprisoned (where many died) as "enemies of the people," while efforts
were under way to exclude them from high party echelons, the state
apparatus, and the army.[123] "Old Bolsheviks," former Bundists, Zionists,
and anarchists were denounced and purged as spies, deviationists, fascists, Trotskyites, Bukharinites, National Democrats, and "hangers-on
of the bourgeoisie." Jewish communist periodicals were shut down and
back issues removed from libraries. From his base in Toronto, Salsberg
picked up on some of these events. In interviews he gave in the late

1970s, he remembered experiencing "a turning point" in his life in 1939 because he realized that during the previous two years, "Jewish institutions began to wither away."[124] The Birobidjan project (to create a Jewish autonomous territory in the far-eastern reaches of the Soviet Union) was faltering, and one of the heads of that community had been executed. And while many Jewish institutions ceased functioning, inquiries from abroad went unanswered.[125]

"So a lot of us began to wonder," Salsberg recalled, "what the heck is going on?" Knowing that he could not raise the matter in the CPC's national executive committee (then called the Political Bureau) because "they would say either I've lost faith or that I am influenced by bourgeois ideas," he decided to go to the Soviet Union to see for himself, revealing his purpose to only Dora and a few friends like *Vochenblatt* editor Joshua Gershman and two other Jewish comrades whom he met in Paris in early July 1939 while on his way to an international congress of communist trade unionists. Proceeding from there to Moscow,[126] he was introduced to Georgi Dimitrov, head of the Third Communist International, probably through Tom Ewen, the CPC's representative at the Comintern.[127]

Professing sympathy for Salsberg's concerns, Dimitrov trotted out the most convenient excuses: the worldwide menace of Trotskyism and other counter-revolutionary forces, besides the possibilities for espionage. He did, however, promise to establish a joint Soviet–United States party commission to investigate these matters, but it never materialized.[128] As well, he promised to look into Salsberg's request for allowing some German Jewish refugees into the Soviet Union, but nothing came of this either. Inquiries that Joe made from two American Jewish communists living in Moscow yielded only evasions. So he got nothing from his trip to Moscow, except the opportunity of seeing his family in Poland on his way back to Canada. Though frustrated and puzzled, he wrote later in his famous nine-article series in the fall 1956 issues of *Vochenblatt*, the weekly serving the Yiddish-speaking segment of the party, that he decided to keep his suspicions "out of the public eye [although] perhaps in retrospect it would have been better if I had spoken out." This was, he said, "a most painful experience."[129]

But what could Salsberg do? Had he left the party in 1939, where could he hang his hat, given that he was a committed revolutionary? Certainly not at the Co-operative Commonwealth Federation (CCF), which he had reviled as "one of the greatest hindrances to the establishment of socialism in Canada" since that party's emergence in 1933,[130] where David Lewis had set his face against any incursions from the radical Left, nor would the Canadian Congress of Labour have welcomed him for similar reasons.[131] Instead, he decided to stay attuned to the situation of the Jews in the Soviet Union. In this respect he was like Jewish communists in the United States, Paul Novick (editor of New York's *Morgen Freiheit*), Reuben Saltzman, and Itche Goldberg; Joshua Gershman (editor of the *Vochenblatt*) in Toronto; and Haim Sloves in Paris, all of whom were hopeful for improvement.[132] Back in Toronto, Salsberg discussed matters with Tim Buck, who remembered that Salsberg "was quite convinced that it was being handled properly because it corresponded with Comrade Stalin's thesis on the national question, and he had confidence in Comrade Stalin." Buck asked him to keep quiet for the sake of the cause.[133] Within the party, however, he encountered considerable antagonism over his daring to address the "Jewish Question" without approval. Such *chutzpah*!!

He stayed silent, but he could well have been puzzled at hearing, while on his way back home, of the recently signed Molotov-Ribbentrop pact, which effectively took the Soviet Union out of the impending war with Nazi Germany. That infamous agreement, historian Gennadi Kostrychenko points out, "contributed significantly to the infection of the [Soviet] state organism with this disease ... [as] new, anti-Jewish tendencies surfaced in the state machinery."[134] These developments were directed principally by Georgii Malenkov, who operated under the guidance of Josef Stalin himself. Although many Jewish communists in Canada and the United States had quit the party over the pact, those who remained "within the fold," Henry Srebrnik points out, "began to reassure themselves that, after all, the Communists had been in the forefront of the battle against fascism for decades," and that the pact was a "brilliant move by Stalin."[135] Articles in *Vochenblatt* hailed the results as highly beneficial to the Jews of eastern Poland, the Baltic states, Bukovina and Bessarabia, now controlled by the USSR.

Following the June 1941 German assault on the Soviet Union, Salsberg, though still in hiding, joined the party's enthusiastic support for the war effort. Writing articles in the party press, he urged labour unity, the utmost in war production, and a second front against the Germans. He served on the Communist Labour Total War Committee, promoting national war production.[136] He wrote for the party press, urging all efforts to destroy the Nazis. He would have been present at the mass rally in Maple Leaf Gardens in early September 1943 to welcome representatives from the Soviet Union's Jewish Anti-Fascist Committee, Itsik Feffer and Shlomo Michoels. They addressed the crowd in Yiddish, urging maximum support for the Russian war effort. Such loyalty to that cause seems to have blinded Salsberg – and most other communists – to the news, deeply disturbing to many like David Lewis who joined the international outcry, of the murder on Stalin's orders in Moscow earlier that year of Victor Alter and Heinrich Erlich, eminent leaders of the Jewish Polish Bund.[137] The successful prosecution of the war took precedence over matters such as these, however, and Salsberg now faced the biggest challenge of his life as member of the Ontario legislature for St Andrew.

All the while, Joe never lost touch with his family, nor Dora with hers. Gatherings at their home and, more often, at his parents' at 59 Cecil Street, took place on Jewish holidays, notably on Passover, the annual festival of freedom from slavery in Egypt. Assembled at the table sat a numerous array of sisters, brothers, their spouses and children, along with invited guests and, likely, a few strangers who had drifted by. Abraham presided as the story of slavery and redemption unfolded according to ancient tradition; he would point to the matzah, the unleavened bread, intoning in Hebrew, "This is the bread of affliction which our forefathers ate in the land of Egypt." Later he would proclaim, "Let all who are hungry come and eat" as the aromas of Sarah-Gitel's wonderful food filled the room, followed by many songs of praise and legend, Joe's melodious baritone in full throat until the ending exhortation of "Next year in Jerusalem!"

Chapter Four

"From a Human Point of View"

Joe Salsberg's twelve-year career in the Ontario legislature from 1943 to 1955 as member for St Andrew gave him ample room to pursue the goals of social and economic justice inherent in his collectivist ideals. Destined to exclusion from a governing party, Salsberg, until 1951 in company with the feisty Cape Breton–born Alexander A. "Alex" MacLeod (1902–70), who represented the neighbouring mixed ethnic riding of Bellwoods, was the government's most dogged critic, the member who with astonishing tenacity and patience single-mindedly pointed out shortcomings in bills before the House, as he once put it, from "a human point of view."[1] His incessant fault-finding was always accompanied by constructive comment pointing to reasonable improvements and helpful clarification in a spirit of concession and conciliation he hoped would win support in the House, despite his minority status there. Once accused of not being able to "take it" from government members irritated by his frequent needling, Salsberg replied: "I have been 'taking it' from honourable members for years and I can 'take it' better than all of them … all seventy-nine of them [who] have to take criticism for a few minutes. So it is time for them to take it now. I have never sat down and been intimidated by them. Their numbers do not overpower me or overawe me so I ask them to have patience for a while and take a bit of criticism."[2]

Salsberg was victorious in St Andrew just five days before Fred Rose, a fellow communist, won the Montreal federal riding of Cartier, defeating incumbent John Judah Glass, a prominent Jewish lawyer who had held the riding for the Liberals since 1934. Salsberg had faced down strong opposition from the Zionist Organization of Toronto, which pointed out that communists aided and abetted Arab terrorists and declared "communism even in its present form … is a calamity to mankind in general

and to the Jewish people in particular."[3] Just as serious was the opposition from Co-operative Commonwealth Federation (CCF) candidate
Murray Cotterill, who had no chance of winning. Hoping for a united
Left, Salsberg had offered to co-operate with the CCF in the legislature
and "in the trade unions, the factories, the mines, the mills, and the
fields to consolidate this mighty progressive force in our province." But
to no avail. Cotterill was put forward, Salsberg believed, as "spite tactics"
to prevent the election of a non-CCFer representing trade union interests, despite countervailing pressure on the party from many, including
the United Auto Workers, who wanted reciprocity from the Labour-Progressive Party (LPP; the new name of the Communist Party of Canada
since 1940) to allow the CCF to win in a Windsor riding.[4] That party
might well have been smarting from Salsberg's attacks on the proposals
to affiliate the Canadian Congress of Labour with the CCF.[5] Still, Salsberg was triumphant, carrying an estimated 90 per cent of the riding's
Jewish vote and over 50 per cent of all votes cast in a four-person race.
He was a popular guy.

His victory in 1943 was very much an ethnic phenomenon. By 1931,
the census of Canada figures showed that the Toronto Jewish community, which was still concentrated in the Spadina-College nexus, was
overwhelmingly working class, with nearly 4871 men and 1814 women
labouring in the city's Jewish-dominated clothing industry that was hidden among the city's factory smokestacks.[6] As well, significant numbers
of Jews worked as furriers, boot and shoe operatives, printers, mechan-
ics, carpenters, painters, hawkers, peddlers, salespersons, domestic servants, and operators of small-scale commercial enterprises.[7] And, given
the general economic downturn during the 1930s, the economic com-
plexion of the community had not improved by 1941, the next census
year. In fact, Jewish and overall employment in the needle trades showed
a significant decline, while the total number of Jews working in manufacturing was virtually unchanged, indicating that economic upward mobil-
ity had levelled off.

Besides living on the economic margins, most new arrivals in the area
felt themselves effectively separated from mainstream Toronto, with its
overwhelming Anglo-Celtic majority, Protestant Orange militancy, and
a prevailing anti-Semitism, along with a general antipathy to all immigrants – even the British. And indeed the Jewish areas constituted an ethnic enclave, with streetscapes that included synagogues, schools, meeting
halls, restaurants, delicatessens, grocery stores, butcher and bakery
shops, and higgledy-piggledy structures housing unions, workers' clubs,

landsmanshaftn, and a wide variety of cultural organizations in which the Yiddish language prevailed. Next to them were enclaves of Ukrainians, Poles, Italians, and other minorities. Thus, while the geographical and cultural separateness of the Jews was not complete, the outbreak of anti-Semitic incidents in the Toronto Beaches area and at Christie Pits in the 1930s, along with restrictive covenants keeping them and other "undesirables" from buying property in most neighbourhoods, and "Gentiles Only" or similarly worded signs at resorts, limited their integration into Toronto society. In his hours-long walks down Spadina and along College Street, and visits to eateries, landsmanshaft meetings, synagogues, and the Labour Lyceum, and out-and-about forays, Salsberg learned of these conditions while offering practical advice, hope, and a twinkly-eyed joke or two. His people just loved him.

What also facilitated Salsberg's victory in 1943 was the campaigning, directed from Moscow through a number of front organizations, variously labelled, that played up the anti-fascist message. Together with the news from the Soviet Union of the Red Army's stupendous victories over the Germans at Stalingrad and Kursk, where the murderers of Jews were at last getting their comeuppance, the Soviet Union and its communist leadership took on a distinctively rosy glow among Jews – and many others. The visit to Toronto in the spring of 1943 by representatives of the Soviet Union's Jewish Anti-Fascist Committee drew tens of thousands of Jews to Maple Leaf Gardens to express their appreciation and admiration for these victories over Nazism. Henry Srebrnik, who studied the communist electoral victories in a Jewish district of London, England, in 1945, notes that the concern of Jews everywhere for the fate of European Jewry made them "amenable to the political entreaties " of Jewish communists who presented themselves as concerned with anti-Semitism and other "items on the Jewish agenda."[8] It was as if only the communists really understood what "Jewish troubles" meant and were doing more than any others to remedy them.

As well, in Toronto Salsberg was correctly seen in the Jewish community as a champion of their detestation of discrimination, which, he stressed, was officially outlawed in the Soviet Union,[9] and thus his campaign was probably unstoppable. Even though the Toronto Yiddish newspaper *Hebraishe Zhurnal* refrained from taking sides in this and most other electoral contests, Salsberg had a well-functioning machine, with dozens of campaigners distributing leaflets, knocking on doors, and organizing street rallies. And, of course, there was Joe himself moving up and down Spadina, across College, and into Kensington Market, greeting, smiling, hugging, and kissing through crowds that seemed to gather around him like flies to honey.[10]

Salsberg's victory was celebrated by hundreds of his supporters. They gathered at the corner of College and Brunswick Streets, where the Jewish left was headquartered, and paraded, gathering hundreds more, a thousand strong – with Salsberg in the lead – towards Spadina. More supporters joined in along the way and the throng moved down Spadina, towards Dundas, with a detour at Joe's parents' house on Cecil Street. Here Abraham – still wondering about G-d's plans for his son's future – thanked them, and Sarah-Gitel, evincing huge pride in her Yosele, bestowed a Yiddish/English blessing: "*Gott zol aich helfen* (May the Lord help you) that you should have such *nachess* (gratification) in your children as we have from our son."[11] "It was late at night," Salsberg remembered. "It was warm, people were sitting outside. They not only applauded ... when they saw me leading the parade, they rushed and we hugged and kissed – strangers. It was a communal affair."

The Ontario legislature at this point was a fractious assembly. Following the 1943 election, which ended the scandal-ridden regime of Liberal Mitchell Hepburn, George Drew's Tories held thirty-eight seats, an increase of nineteen and enough to form a minority government. The CCF, headed by E.B. (Ted) Joliffe, had gone from nil to thirty-four seats, while the Liberals, headed again by Hepburn, came back with fifteen – down from fifty-nine; and the LPP, whose leader was Alexander A. MacLeod, got two. The CCF, which had gained 32.7 per cent of the provincial vote, was now the official Opposition,[12] but was unable to capitalize on its huge success, partly owing to the party's unwillingness to bring down the Drew minority government. The Liberals, having been defeated, were similarly weak and tried to form a "matrimonial relationship" with the two LPP members.[13] In this uncertain parliamentary scene, Salsberg and MacLeod exploited their leverage, however limited, to greatest advantage, focusing on labour and human rights issues.

Although willing to cooperate with the CPC in 1937,[14] David Lewis, the CCF's leading organizer, had no love for the communists, labelling them "not a Canadian party in any real sense but one of Stalin's puppet instruments for the defence of the Soviet Union and of its brand of Communism around the world."[15] As noted above, Salsberg, however, showed few overt signs of being a Stalinist, except in the remotest sense. While he spoke at party rallies that celebrated the Soviet Union, none of his published writings during the 1930s mention Stalin, nor do they champion that country's dramatic social and economic transformations celebrated by so many non-communists; his electioneering literature was also free of this. Even during his 1943 and 1945 campaigns, when sympathy with the Soviet ally and admiration for its astonishing military assault against Nazi Germany were widespread, Salsberg's publicity carried little of it – and no adulation of Stalin, who was recognized as the pivotal figure in the "Great Patriotic War."[16] Salsberg was dubious of the marriage between the CCF and the Canadian Congress of Labour, arguing that the CCF was not interested in giving labour its due weight within the party. It is clear that by the end of the war, Salsberg's party was deeply at odds with the CCF.[17] Lewis by then believed that Salsberg and MacLeod were in a "matrimonial relationship" with Mitch Hepburn's Liberals in the run-up to the 1945 Ontario general election and were part of the communists' "deliberate actions" to undermine the CCF.[18] But this view was not shared by E.B. Joliffe, who recalled that the communists "were not in a position to do anything much except concentrate on getting MacLeod and Salsberg elected ... and I don't recall them playing any real part anywhere else."[19]

Salsberg's first major concern after taking his seat in the legislature was not labour issues, his forte after all, but human rights concerns, specifically discrimination against minorities. Visibly, or otherwise easily detected (by skin colour, names, religion, or command of English), some minorities were having a hard time of it.[20] In southwestern Ontario, white residents of Dresden kept the town's Negro (then the term for African-Canadians) population out of their stores, barbershops, churches, and restaurants; meanwhile, restrictive covenants were employed to keep such "undesirables" from purchasing real estate in certain areas of Canadian cities.[21] Germans, First Nations, blacks, and Asians generally met with the most severe discrimination, but people of east or south European background were frequently subjected to abuse, especially during the 1930s, when "popular opinion blamed immigrants for stealing jobs from Canadians."[22] Jews were singled out for special discrimination. "Gentiles Only" signs often appeared at beaches and resorts; others proclaimed: "No Jews Wanted" or "Restricted." Advertisements for jobs might specify "Christians Only Need Apply."[23]

Sneers and imprecations let Jews and other "foreigners" know where they stood with white Protestant Ontarians; name calling and fistfights in school playgrounds and neighbourhood parks told Jews and other minority children that they were not the equals of the MacGregors and Joneses. Roman Catholics, though hardly a small minority, were not immune to discrimination. The Orange Order still thrived throughout Ontario during the interwar period as the defender of so-called British Protestant values, which often meant discrimination against Roman Catholics; July 12th commemorations of the Battle of the Boyne were often occasions for the expression of hate. Even during the Second World War, when Canadians were fighting to defend freedom and democracy, as Carmela Patrias demonstrates, there was plenty of race hatred and discrimination in Canada.[24]

Salsberg knew about these matters, and many minority members – not just Jews – sought his help, either buttonholing him on Spadina, or showing up at Abella's Lunch or at his office on Saturdays. One such case led to an important outcome. Because he was a Negro, Harry Gairey's son was refused admission to the Icelandia Skating Rink in November 1945, and believing that "the Jews will fight," Gairey went to Salsberg's office (then at the corner of College and Spadina) and told him the whole story. The next day Salsberg accompanied Gairey to a meeting of city council to make his case, and he led a demonstration outside the rink a few months later.[25] In January 1947, Toronto banned discrimination at public recreation and amusement places.[26] Thereafter, Salsberg was a hero to many in the Negro community; supporters campaigned for him and marched with him, proudly under their own banners, in May Day parades.

Salsberg never tired of patrolling his turf. On College Street early one Sunday evening he noticed two young men leaving Becker's Delicatessen and getting into a car with California licence plates. "Wow!" he said to them. "You drove all the way from California for a Toronto corned beef sandwich?"[27] But he sought out his people everywhere, even, according to legend – which cannot now be verified but is eminently believable – by slipping into one or other Spadina-area synagogues on a Sabbath or holiday to join in the singing. He would happily serve in a *minyan* (quorum for prayer), especially if a tenth man was required for the recitation of the *Kaddish* (memorial for the deceased). In his mind, obviously, there was no inconsistency in being a communist and raising his voice to praise the Lord in supplication through ancient Hebrew prayers, even though he did not believe a word of them. Salsberg was a Jew; he enjoyed singing, meeting people, and, possibly, the traditional shot or two of whisky, pieces of herring, and helping of sponge cake after services. And if ever challenged by a party purist for such "deviant" behaviour, Salsberg would likely have replied in his deep baritone – with his massive eyebrows arched theatrically over twinkling eyes – "What's wrong with singing, comrade? We all seek redemption, don't we?"

As a Jew, Salsberg was no stranger to discrimination. At the downtown Lord Lansdowne School he had attended as a boy, and in the
shops where he had worked since age fourteen, he would likely have
witnessed plenty of fights, verbal and physical, and heard the tales from
Jews and members of other minorities of various forms of persecution.
"I am probably the only member of this House who has experienced
discrimination," Salsberg said in the legislature in March 1951 in favour
of the bill to ensure fair remuneration to female employees. "I have experienced the indignity, and very often the disadvantage of being discriminated against."[28] He would have known of treatment meted out to
Toronto Maple Leafs defenceman Alex "Mine Boy" Levinsky and professional boxers Sammy Luftspring and "Baby" Yack, who regularly received
anti-Semitic hoots and jeers from the stands, while Negro athletes had to
endure even worse harassment from Toronto sports fans.[29]

Racial discrimination did not stop there. It was present in employment, housing, and university admissions too. Meanwhile Negroes,
Asians, Jews, Italians, and East Europeans lived in their own enclaves,
often, but not always, out of choice. They sometimes could not get jobs
in certain occupations – even during the Second World War labour short-
ages – and were often relegated to low-level occupations or to precarious
self-employment.[30] Discrimination was routinely practised by insurance
companies, banks, and department stores on the basis of religion and
nationality. These matters were of serious concern to Salsberg, who
together with MacLeod campaigned vigorously to have such practices
banned. They would have been well aware of the efforts mounted since
1938 by the Joint Public Relations Committee of the Canadian Jewish
Congress and the Anti-Defamation League of B'nai Brith to combat anti-
Semitism and other forms of discrimination in Ontario.

Having just taken his seat as the legislature opened in early February
1944, Salsberg set out his position on discrimination of all kinds in a
lengthy letter to Premier George Drew on the "urgent need for provincial legislation" to outlaw these practices in Ontario. Referring to the
current wartime battle against Hitlerism, Salsberg asserted: "History is
filled with evidence that the fight against such forms of discrimination
and persecution is not merely a requirement of the persecuted but a necessity for the well being and progress of society as a whole."[31] This was a
broad-based attack on a multifaceted problem of exclusion on grounds
of race or creed in housing, employment, and education, but Salsberg's
main concern at this point was employment.[32]

To drive his point home with the premier, who seemed inclined to listen because he did not command a majority government, Salsberg attached a memo to his letter citing ten specific instances of recent blatant anti-Semitic and anti-Negro incidents, including a by-law introduced in 1943 at the Port Elgin town council proposing to bar Jews from local hotels and tourist homes.[33] Drew replied, offering to meet Salsberg and MacLeod, but warned that "enlightened people everywhere ... are not agreed that tolerance can be created by compulsion."[34] A few days later, Salsberg handed Drew yet more documentary evidence of discrimination and proposed specific measures to prevent such practises in employment at hotels, restaurants, and recreational facilities,[35] emphasizing that racial and religious restrictions, especially employment, should be given the highest priority.[36] Hoping for Labour-Progressive help to keep his government afloat, Drew acted quickly, despite strong opposition from certain church groups and individuals defending "freedom of Speech" and "Anglo-Saxon rights." In the Speech from the Throne two weeks later, his government committed itself to enact anti-discrimination legislation, which appeared on 3 March as the "Act to Prevent the Publication of Discriminatory Matter Referring to Race or Creed."[37]

Even with this major human rights breakthrough, which was the first legislation of its kind in Canada, Salsberg was not satisfied because the act banned only the dissemination of discriminatory publicity while saying nothing about employment or housing. Speaking in the ensuing debate, Salsberg declared it "criminal for an employer to refuse a man a job because of race or nationality" and demanded appropriate amendments to the act,[38] which was full of enough weasel words to "render negative some of its positive prohibitions"; but Salsberg's proposed amendment went nowhere. Despite his misgivings about its weaknesses and opposition from the Orange Lodge and the *Globe and Mail,* who saw it as an infringement on free speech,[39] Salsberg knew that this was a significant advance, even though the bill, which had near unanimous support in the legislature, "does not enable us to prosecute an employer who refused to give employment to anyone because he is a Jew ... [nor provide] the legal grounds for prosecution when we are denied the right to purchase land or homes in those areas where ... landowners place restrictions against Jews." But it is, he asserted in a lengthy explanation to the Ontario Jewish community, "the first step ... forward in the fight to place anti-Semitic and other discriminatory practices beyond the pale of the law."[40] Having received numerous letters and telephone calls, many of them "abusive and threatening," complaining of discrimination, he felt it necessary to correct "unjustified interpretations of the legislation."

Enforcement, however, soon became a problem and Salsberg picked up on this quickly, as "discriminatory acts ... to our sorrow ... are not diminishing but are actually on the increase."[41] In September he secured an injunction against a resort owner who displayed a "Gentiles Only" sign and joined the protest against the ban on Jews renting premises on the Toronto Islands. In March 1945 he informed the House that a woman sent to a job opening at a Toronto firm by Selective Service was told that "We do not employ Jews, and I told [them] not to send me any Jews. It would not promote the best interests of the company to employ Jewish salesmen."[42] A young black woman who was denied entry to an Ontario nursing school was advised by a government official(!) to go to the United States for training.[43] Outraged by these and other complaints, Salsberg teamed up with Holy Blossom's Rabbi Abraham Feinberg to mount a campaign for provincial legislation ensuring fair accommodation practices. In the House he rose repeatedly to urge action on equal rights and anti-discrimination legislation, including a bill he authored in 1950 regarding fair employment practices.[44] He served on the Joint Public Relations Committee of the Canadian Jewish Congress and B'nai Brith, visited the western Ontario town of Dresden to lend his support to its beleaguered black community, and kept a watching brief on enforcement of the 1951 Fair Employment Practises Act.[45]

Civil rights aside, labour was Salsberg's primary focus throughout his twelve years in the legislature. Barely seated, he called for a government-sponsored conference of labour leaders to discuss an agenda for the future, pointing out that the Drew government's new bill creating a forty-eight-hour work week, while commendable in theory, would be "valueless" without minimum-wage laws.[46] Urging a provincial public inquiry, Salsberg offered assurances that "the trade unions had no desire to wage war against the Government or against employers," but wish "to work in harmony and cooperation with all bodies and individuals." He spoke at length of the need for national labour legislation, amendments to the Workmen's Compensation Act to provide 100 per cent coverage, a minimum wage for women, and postwar labour planning.

Few details affecting labour issues, however minor, escaped Salberg's attention. He noted disapprovingly in the House that Queen's Park building staff were often required to work extra hours for no additional pay[47] and that workers generally perceived that the Ontario Provincial Police were being used as an "instrument ... against them" in recent industrial disputes at Hespeler and Kitchener factories. The minimum wage was a major concern and he proposed that the labour committee Drew had promised propose a new scale.[48] He urged streamlining the 1944 Labour Relations Act and the Collective Bargaining Act to better protect workers and pointed out that the provision for a week's paid vacation for every fifty-one weeks of employment per year was not inclusive – because workers in some industries did not work that many weeks per year! In March 1944 he charged that six Ontario firms (namely, Ford Motors, Canada Bread, Imperial Optical, Westinghouse, Sylvanite Gold Mines, and Electro-Metallurgical) were violating the spirit of both dominion and provincial labour laws by refusing to recognize unions and collectively bargain with their workers. Ford and the gold mining companies were blatantly obstructing their unions and taking unfair advantage of union no-strike policies during wartime.[49] Meanwhile, Ontario Hydro was preventing the Electrical Workers Union from organizing its workers.[50]

The following year, while condemning the "steady deterioration of labour relations," he again pressed Drew to appoint a select committee to draft a new act "which will establish the basis of justice, co-operation and responsibility which is so necessary for the welfare and security of all our people."[51] A harsh critic of the shortcomings of labour measures under the Hepburn government, Salsberg pestered the Conservatives for years on this matter. Meanwhile, he pointed out problems in workmen's compensation practices, at the same time stressing that the trade union movement sought to "work in harmony and co-operation with all bodies [including the provincial government] and individuals." During periods of serious unemployment, like the winter of 1950, he called for cash relief – without success.[52]

Like many others on the left he was concerned that wartime harmony would deteriorate after 1945 as capital sought to return to the "good old days." He charged that "reactionary industrialists are not averse to promoting strife ... [through] an organized attack on existing labour legislation."[53] Ford's attitude was especially egregious, as the company tried to terminate its wartime agreements with the United Auto Workers and refused demands for union security, precipitating a bitter and lengthy strike at its Windsor plant.[54] After police intervened, Salsberg threatened to join the picket line and on several occasions spoke to the strikers, alleging that the Drew government deliberately created panic to justify sending armed police to bolster the company's resistance to the union.[55]

Salsberg and his mother, Sarah-Gitel, in Lagov, Poland, 1912. Queen's
University Archives, V101.27 SE.

Lagov before 1920. Harvey Spiegel.

Dora Wilensky's graduation portrait, McMaster University, 1924. Queen's
University Archives, 2303.36/21/27.

Joe, Dora, and friends, 1928. Queen's University Archives, 2303.36/21/18.

Salsberg at Achdud Avodah Poale Zion convention, Boston, 1923. Ontario Jewish Archives, Fonds 92, series 2, file 2.

United Hatters, Cap, and Millinery Workers International Union executive
board, Montreal, ca 1923. Ontario Jewish Archives, 6023.

Salsberg being arrested, Toronto, October 1929. City of Toronto Archives, *Globe*, 19 October 1929.

Salsberg. Late 1920s. Queen's University Archives, 2303.36/21/26.

Joe and Dora on holiday, late 1930s. Queen's University Archives, 2303.36/21/18.

Joe and Dora at home, ca 1936. Ontario Jewish Archives, Fonds 33, series 4, item 9.

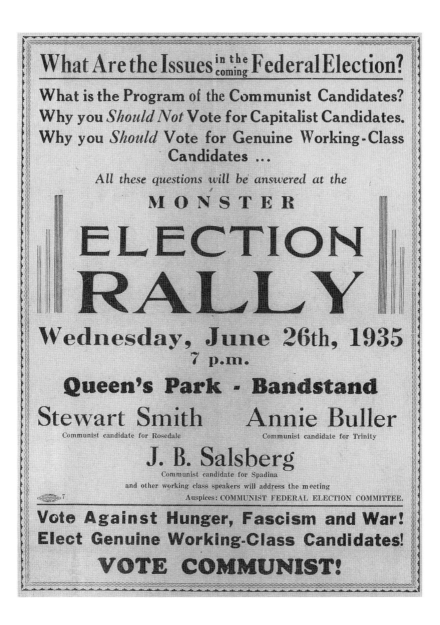

Dominion election rally for Salsberg and other communist candidates, 1935.
Queen's University Archives, Salsberg Fonds, box 9, file 6.

Salsberg campaigning, 1943. Ontario Jewish Archives, Fonds 92, series 3, file 6.

Toronto clothing workers in May Day parade, 1935. Queen's University Archives, 2303.36/21/18.

Salsberg visiting family in Lagov, Poland, August 1939. Queen's University
Archives, 2303.36/21/27.

Salsberg at the former family home in Lagov, Poland, 1947. Queen's University Archives, Salsberg Fonds, box 9, file 15.

• אַ גרום פון אייראָפע . . .
• • אַ גרום פון די אידן אין פוילן . . . .
• • • אַ גרום פון אייערע שוועסטער און ברידער
• • • • אין די די. פי. לאַגערן אין דייטשלאַנד . . . . .
• • • • • אַ גרום פון שלאַכט-פראָנט אין ארץ ישראל . . . . . .

י. ב. זאַלצבערג

באַליבטער אידישער ארבעטער-פידער און מיטגליד פון אָנטעריא פּאַרלא־
מענט, האָט זיך ערשט אומגעקערט פון א לענגערער רייזע איבער ענגלאַנד
פראַנקרייך, די. פי. לאַגערן אין דייטשלאַנד, פוילן, טשעכאָסלאָוואַקיע און
ארץ ישראל.

ער וועט ריידן בײַ א

מאַסן פאַרזאַמלונג

זונטיק אָוונט, פעברואַר 8-טן, 1948

וויקטאָרי טעאַטער

ספּעדײנע און דאָנדעס

אַראַנזשירט פון:
קאָונסיל פון לינקע אידישע אָרגאַניזאַציעס
אין טאָראָנטאָ

טירן אָפן 7 אזייגער

Notice of a mass meeting in Toronto where Salsberg was to report on his 1947–8 trip to Europe and Palestine. Queen's University Archives, Salsberg Fonds, box 9, file 6.

Election campaign poster, early 1950s. Ontario Jewish Archives, Fonds 92, series 3, file 6.

Salsberg voting in 1948 provincial election. Queen's University Archives, 2303.36/21/18.

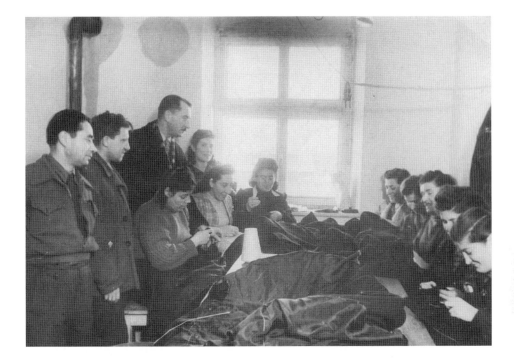

Salsberg in a Polish clothing factory, 1940s. Queen's University Archives, 2303.36/21/18.

Salsberg campaigning, 1948. Queen's University Archives, 2303.36.21/18.

Salsberg in the Ontario Legislature, 1950 (third person from bottom of picture in the second row). Ontario Jewish Archives, Fonds 92, series 3, file 15.

Salsberg with David Ben Gurion, Sde-Boker, Israel, 1970. Ontario Jewish Archives, Fonds 92, series 1, file 15.

Opening the J.B. Salsberg Medical Centre in Israel, 1980s. Queen's University
Archives, 2303.36/21/22.

Salsberg addressing a gathering, 1984. Queen's University Archives, 2303.36/21/21.

Despite Salsberg's generally courteous and conciliatory parliamentary style, anti-communist rhetoric, directed mainly against A.A. MacLeod, a feistier man, erupted often. In March 1945, Labour Minister Charles Daley labelled MacLeod "a little pipsqueak Communist," wondering how he could get elected by "the Jewish people of Bellwoods."[56] The premier, who accused Mitch Hepburn and MacLeod of forming an alliance, "a Liberal-Communist tie-up," to create disunity in the province, "was in the forefront of the red paint brigade," in Reg Whitaker's felicitous phrase.[57] Drew was not wrong. In March 1945 MacLeod proposed that all parties in the Opposition, commanding a total of fifty-two seats, unite to defeat the minority government – in his words, "a disaster looking for a place to happen" – which held only thirty-seven seats in the House, and form a coalition government uniting all Opposition parties.[58] Meanwhile, anti-communist diatribes in the legislature, in the press, and on the hustings at election times, were indicative of the vilification that prevailed widely in Canada during and after the Second World War. Despite the fact that from late June of 1941 the Soviet Union was an ally fighting against Nazi Germany, there was, as Whitaker explains, "a continuity of State coercion against the communist left" under the Defence of Canada Regulations, including press censorship, preventive detention, outlawed associations, attacks on unions, and persecution of the Left Ukrainians. Meanwhile, despite the Soviet military successes that had decisively turned the tide of war in favour of the Allied cause by the summer of 1943, there remained a substantial body of fear and distrust of the USSR that continued throughout the postwar era, especially after the Gouzenko allegations that members of the LPP were spying for the USSR, later proved to be correct in the case of Fred Rose, the Member of Parliament for the Montreal riding of Cartier.

Anti-communist attacks on Salsberg and MacLeod came from government front benchers who let few opportunities pass for condemning communists as threats to democracy and Canada's way of life. Salsberg sometimes would counterattack by accusing Premier Drew of "red baiting," and labelled Charles Daley's barbs as "a shameful display of the susceptibility of the Tory mind to the reaction of fascist propaganda." "Communism," Salsberg went on, "means the thousands of Canadians who went to fight against Franco and the Fascists in Spain. It means the Communists also fought the Germans."[59] Drew nevertheless kept at it, especially in debate with MacLeod, who seemed to delight in baiting the premier. In March 1946, quoting Tim Buck's statement that "the general strike during a political crisis is the gateway to revolution," Drew exclaimed: "There, gentlemen, you see at last the admission of support of the vile principles of Lenin and Marx,"[60] and called for the removal of communists and "their vile anti-Christian doctrines" from the legislature. MacLeod retorted that such talk was reminiscent of pre-war Nazi rally speeches in the Berlin *sports-palast* and reminded the House that before 1939 Drew had written that fascist states were not seeking war; Drew had also assailed Russia early in the war and only recently stated that Russia threatened Canada.[61]

In the wake of the Gouzenko allegations and the conviction of MP Fred Rose for espionage, such beliefs were widespread, even prompting the Toronto Board of Education to ban the use of school premises to communists and to bar them from employment as teachers.[62] Cold War anti-communism inspired A.H. Cowling (High Park) to inform the House in March 1952 that "it is a tradition here to refer to all hon. Members as 'honourable,' but in regard to the member for St Andrew (Mr Salsberg), I will have to skip that in making reference to him. Anybody who represents the way of life he does should not even be here in the first place and to be termed 'honourable' is just too much."[63] Salsberg let it pass. When another MLA responding to Salsberg's complaints that Canada was threatened by United States economic imperialism said that Canada "would not be annexed to Russia," MacLeod retorted: "Now listen to the hon. Member ... who has been in this House for seven years and all he does is sit in the back row and chew gum. Just look at him."[64] On one occasion, anti-communist attacks drew criticism from an Opposition member who urged the premier to fight communism with "adequate social legislation ... There are too many men in public life today who forget the poor. Pass the proper legislation ... and we won't have to bear communism."[65]

Salsberg was returned in 1945, defeating lawyer Edwin Goodman, his Progressive Conservative opponent with a distinguished record as a combat soldier in the recent war.[66] Salsberg was re-elected again in 1948, defeating long-serving Ward 4 alderman Nathan Phillips, a well-known lawyer and seasoned politician, who ran a strong anti-communist campaign.[67] Salsberg won again in 1951, even despite the rising crescendo of anti-communism prevalent during the Korean War.[68] This electoral strength is one measure of the widespread respect, even love, for Salsberg among his constituents, especially among the large Jewish population in his riding. He spoke to the immigrants in their Yiddish. He regularly walked the streets, even in the early evening when people went out to stroll, in the hope of meeting friends and schmoozing with them. He was consulted on personal matters and about employment possibilities and, famously, by Toronto's kosher ritual slaughterers about forming a union.

He was also earning respect in the legislature. While serving as Ontario Premier (from 1949 to 1961) Leslie Frost had such high regard for Salsberg's and MacLeod's effectiveness in the House that he was heard to say that "those two honorable gentlemen on opposite have more brains than my entire backbench put together"[69] and "Salsberg's the only real opposition we have around here."[70] On another occasion, Frost said, "Those two [Salsberg and MacLeod] had more brains between them than the rest of the opposition put together ... I'd listen to them. Often I'd just grab one of their ideas."[71] The premier especially admired Salsberg, even to the extent – legend has it – that he offered him a cabinet post if he would jump ship. On occasion Frost complimented Salsberg in the House, as he did during the extended debate on the government's fair employment practices act in late March 1951. In response to Salsberg's suggestion that the bill provide for education so that enforcement would have to be applied less frequently over time, Frost said: "I want to compliment the hon. Member for bringing this up, for stating his case in a very reasonable and proper way ... The fact is the point he raised is perhaps the most important point in the whole thing."[72] Frost was seen walking down a Queen's Park hallway with his arm over Salsberg's shoulder, possibly consoling him, shortly after the bitter 1955 St Andrew election campaign in which Salsberg was defeated by the Conservative Alan Grossman.[73] The relationship continued. As late as 1969, both of them long retired from political life, Salsberg wrote inviting Frost down from Lindsay to have lunch with him in Toronto. "As far as I am concerned you are still my Premier, for I recognize no other, and with good reasons," Salsberg began, suggesting that "we could, in addition to consuming some food, also talk about this, that and other things," including, he added mysteriously, "something that has been on my mind for four years." For his part, Frost had enormous admiration for both Salsberg and MacLeod, stating to one correspondent, "I did befriend them and had for many years and even to date the most friendly relationships with them," and continuing, "I never counted [them] as true Communists. I think that they were men who were dissatisfied with the way of things ... This pair were actually very brilliant brains ... In the great mill run of things they were very interesting and stimulating Opposition Members."[74]

The legislative debates reveal the broad range of topics Salsberg was interested in regarding public and individual human welfare. The issue at hand might have been the management of forestry or other natural resources, health care, hospital financing, the monopoly enjoyed by Consumers' Gas Company in Toronto, the powers of the Ontario Municipal Board, or the educational services for handicapped children. It could have been the Ontario Milk Board, facilities for cancer patients, the public use of loudspeakers, birth certificates stamped "Illegitimate" for children born out of wedlock, day nurseries for children of working mothers, highways, government publications, commissions of inquiry. The proposed legislation would have touched on education, pensions – not to mention labour issues like employment practices, workmen's compensation, and the rights of civil-service workers to organize unions and be certified under the law – and Salsberg was up on his feet, before or after MacLeod, with searching comments, penetrating questions, or well-prepared amendments to bills under discussion.

Although it has been asserted that Salsberg used "his great talent to deceive his fellow Jews into becoming dupes of Soviet tyranny" or to "propound ... his [communist] ideology in the Ontario legislature,"[75] no record exists of Salsberg ever mentioning communism in the House. Nor did he once extol the Soviet "workers' paradise," communist beliefs, or, during the Second World War, Soviet military victories. His comments, questions, critiques, and assertions were those of a committed reformer, or progressive, and probably would have been shared by other members of the legislature who approached specific nuts-and-bolts issues with a genuine concern for the public interest – regardless of party affiliation.

Salsberg and MacLeod performed like a well-matched wrestling tag team, the one picking up where the other left off, relentlessly questioning a minister or government member or responding either to an evasive or limited answer or to a crude anti-communist barb. Their performances might have seemed rehearsed. They would, for example, start the attack with one or the other questioning, possibly, the taxation on mining profits, as they did in March 1950, when Salsberg inquired whether special status for nickel producers was improperly denying the province revenue.[76] When the minister, W.A. Gemmell, stoutly defended the policy and praised Inco's current president, MacLeod queried whether the man was going to be awarded an honorary degree, then launched into a scathing attack on the generous concessions granted to United States entrepreneur Cyrus Eaton at Steep Rock, "where there are perhaps one billion tons of ore," for his company's right to mine "for ever and a day."

When Frost responded that such mining concessions produced wealth and jobs, MacLeod commented that "the policy he is defending actually caused that whole area to be annexed to the United States," pointing out that the deed on the property was held by an American corporation.

The growing influence of United States interests in Canada carried other dangers. In February 1951, at the height of the Korean War, MacLeod stated that "it is unquestionably true that most of the problems that confront this Legislature at present have their roots in or grew out of the international situation. The grave danger of war which faces the people of the world is certainly affecting government policies and ... legislation."[77] Pointing to the "war machinations of [certain] circles in the United States, ... the present trend endangers the sovereignty ... as well as the peace of this country," including its economic well-being. There is "the danger of turning [Canada] into an economic and political satellite of Wall Street" with American monopoly capital. Salsberg repeatedly underscored the extent of American economic penetration into Canada, notably in the development of the St Lawrence Seaway, which would facilitate the export of Canadian raw materials for processing in the United States rather than in Canada: "Canals should not become speedways for carrying out our nation's wealth."[78]

Salsberg on occasion actually complimented the government, as he did when the Frost regime brought in legislation in late March 1950 to ban discriminatory covenant deeds; Salsberg commented that "even with its shortcomings ... this [bill] will be acknowledged throughout the length and breadth of the continent ... and will be to the credit of the government."[79] During the same session, he praised a Conservative member of the House for excellent work in a committee on resources, taking the opportunity to explain the Jewish spring festival, "the new year of the trees" (*Tu Beshvat*, the fifteenth day of the Hebrew month of *Shvat*), which, he explained, was only one aspect of Jewish prayers for the preservation of the soil, the forests, and water. But in Ontario, he continued, we have "the rivers and streams and the wholesale devastation in forest areas in our province, ... acres and acres of land already wasted."[80] This reference in the House to his Jewish identity was rare for Salsberg and he might have done so deliberately, knowing how it could irritate (in private, of course) other members. But it was more likely a reflection of his unceasing ethnic pride and his ability to draw universalistic meaning from his religious knowledge.

He was sometimes biting. After receiving a gibe from Attorney General Dana Porter, he observed that "in view of the physical condition [drunk?] I do not wish to aggravate him now and I will postpone my question."[81] He needled Leslie Frost so much on health legislation that the premier got up and left the House. In another sharp-tongued contretemps, Salsberg called Minister of Labour Charles Daley "a toad on a log" and berated him: "You are scared of everything. You do not do anything at all."[82] And Salsberg was so outraged in the wake of the tragic fire at a building housing two clothing factories on Toronto's Richmond Street, in which nine workers were killed, that he shouted: "Are we going to wait until the lives of hundreds of people are lost before we do anything?" Remembering his own experiences in these sweatshops, he roared: "Is the Minister of Labour waiting for 200 people to lose their lives before he will move?" To which a government frontbencher interjected: "Why do you not go back to Russia?" Salsberg ignored the insult, focusing instead on Daley, whose department had allowed the factory windows to be fitted with the bars that had trapped the victims in the basement inferno. Such practices, Salsberg continued, must be stopped: "There is no law or regulation on our books ... to make such practices unlawful ... We cannot wait until more people die before this is rectified." "The building in which the fatalities occurred was inspected and everything was legal, i.e. the window bars were legal," Salsberg roared, "but nine people died there, and that proves that the laws are inadequate and we must change them. This deals with the life and health and limbs of people, and I say to the government that if we are to be guarded by this hon. Minister (Mr. Daley) and if there is no change made, then we will be confronted with a tragic experience." In white heat he demanded, "Are we going to wait for more people to die before we do anything?" Pointing across the floor, Salsberg exclaimed: "He [Daley] is scared. He is like the devil who is scared of holy water. To which Daley replied: "What do you know about holy water? ... I think that you are a nasty piece of goods." Again ignoring the minister's anti-Semitism, Salsberg revisited the safety standards issue a week later, but to no avail.[83]

In debate, Salsberg sometimes cut loose with accusations that an honourable minister was full of hot air. Thus, he told the House, Attorney General Dana Porter "exposes a bag full of wind, and not a single sound argument"[84] over the question of allowing exemptions from contracts for homeowners, who because of unemployment, sickness, or other disasters were not able to meet their obligations: "I am not advocating the violation of contract, but I do advocate the defence of the family and its interests, which are more serious and more important than my formal contract made for any purpose. It is the sanctity of the home that I place before the abstract contract."[85] "Those of us who are old enough to re-member the tragedy which occurred in many homes in working-class areas will agree that such legislation is necessary." In the ensuing debate, MacLeod stated heatedly that Porter was "obviously incompetent and ut-terly unable to deal with the subject matter of the legislation," this after Porter accused Salsberg of not believing "in the sanctity of a contract and, as far as he knows, does not believe in the sanctity of anything."

Any health issue before the House, especially involving children, got Salsberg – no doubt well informed over the breakfast table on these mat-ters by his wife, Dora, who headed Jewish Family Services and had a wide reputation as a progressive thinker in this field – up on his feet. In March 1950 he said: "It is ... necessary, ... vitally necessary for the Opposition to shock the government into the realization that they have not lived up to the responsibilities which faced them. Furthermore, they have not lived up to their promises ... in regard to health protection."[86] He was in-censed that the government's promise that "steps will be taken to insure that every child is given the greatest possible opportunity to face life with a healthy body and mind" had not been met.

Salsberg's and MacLeod's contributions to debates in the House are a bellwether of the times, a reflection of the social and economic condi-tions afflicting the poor and the not-so-well-off in Ontario in the 1940s and 1950s. Of course, the CCF was usually on the same page. But Sals-berg and MacLeod were in some ways really the conscience of the House. They never allowed any issue to escape their intense scrutiny and criti-cism for its failure to meet the test of what was best for ordinary people. It was more than the public interest they sought, it was, more broadly, the people's welfare. And in pursuit of this goal, they were unrelenting. They behaved as if there was no time to lose, that no opportunity to improve should be missed, and no effort to do so should be spared. Sals-berg once advised his colleagues on the Opposition benches: "We are now in a position where we have Conservatives to the right of us, Conser-vatives to the left of us, and Conservatives in front of us, and under such circumstances, there is only one thing to do, attack, attack, and attack."

His fire was not always directed at the government benches. Salsberg once criticized CCF leader Ted Joliffe, with whom he seemed generally to be on good terms, during an exchange about "red baiting." Accused by Joliffe as "one who has tried to besmirch the labour movement," Salsberg pointedly replied: "I have been in the labour movement much longer than [Joliffe] ... and I am not going to take any lessons from [him] on labour questions." And when Eamon Park, CCF member for Dovercourt, accused the LPP of trying to exploit the issue of unemployment by creating animosity towards "Displaced Persons" of certain national origins, Salsberg exploded, calling the charge "an absolute lie."[87]

In February 1951, Salsberg and MacLeod introduced no fewer than five bills: "An Act Respecting Fair Employment Practises," "An Act to amend the Minimum Wage Act," and "An Act to Amend the Hours of Work and Vacation with Pay Act," as well as two other measures dealing with elections and public schools. In the same session, Salsberg also spoke at length about workmen's compensation, citing hardship cases which had come to his attention and required review by the Compensation Board, which, he argued, "should have the authority to classify certain occupational illness as industrial diseases and enable workers ... to receive compensation." As well, he noted that the legislation omitted recommendations by the Roach commission to amend the existing act and cover workers for health problems incurred in certain industries, like Consumers' Gas Company, where lung cancer was affecting large numbers of them. But the Frost government refused the amendment. In the ensuing debate Salsberg cited an instance of a New Canadian workman whose claim was unfairly denied[88] because he had no acceptable proof of age; he reminded the House that this would be true of many, given circumstances in the countries they left.[89] He returned to problems with workmen's compensation repeatedly over the years.

In the February 1951 debate on the "Vacation with Pay" bill to amend the legislation of 1944, Salsberg again proposed a two-week vacation with pay period and other amendments for all Ontario workers. The premier had labelled these efforts as "perennials" from Salsberg and MacLeod. Salsberg interjected heatedly: "I want to remind the government that ... it is the continuous hammering for reform legislation which Opposition groups introduce ... which ultimately result in their adoption, their enactment, or in the adoption of something similar to them."[90] He stressed that "while certain pieces of progressive legislation were introduced by this government, or, rather, by the Conservative governments since 1944, that was the result of irresistible pressure which came from this side of the House ... What is necessary to remember when we discuss legislation of this type is that ... vacations have become absolutely necessary ... It is a necessity for the preservation of the mental and physical health of industrial workers [who] feel exhausted physically and mentally at the end of a day's work." The social costs of not having these provisions result in increased liquor consumption and mental illness, and in the undermining of family life. "This legislation is good social legislation" and would allow Ontario workers and their families to enjoy the province's recreational facilities. Referring to a streetcar driver he knew who experienced such on-the-job tensions that he could not enjoy his life, Salsberg continued: "That is true for tens of thousands of workers employed in modern industry ... We should think of those people when we are dealing with legislation of this sort." When Labour Minister Charles Daley said that he, too, would like a couple of weeks off, Salsberg shouted: "Organize for it, organize the Cabinet and fight for it." The government benchers were not amused!

On old age pensions, Salsberg supported the government view that means tests still imposed by the dominion government be abolished as soon as possible, and he referred – as he always did – to constituents who came to see him about their hardship under this requirement with questions such as: "Well, the [news] paper says no more means test, can I now apply although I've got a house?" "I shall never forget that Saturday morning," he continued, "when my office was literally crowded with old people who came in with letters they had received from the provincial Minister of Welfare [William] Goodfellow's department, having their pension either cut [off] completely or reduced to fifteen dollars a month because of the supposed income which, in reality, they never had." When the provincial government eliminated its supplements to boost the pension of forty dollars by ten dollars per month,[91] Salsberg was livid: "This government should be indicted before the bar of public opinion as being guilty of moral indifference to the suffering of thousands of aged people in this province." He argued that the provincial government should supplement the federal old age pension by ten dollars per month, mentioning that three other provinces were providing such payments.

The House had heard the same refrain from Salsberg since 1943, but he was unrelenting, accusing Frost of having "a blind spot" on the issue. In April 1952 he promised to "continue to make the same speech until we get some monthly allowance for our pensioners who are not given enough to live on and not enough to die on ... I shall speak as often as I think necessary until this injustice is corrected."[92] "Nonsense," Frost replied, "He is just specializing in what he talks [about] here perpetually. Nonsense, that is all." "This is one subject on which I will not be silenced," Salsberg retorted, before launching into a lengthy lecture on the pension issue. When interrupted by Dana Porter, Salsberg struck back with "Let not the Hon. Attorney General try to make trivia out of such a serious question. Let him not try to be a 'smart alec,'" and offered to publicly debate the matter with him in Porter's own constituency of Oxford. Porter demurred.

Alone in the House after MacLeod's defeat in the 1951 election, Salsberg remained unrelenting, never tiring of his role of gadfly and, despite numerous provocations, seldom losing his temper, though when responding to Opposition barbs he could be tough and acerbic. He often had words with Attorney General Porter, but there seems to have been an underlay of mutual respect in these exchanges, Porter perhaps recognizing Salsberg's remarkable persistence, outstanding eloquence, and mastery of detail, and Salsberg realizing that he was up against an able and dedicated, though haughty, public servant. Verbal fisticuffs erupted often. When Salsberg opposed corporal punishment at the correctional facility at Guelph, CCF member William Grummett (Cochrane South) interjected, "You'd have them shot," a reference, no doubt, to the brutal Stalinist repression of dissidents in the Soviet Union.[93] During debate on housing, Salsberg was asked by a member who was exasperated by Salsberg's incessant questions whether he knew of any better place to live than Ontario. When Salsberg replied that as one of the Opposition members his job was to "pressure the government into doing more than it is doing in every field, particularly the field of human welfare," a government member exclaimed: "The honourable member knows that there is no gas chamber in Ontario."[94] Salsberg let the anti-Semitic slur pass, saying only: "Let us be adult ... We are tackling an important social problem."

When, in March 1952, the minister of health, MacKinnon Phillips, made derogatory remarks about some of the early-twentieth-century immigrants, using the term "infidel," an obvious reference to Jews and to Salsberg, whose family had arrived in 1913, he replied softly: "I am extremely sorry that he thought it necessary to do that. It would have been far better had he left matters outside of his jurisdiction and his ken, to other honourable members of the Cabinet who are better suited for it, and have more knowledge of the subject."[95] When a government member opined that all communists be disenfranchised, again Salsberg stayed silent. Nor did he reply to Liberal leader Farquhar Oliver's condemnation of Salsberg's support of communism, in view of Moscow's persecution of Jews, except to suggest that people should not believe information disseminated by the United States State Department. This was dishonest because by that time he knew full well that Jews were being persecuted.

Two weeks later, on the news of Stalin's death, he reluctantly acceded to pressure from the Labour-Progressive Party leadership and praised the late Soviet leader to a silent House as "one of the greatest personalities of our time" and his demise "as a severe loss ... to all who strive for a peaceful world."[96] Then waxing rhapsodic in praise of Stalin's military genius and theoretical writings, Salsberg proclaimed: "I am confident that the calumnies which have been directed for so long against Stalin will, as time goes on, sink into oblivion and the figure of Stalin will emerge and remain in history as one of the greatest among the great of all times."[97] Having been challenged to "love the land, or live in the land you love," Salsberg went overboard to defend the reputation of one of history's greatest criminals.[98]

His critiques often enraged the government front benches. After impugning some "questionable" appointments to the Labour Board, Salsberg was asked by Minister of Public Works William Griesinger "what he has ever contributed to this province or this country, outside of criticism?"[99] Salsberg responded: "I have contributed as much as any hon. Member in this House of many years, as a worker ... and as a member of a union ... I was secretary of my union when I was still in short pants," dodging inspectors because he was below legal age. Proudly admitting to being a gadfly, he said his purpose was "to stop [the government] from falling asleep, and wake them up when they begin to snore, and get them into action, in order that they will do things." The same day, while addressing weaknesses in current labour laws concerning procedures for conciliation, Salsberg was asked: "Does the hon. Member think that there are boards in Russia?" Salsberg responded only by observing that "one of the big troubles with this Government is it always jumps to a defensive position even when it is not attacked." He went on to the need for remedying dangerous conditions existing in grain elevators, noting the deaths of six men in Port Arthur in September 1952. He then spoke at length on problems in the audit of Ontario Hydro, and the lack of a labour representative there, a subject to which he returned repeatedly over the years.[100] Sometimes, Salsberg's passion outran his better judgment; in March 1953 he interrupted proceedings of a legislative committee – of which he was not even a member – so often that he came close to being physically attacked by an irate fellow MLA.[101]

In March 1951, Salsberg repeated at length and with great heat his yearly refrain for a provincial supplement to the inadequate federal old age pensions that left 81 per cent of Ontario recipients destitute, some of them "literally starving."[102] Response from the government benches, chiefly Charles Daley, on this occasion was so callous that Salsberg blew up: it would be "hypocritical for the hon. Minister, Daley ... to go back to his constituency at Easter and walk down the street with his self-satisfied feeling and with a smirk on his face when there are old people in his town who are not able to enjoy food at Easter." Let Premier Frost supplement old age pensions and "he would really emerge in the role of a social reformer who is utilizing his high office" to pressure Ottawa to implement relief for all provinces doing the same to help their pensioners. He called on Frost to "utilize this tribune ... to thunder at Ottawa after he will have announced an emergency supplementary allowance." His voice will be heard from one end of the country to the other ... He would really emerge in the role of a social reformer."

In April 1952, after speaking about inadequacies in health services, housing, and forestry management, Salsberg was accused of getting up too often. "I do not want to apologize. I never do anything in this House that calls for an apology," he said; "but I want to remind hon. Members that the Opposition has a duty to perform ... even if it causes discomfort occasionally to the Government ...You are so many and we are so few."[103] However good-humoured and restrained, Salsberg was not without hubris. In a wide-ranging attack on government ineptitude in February 1953, accusing them of being "grumpy, sour, jumpy, and filled with political stomach acidity, which comes after overeating," he continued: "It takes the government a long time to accept some of the very constructive and progressive proposals which I make."[104] But he recognized his own vulnerability too, especially after the reaction to his eulogy for Stalin and the narrowness of his win in the 1951 election. After a long speech on the costs and the benefits to bondholders and speculators of the bill to amalgamate Toronto municipalities under a metropolitan government, he allowed, prophetically, that "elections and defeats are not the greatest things in a man's life ... I have been defeated before and I will be defeated again."[105]

At every opportunity, Salsberg proposed increased compensation for Ontario government civil servants, who were denied the right to collective bargaining. As well, he promoted equal pay for equal work for female employees. When the Frost government first brought in its bill in 1951 Salsberg demanded that "fair" be changed to "equal" to make it "a more perfect piece of legislation."[106] "I have experienced the indignity, and very often the disadvantage of being discriminated against," he said. Discrimination harms those who practise it; "it degrades them; it reduces the degree of decency which must express itself in all their relationships." He angrily pointed out that he had recently been approached by a second-generation Canadian of Ukrainian origin who could not get a job because of his foreign-sounding name.

Concern for the disadvantaged was uppermost in Salsberg's mind. When Consumers Gas Company rates were increased, he was on his feet protesting that consumers were being forced to pay for speculation in the company's stocks. "I say that it is almost criminal," he averred, "to insist that a widow who is living on mother's allowance, that puny allowance that they receive from the province, should pay through their gas rates a higher interest because somebody speculated in the market and bought a $100 share for $200." He demanded that Consumers Gas be turned into a publicly owned body.[107] On unemployment Salsberg never rested, nor did he forget the need for low-cost housing. He once appealed for those about to be evicted on Saturday, though he would not mind "the Government being in office on Saturday if I could get them out of office the rest of the week."[108] The cost of milk was too high for working-class families and should be subsidized, he asserted in debate on a bill amending the Ontario Milk Board: "This great province, this rich province, and this government which enjoys the fruits of the prosperity in this province, must assume that responsibility."

Restrictions on the use of loudspeakers, he pointed out, would seriously disadvantage trade unions and labour and political groups – which do not get adequate exposure in the press – and religious minorities.[109] Recalling that he was once arrested at the corner of Dundas Street and Pacific Avenue in Toronto for using a loudspeaker at a political rally, Salsberg proclaimed: "The rich must understand the difficulties of the poor." Municipalities, he stated, should not have the power to restrict the use of loudspeakers, which are used "to bring a reasonable and common sense point of view to the workers, whom you cannot reach otherwise, because you have not the daily papers to support you" and no money for advertising, "and that is the only way we can find to reach our fellow citizens by direct contact ... which was the first accomplishment for political free speech, and political labour representation."[110]

Numerous social and health issues drew Salsberg to his feet during these years, even ragweed. Drawing the attention of the House to the "suffering of so many people" during ragweed season, he opined that "if all the people should sneeze together, they would shake the foundations of this building, and perhaps get some results."[111] He urged sufferers to "storm the very heavens to defeat this government for its failure to take

care of what, to them, is a most important problem at that time of year."
When amendments to the Parole Act came up for discussion in early
March 1952, Salsberg praised them as a "progressive step," but noted
that they were only "a piece-meal approach to an important social problem."[112] He reported that numerous ex-prisoners at Burwash had complained to him of floggings, bad food, and general brutality, especially
towards the mentally ill. Some inmates, because of overcrowding there,
were sent in chain gangs to local jails, where conditions were even worse.
He demanded a royal commission or a select committee of the House to
investigate and report.

Salsberg also supported the arts, often calling on the government for
an annual allocation to buy paintings by Ontario artists for Queen's Park
and to encourage the province's creative talent, although he admitted
that he "admired Picasso politically but not artistically."[113] And he rec-
ommended government-sponsored evening courses to enable workers
to complete secondary education.[114] Reflecting a strong interest in social work, he argued for better social services for handicapped children,
whose experiences in the regular schools were often unhappy and un-
fruitful.[115] He called for provincial grants of up to 50 per cent to the municipalities towards the costs of education[116] and for better facilities for
cancer treatment.[117] He argued strenuously for day nurseries[118] for children of working mothers and warned that he would urge these women
to come to Queen's Park to present their case.

Delays in the printing of Hansard and of bills and reports needed by
MPPs drew Salsberg's repeated criticism and his concern that such work
be contracted out in union shops only after implementation of a proper
bidding process.[119] Inflated municipal tax assessments on many of Toronto's working-class homeowners was an issue requiring a fair and eq-
uitable assessment yardstick. Amendments to the provincial elections act
were needed, he pointed out, to allow workers three consecutive working hours to vote: "You do not move very fast or very far; you move only
by inches, and unless we prod you, you will not move at all."[120]

By 1955 the anti-communist heckling directed at Salsberg had not
abated. As the session was coming to an end in late March, he seems to
have had a premonition of the electoral defeat he would soon suffer. In
a debate touching on five deaths that occurred in slum housing in Toronto, Salsberg said: "I do not apologize for taking the time of the House
in discussing what I consider to be critical and urgent social problems
affecting the lives of human beings, and the future of children raised
in dilapidated, overcrowded, unsafe housing conditions, ... I am sorry

to have to repeat what I say on housing, on unemployment, and on relief."[121] Taunted that he was speaking "on behalf of the communists,"
Salsberg let it pass and stressed that "tens of thousands of families are
living under these conditions ... I am not apologizing at all when I speak
about these conditions." Interrupted by a request that he "tell us where
[Soviet Premier] Mr. Malenkov is?" Salsberg calmly continued, quoting details of the seriousness of Toronto's housing ills and pleading for
"a proper approach to this problem, a social consciousness in the first
place, and a feeling of responsibility." Then, after outlining eleven points
on relief, unemployment, health care, housing, rising American owner-
ship, trade, forestry, natural gas pipelines, taxation, and mining royalties
needing urgent attention, he sat down for the last time and went out of
the legislature to face the election campaign, the bitterest he had faced
and one which he lost to his opponent, alderman Allan Grossman, a
staunch Conservative who campaigned on the slogan "Beat Salsberg."

Besides having to face powerful anti-communist rhetoric and Grossman's rough-and-tumble campaign tactics, Salsberg's previous electoral
strength was undermined by the demographic results of postwar prosperity, as a significant proportion of the Jewish population had moved from
the St Andrew area to new homes being built in northern suburbs along
north Bathurst Street. Among those moving into the riding were recent
immigrants from Eastern Europe, many of whom had suffered under
Stalinist oppression. The campaign leading up to the 9 June election was
hard fought, bitter, and extremely nasty, with one veteran campaigner
describing this as "the dirtiest campaign of them all ... a new low." Grossman vigorously championed an anti-communist and anti-Salsberg crusade. "The time has come," he asserted, "for this riding to rid itself of
Communists and Communism." *Hush*, a Toronto tabloid, waded in with
a screed stating that "Joe Salsberg has done more harm to the people of
Ontario than any person in the Province of Ontario."[122] The *Hebraishe
Zhurnal*, Toronto's Yiddish newspaper, was no help to Salsberg, featuring
editorials favouring Grossman – "alderman alan grosman darf dervilt
veren" (Alderman Grossman must be elected), "far voss yidn darf shti-
men far alan grosman" (Why Jews must vote for Allan Grossman) – and
condemning "Moscow."[123] Salsberg's campaign was directed by Robert
Laxer and backed by numerous youthful enthusiasts who plastered the
riding with posters, pamphlets, and poems ("Needing his help we didn't
vote blind / We put in Joe cause he's our kind / Sent up to parliament
the best we could find / A union man with a union mind"). Meanwhile,
truckloads of others moved up and down Spadina singing, to the tune of

"Skip to My Lou," lengthy ditties punctuated by the refrain "Vote, vote, vote for Joe / Vote for the man you know." Joe and his campaign workers worked the Spadina/College nexus, and campaigned on the radio and in newspapers. It was a tight race and he realized that he might not win again. As the election results came in on 9 June, the tally for Grossman mounted steadily over Salsberg's, until by 9:00 o'clock, having been beaten by a margin of 680 votes, he was ready to concede defeat; it was a hard blow. "Don't worry," he said to one well-wisher, "I'll be back." One campaign worker wrote to him: "I am satisfied that we did everything we could to rally our support. Our campaign was a good, clean fight ... You are well aware of the warmth & esteem people have for you ... We are all proud of you."[124]

How does one assess Salsberg's legislative career, the record of a communist House member who had no prospect of ever being a member of the government caucus, of serving on its front bench, of being a minister, of formulating and carrying out government policy, of even getting appointed to important legislative committees, and defending against Opposition criticism?[125] Despite those limitations, he tried to improve life in Ontario, especially for the socially and economically disadvantaged. While the postwar era saw unparalleled expansion of the provincial economy, Salsberg defined his role as spokesman for the poor, the unemployed, and the pensioners, and as the advocate for fair employment practices and general improvements in the public welfare. After he was defeated in the hotly contested 1955 election, therefore, he could realistically survey his twelve-year career with a genuine sense of accomplishment. He had spoken often on most major issues before the House, eloquently, usually passionately, and always knowledgeably. But to what practical effect? he must have wondered. Could he point to many or any bills that had been modified as a result of his criticisms or suggestions? Despite their interest, occasional brilliance, and persistence, were his contributions to debate of any measureable utility? Given the circumstances of Cold War Canada and the bitterness of those times in which Soviet espionage had been proved, it is noteworthy that a fervent and proud communist significantly influenced the course of Ontario's human rights, social, and labour legislation.

And yet, contemporaries, however justifiably sceptical of this man who remained loyal to communism despite undeniable evidence of odious Stalinist mass murder, torture, and imprisonment, could not help but pay attention to Salsberg's eloquence, persistence, and social conscience.

Like many outstanding personalities, he was a flawed man, but he had a perpetual "fire in his heart" for social justice, not just as a prelude to revolution, but as an end in itself, not unlike his contemporary Yiddish radical socialists beyond Toronto.[126] It is not a mere legend that some students from the University of Toronto would cut classes and rush to the legislature's galleries when word came over from Queen's Park that Salsberg was on his feet. It is certainly no myth that he spoke up repeatedly and passionately for the disadvantaged. Nor is it mere fancy that knowledgeable contemporary leftists like Pat Walsh, a Quebec labour organizer, considered Salsberg one of the "real" leaders of the Labour-Progressive Party (along with Stanley Ryerson and Harvey Murphy).[127] And it is on record that, though irked by Salsberg's stings, Leslie Frost let it be known that he admired him, although some front-bench Tories obviously did not. In sum, Salsberg might have reflected with some self-satisfaction on a passage in the Talmud, the tomes he had studied so fervently in his religious youthful years: "You are not obliged to finish the work, but neither are you free to desist from it."[128] He did his job, as he once put it in the House, despite the fact that "you [the Government] are so many and we [the communists] are so few."[129]

His twelve-year legislative career at an end, Salsberg would run for office again only four months later, in the federal riding of Spadina (recently vacated by David Croll, who had been elevated to the Senate),[130] only to lose once more to another Tory, Ted Rea, who enjoyed the benefits of Allan Grossman's electoral machine. But that time Salsberg was facing a crisis of faith in the very cause he had embraced and served for the previous thirty years.

During these years Joe and Dora faced profound personal disappointments: they would never have children, all attempts having ended in failure, heartbreak, and mourning. Their feelings of loss were partially alleviated by their continuing closeness to family. In summers they frequented the family encampments at Agincourt and Wilcox Lake where Abraham's and Sarah-Gitel's warm love and bounteous good food bestowed comfort and joy. They were especially attached to the numerous nephews and nieces in the Salsberg-Wilensky clans. Dora and Joe's annual Hanukah party at their triplex on Madison Avenue included mounds of latkes and other delights from Sarah-Gitel's and other relatives' kitchens, gifts including *Hanukah gelt* (holiday money) for the children, the traditional lighting of candles to commemorate the ancient Maccabean revolt against religious oppression, and, without doubt, a lengthy disquisition by Joe on the broad social and political significance of those ancient events that ensured the survival of Judaism. These evenings would end after singing, Joe's baritone soaring in full voice, followed by a lengthy round of hugs and kisses. And then Joe and Dora would be alone.

Chapter Five

Family Quarrel

By the mid-1950s, then, Joe Salsberg was at a crossroads. His political career had been terminated, never to be renewed. And although this must have been a serious disappointment in one who felt that he had given so much to the public welfare, he was more concerned with anti-Semitism in the Soviet Union and throughout the communist block in Eastern Europe. Not only had Jewish culture been suppressed under Stalin, but his successors seemed determined to continue that policy. Salsberg believed that the communist family had rejected him and other Jewish devotees of the great cause – and it broke his heart. Why it took him so long to publicly acknowledge what he knew had been happening to Jews in the Soviet union under Stalin's brutal regime lies in large measure in Salsberg's continuing commitment to socialist ideals, Bryan Palmer advises, and in his failure to "appreciat[e] the full extent of other developments [such as the repudiation] of proletarian internationalism [and] the unleashing of Great Russian chauvinism, antisemitism, etc."[1]

The post–Second World War attacks on Jewish cultural expression in the USSR, sparked by a resurgence of traditional East European anti-Semitism and war-inspired Russian chauvinism, certainly would have brought Salsberg no comfort. Publicly, however, he continued to hold his peace through the late 1940s, even when, in November 1948, the Jewish Anti-Fascist Committee was suddenly abolished and its printing plant and library shut down. Established in 1942 to mobilize support in the USSR and in the West for the war effort, that institution had been valiantly attempting to rebuild Jewish cultural life that had been decimated by the Germans. This blow was followed by the closure of virtually all Jewish cultural institutions, the suspension of Yiddish publications, and the arrest, imprisonment, and execution of writers, actors, and intellectuals.[2] Meanwhile, Jews had been eliminated from diplomatic and military academies.

Salsberg's concern over the fate of Jews in the Soviet Union was sharply accentuated by the Holocaust. When he travelled to Europe in late October 1947 to observe its aftermath first-hand, often accompanied by local Communist Party officials, he spent most of his time in Poland, where nine-tenths of the Jewish population had been murdered, and Germany, where most of the survivors were housed in displaced-persons camps. The effect on Salsberg of what he saw was devastating and his impressions recorded in *Vochenblatt* were highly emotional. "Shreibt tsu eiyere kroivim und freind in die d.p. lagern" (write to your family and friends in the DP camps), he beseeched readers in one article, explaining that survivors were desperate to reconnect with loved ones in Canada.[3] At the same time he wrote at length to Saul Hayes, executive director of the Canadian Jewish Congress, asserting that Jewish refugees faced bald-faced discrimination from Canadian immigration and RCMP security officials in Germany, chiefly Vincent Cormier. Salsberg alleged that "the chief difficulties stem from Ottawa where policies are made and from where instructions are issued."[4]

"After a month among Jewish refugees, in the DP camps of Germany," Salsberg wrote, "[I] feel compelled to set everything else aside in order to write this appeal to the Jews of the world. Time and again I was put to shame by the justified complaints and accusations which the Jews in the detestable camps levelled against their relatives abroad for their failure to write to them. One has to meet and speak with these martyred people to appreciate what a relative and some tangible contact with such a relative means to them. The survivors feel that Jews abroad do not try hard enough to get them out of the camps in Germany and reunite them with family."[5] Like his contemporary, Hananiah Meier Caiserman, executive director of the Canadian Jewish Congress, Salsberg was disgusted by the apparent lack of empathy from Canadian Jews for their own family members who had survived the Holocaust.[6] Joe wrote often to Dora, who meanwhile was heavily involved in the settlement of refugee children, during this trip and, though his letters have not survived, she chided him for hiding his deepest feelings about his experiences.

Probably the most poignant part of Salsberg's 1947 Polish tour was his visit to Lagow, his hometown. He had last been there in late August 1939, when on a trip to Moscow he had gone to visit family and friends he had not seen since emigrating to Toronto in 1913. Now, in the wake of the

Holocaust, the town presented a picture of desolation and despair. The cemetery had been vandalized, the gravestones used for local paving. "I looked at the synagogue," he recalled, "and it was a grotesque sight ... [It] looked like the broken back of a camel ... blackened by what obviously [had been] a fire inside and the flames licking up the walls." He went over to his boyhood home, but the occupant would not allow him to enter, and he stood on the steps forlornly facing a camera that recorded the scene.[7]

In his own notes Salsberg wrote: "Farmers Ragged walk back from market carrying 3[?] on strings, canes, or hand. Mudd and Mudd, Poverty on all sides ... Dark afternoon ... Ghastly appearance of town. Burned skeletons, fields where once houses. He observed that "houses once inhabited by Feter [uncle] Fishel was, like others gone. But the "bath house [was] saved. Shule – Burned. Roof half gone." He found his old house: "It was [made] of bricks," but was overcome by the "Frightfulness of [the] whole thing." One of the few surviving Jews, "Garbatsky leads me [to his] House and family."[8] "I left town that night in an extremely emotional disposition," he remembered. "It was the first time I've ever lost control. I cried like a child."[9] If he did not know earlier, here he would have learned the fate of Lagow's Jews: they were herded in June 1942 by German forces into a ghetto, many of them murdered there or in the countryside, and in October the remnants marched to nearby Kielce, where they were forced onto trains which took them to the gas chambers at Treblinka.[10] He was told that his grandmother had been "taken away in a cart – she was a little thing and far too old to walk – and they shot her on the side of the road. Nobody knows where she's buried."

Salsberg applied to visit the Soviet Union to view the Jewish situation there as well, but was refused entry, Larry Black points out, "at an extraordinarily high level" in Moscow on the grounds that his entry would risk "attracting the attention of Anglo-American intelligence ... and could risk making the situation for Communists in Canada even worse than it already was." Now that Moscow had openly declared its support for the establishment of a Jewish state in Palestine, it was "kosher" for Salsberg to pay a visit there. Thus, he went over from Europe in January 1948 and remained for two and a half weeks, only six months before Israel was proclaimed with full Soviet support.[11] "I landed on a Friday, late ... afternoon," he recalled. "When we arrived in Tel Aviv it was warm. Trees were green, leaves were out, and people were walking in the streets ... I was very excited ... Jews were talking in Hebrew and in Yiddish on the streets, and I was so taken by it." He met with some local communists and, possibly,

with a few old Toronto Labour Zionist *chaverim* (close friends), including the remarkable David Mangel, veteran of the Mackenzie-Papineau
Battalion. After two weeks Salsberg was summoned back to Toronto for a
special session of the legislature and he reluctantly cut his visit short. His
Zionism seems to have been rekindled, however, and he reflected that
"[the] perpetuity of a nation, national culture and social historic life [is]
possible only under conditions of spaces, where it constitutes a majority
of people, and neither you nor your national tapestry are as that of any
other nation." He rejoiced in the new vibrant spirit of the Jews in Palestine: "They say … I am here, this is our home, and so what?"

Salsberg seems to have regarded this as a private side trip and published
little about it in *Vochenblatt*, though he did speak to party gatherings,
where he called for "Jewish unity in the fight for the solution of Jewish
problems and the establishment of the Jewish state in Palestine under
the terms of the [1947] UN decision."[12] While it is not clear whether
he got to meet any prominent Arabs during these tense times, he saw
"numerous examples of peaceful and friendly relations and co-operation
between Arab and Jewish farmers and workers.[13] But for British machinations intended to undermine the two-state solution proposed by the
United Nations and the nefarious activities of a tiny group of super-rich
Arab Nazi sympathizers, all would be well. Meanwhile, Salsberg asserted,
arms shipments to the Jewish defenders of the Yishuv were essential; and
their victory was assured: "the Jews will win" if conflict breaks out. In the
meantime, he observed no panic. In Palestine, "life goes on." He advocated the presence of a UN force to foster cooperation between the two
states "without which full progress will be extremely difficult for both."[14]
Was he returning to Zionism? Had he ever really left it?

In the Soviet Union, by the end of 1948, more than four hundred
members of the Jewish intelligentsia had been arrested on charges of "espionage, bourgeois nationalism, 'lack of true Soviet spirit,' including a
plot to hand the Crimea over to American and Zionist imperialists."[15] Actors, a former deputy foreign minister, a scientist, a general, and an array
of writers and poets were arrested and thrown into Moscow's dreaded
Lubyanka prison, where they were to languish until fourteen of the poets
were executed on the night of 12–13 August 1952. Between 1948 and
1950, *Izvestia* and *Pravda* carried stories almost daily of "transgressions"
by Jewish officials, "with heavy emphasis," Gregor Aronson writes, "laid
on their Jewish names, comprising nicknames, patronymic and family names."[16] Labelled as "cosmopolitans," these Jews were accused of
"toadying to the West" through connections to Tel Aviv and New York.

Most menacingly of all Soviet measures against Jews – and they were not the only minority to suffer from cultural aggression in the USSR – was the "doctors' plot" of August 1952 (of mostly Jewish defendants who had been arrested in 1948) and the start of an unrestricted anti-Semitic campaign in *Pravda, Izvestia,* and *Meditsinkaia gazeta* accusing Jewish doctors of incompetence and malpractice.[17] This was followed by the blatantly anti-Semitic allegations inspired by Moscow against Rudolph Slansky (who was convicted in November 1952 and executed) in Czechoslovakia. Many Jewish communists and sympathizers in the West were shattered.[18]

Smarting over the Soviet Union's refusal to allow him entry, Salsberg concluded that "a fog seemed to descend" over Soviet Jewry in the postwar era.[19] Not only were Jewish cultural institutions boarded up, but outside contacts between communal leaders and artists were also terminated. Unwilling to stay quiet, at least within the party, where years beforehand "he was already suspect for his known Jewish 'nationalist' sentiments," Salsberg went before the national executive in 1949, appealing that Moscow be asked to explain its actions.[20] But this was rejected. Rumours of anti-Semitic policies and actions persisted, but Salsberg would not go public, not wanting to supply ammunition to the anti-Soviet cold war chorus: "I did not make my own views – which differed from that of my party – public property and did not defend them before the bar of public opinion. I simply refused to speak or write about Jewish life in the USSR."[21]

Within the communist family, however, he continued efforts to convince the party leadership to examine the Jewish question in the USSR. He failed. The "Stalin cult" was too strong, he concluded, and leading communists "lacked that measure of real independent thinking in relation to the Soviet Union that was required ... to save the executed writers Jewish and non-Jewish." He claimed in a 1991 interview that he even made a "personal inquiry" in 1948 when he met with Jewish leaders and "widows of writers ... Bergelson's widow ... And she cried and I cried. She told me how they came and took Bergelson away."[22] As to why he did not quit the party after this, Salsberg stated in the interview that as "the powerful and influential number two man in the Communist Party," he believed that he could convince members to accept his views and thus weaken the CPC's ties to Moscow.[23] Pressed strongly by Buck, Salsberg retreated, although he believed that his leader "would have voted for my slaughter, if [the order] came from Moscow."[24] Buck soothed Joe by claiming that he "could provide desperately-needed help and aid to a

Soviet Jewry trapped behind the Iron Curtain ... [by] asking tough questions ... within powerful communist circles everywhere."

According to fellow Toronto communist Sam Lipshitz, immediately
after the November 1948 arrests "Joe Salsberg began to press the political bureau, of which he was an important member. We have to find out,
we have to give answers. People are asking us what happened. And he
kept fighting on this question, really battling within the Party, everybody
knew, when he was finally removed from the political view."[25] Publicly,
however, Lipshitz hewed close to the party line. In an article he wrote
in 1953 for *National Affairs*, he waxed rhapsodic on the Jewish situation
in the Soviet Union and the "People's Democracies" in Eastern Europe,
"who have fully and completely eradicated anti-Semitism and racial discrimination ... The Jewish citizens ... enjoy full and complete equality
and unlimited opportunities for the building of a full, free and cultural
life." At the same time, he slammed Rudolph Slansky, a Jew who headed
the communist party in Czechoslovakia and was arrested for "crimes"
including "conspiring with Zionist agencies." "Zionism," Lipshitz thundered, "is the ideology of Jewish bourgeois nationalism," the tool of
Western imperialism and the real enemy of the Jewish people.[26]

In public, Salsberg manifested loyalty. It was a matter of faith to him.
In early 1950 he had delivered a lengthy *tour d'horizon* to the party's conference plenary of the National Jewish Committee, condemning the
"manifestations of bourgeois nationalism [which] came to the surface
in the work of several persons who formerly held positions in the Jewish
Anti-Fascist Committee and in literary circles." "The harmful effects of
these false anti-Marxist positions," he asserted, would be overcome by
the "discussions in the Soviet Union on ways and means how best to utilize the great opportunities that exist for the development of the culture
of the Jewish masses." A few years later, however, he was more honest and
forthright in higher party circles. At a meeting of the national executive committee in 1955, he charged that the Soviet Union was practising
overt anti-Semitism.[27] Unwilling to retract his comments, he was expelled
from the executive the following year.[28] His agitation did cause some debate within the party, however, notably in the National Jewish Committee
(NJC), which, since 1925, had advised the executive on Jewish affairs.
At a meeting on 18 April 1954, the NJC had objected to "opportunist
theories of exceptionalism ... to the effect that the Jewish people of the
world – all Jews – are some kind of a third force between the East and the
West." This was followed by a warning against "the dangers of bourgeois
nationalism and cosmopolitanism."[29] The following year, the NJC issued

its guidelines, including the statement that deepening "the practise of proletarian internationalism, recogniz[es] that ... the danger is always of bourgeois-nationalism *in one guise or another*" (my italics).[30] Two years later, however, the NJC changed its tune.

While grumbling inside the party, in public Salsberg remained loyal, even labelling the growing allegations of anti-Semitism in the USSR, in what he called the "reactionary press," a "big lie." At a mass meeting featuring the Very Reverend Dr Hewlett Johnson, dean of Canterbury Cathedral, at Massey Hall in February 1953, sponsored by the Canada-Soviet Friendship Society, Salsberg condemned the "phoney protest rally" held two weeks earlier by the Canadian Jewish Congress.[31] So-called Soviet anti-Semitism, he exclaimed before the packed hall, was a "trumped up charge" that could only bolster US Secretary of State John Foster Dulles and his plans for aggression against the Soviet Union. Jews, he said, should be wary of backing from reactionaries who, like WASP members of some Toronto golf clubs and a St Clair Avenue dining club, were themselves anti-Semites and by no means friends of the Jewish people or other minorities. Salsberg chose to lie to cover up what he then knew to be horrible truths about Stalinist anti-Semitism – and, no doubt, its other crimes as well. Was it out of blind loyalty to the "cause"? Was it hubristic unwillingness to admit that he was wrong? Was it a wildly naive expectation that he could reverse these Soviet policies? Perhaps all three, though he did not explain himself at the time.

Salsberg's next major opportunity to confront the Soviets directly came after his trip to Helsinki in June 1955 as the United Jewish People's Order (UJPO) delegate to the World Peace Assembly in Helsinki, then to the World Jewish Conference Against German Rearmament in Paris, and, finally on to Moscow. Here officials told him that the Jewish Anti-Fascist Committee had been dissolved because, by 1948, it had outlived its purpose and, in any case, included members who "had developed bourgeois nationalist tendencies."[32] Salsberg may not have known for certain that this was an outright lie (although he probably had his suspicions). It was later revealed that the secret decision to close down the committee was – according to the official, though then secret, record – based on false charges that "as the facts show, this Committee is a center of anti-Soviet propaganda and regularly submits anti-Soviet information of foreign intelligence."[33]

Yes, Jewish writers had been arrested, Salsberg's interlocutors admitted, but that was the work of the discredited Lavrenti Beria (former secret police chief, executed in 1953) "and regrettably innocent people were among his victims."[34] In any event, not only Jews, but also writers of many nationalities had suffered. "I was urged to be patient," Salsberg reported. "All those falsely arrested were being freed and rehabilitated." When he inquired about the fate of intellectuals, artists, and actors like Bergelson, Feffer, Markish, Kvitko, Hofshtein, and Der Nister he was told again that "innocent people had been killed." And in response to his concerns about the crushing of Yiddish culture, he was assured that some concerts were being planned for ten cities.[35]

Salsberg did not publically discuss overt anti-Semitism in the Soviet Union, some of it emanating from Stalin himself, who began to conceive of an "international Jewish conspiracy" against his country.[36] The ensuing campaign against "cosmopolitanism," Zionism, and the State of Israel was nothing less than full-scale anti-Semitism, which was only thinly masked by assertions of a need to expose enemies of the state. Stalin's system, as Jonathan Brent and Vladimir Naumov conclude, "required enemies who would destabilize social and political conditions so that power could be seized and held. Political stability depended on crises."[37] But Salsberg likely realized that pressing the point would only have aroused hostility and, quite possibly, even worsened the suppression of Jewish culture. Even if he did not believe what he was told, he did not protest, probably because his goal was to push for the survival of a language and a culture.

It is now known – thanks to recently released documents in Russian archives – that Stalin's persecution of these Jewish poets, writers, and actors was tantamount to a pogrom, but in the early 1950s much was hidden. It was perhaps naive to avoid public debate, but not unreasonable, in the circumstances, for Salsberg to accept what he was told in Moscow and to regard the annulment of the sentences (on 22 November 1955) as an end to the entire affair.[38]

During his Soviet Union visit, Salsberg tried to get information and impressions from Jews he met in Moscow restaurants, stores, and streets, but had only limited success. Even though the situation seemed to be improving somewhat, he came away with the impression that concerning "Jewish cultural – communal activity ... the basic approach of the Party in the Soviet Union was still negative and inconsistent."[39] He reported this to the national executive on his return to Canada in August and insisted that the party admit that it had been wrong and confront the CPSU's top leadership on it. The executive baulked, but agreed to have Buck, who was about to leave for Moscow on party business, revisit the question with officials there. Salsberg agreed to wait for his report.

Publicly, he still continued to toe the party line. Writing in *Vochenblatt* about his trip, he simply glowed with enthusiasm for the progress he witnessed in the Soviet Union. "The tremendous rate of construction and the universal desire for peace – these two manifestations of life in the Soviet Union – constitute the major impressions of life there."[40] He gave no hint of his rising angst. In fact, he stated that he was "impressed by the signs which point to a renewed extension of Jewish cultural and religious endeavours" and reported that concerts of Yiddish folk songs in Moscow and other major cities (where there were packed houses) were in progress. Moscow had no less than three synagogues, two of them with full-time rabbis! The city's Rabbi Schleiffer, supported by synagogue officials, waxed enthusiastic about government approval for a new prayer book – to be printed on the finest of paper – and the promise of a new rabbinical seminary.

While the situation in the Soviet Union remained unchanged following Stalin's death in 1953, the Khrushchev revelations of "Stalin's crimes" at the CPSU's [Communist Party of the Soviet Union] twentieth congress in February 1956 put virtually all such questions on hold until the bombshell could be absorbed. In April, the ever-loyal National Jewish Committee issued a lengthy document addressing the "profound" effect of the revelations on Canadian Jewish comrades who were "shocked and grieved at the news."[41] These powerful sentiments, it was reported, were being fanned by the right-wing Yiddish press, whose red-baiters now took to the offensive, deliberately adding further bitterness and confusion. In the face of this assault, the NJC pressed for clarity among the faithful through seminars and discussions, although the "crimes" were, undoubtedly, chiefly the work of the "Beria gang" in the Kremlin, "and the ravages of Hitlerism." "While we were unhappy with the dissolution of the Anti-Fascist Committee in 1948," the document continued, "most of us had such implicit faith in the workings of socialist justice that we emphatically rejected any serious questioning of what happened." But we were in error by not listening to the "anti-Soviet slanders of the bourgeois press, including the campaign of reactionary elements in the Jewish community," because the wrongs were now being corrected. Nevertheless, they needed to press Moscow for explanations and for information on steps being taken to make amends and eliminate the possibilities for "further violations." This, the NJC insisted, must be accompanied not only by patience and faith in socialism but also with confidence that "discussions around the 20th Congress will stimulate improvements on every front." In a mid-April issue of *Vochenblatt*, editor Joshua Gershman attacked those who rushed to judgment, saying that while Jewish culture had been undermined, this was the unlawful work of the "Beria clique" and was since being corrected, especially in the field of Yiddish literature, "irrefutable evidence of the full and untrammelled opportunities made available to Jews by the Soviet state." "Let us not forget," he correctly pointed out, "that it was the Soviet Union that saved millions of Jews from Nazi extermination."[42]

In May the LPP admitted its error in expelling Salsberg from the National Executive Committee in 1953 and reinstated him.[43] It also voted to send him to Moscow on a special mission to reopen the matter; at the same time it issued a resolution admitting its error in not raising "the issue with ... the CPSU, in regard to the case of the Jewish writers in the U.S.S.R. and the dissolution of Jewish cultural institutions ... by arbitrary measures ... despite the fact that there were requests voiced in the LPP that the National Committee seek to ascertain the facts."[44] The party later decided only to include Salsberg as part of a four-person delegation – including William Kardash, Sam Lipshitz (accompanied by his wife, Mania), and Tim Buck – to raise a number of issues, not just the "Jewish question," with the CPSU's central committee.[45] The delegation, nevertheless, was not the only communist party to place the issue before the top Soviet leadership.[46] In early May, leaders of the communist party held a lengthy discussion on the issue with Khrushchev and Anastas Mikoyan in Moscow.[47] The Canadians arrived in late August and Salsberg and Buck met with Khrushchev and Mikhail Suslov soon afterwards. Salsberg conveyed the gist of the meeting in his *Vochenblatt* articles. But the tone of the encounter is best captured in his careful notes of those meetings.[48]

The Soviets were adamant and dismissive. All of the concerns Salsberg had raised in 1955 were reiterated – and the same explanations offered.[49] When asked why there was so much anti-Semitism there, Khrushchev bluntly replied that there was none. On the contrary, he asserted that there were "Jewish ministers, party deputies, writers, scientists, musicians, etc." "His own daughter-in-law was Jewish and Jews had their own territory in Birobidjan." "Where one Jew strikes [anchor?] there he establishes a synagogue, ... Rabbis made reactionary speeches ... [stressing that Jews] must always remain Jews. Have to take it from Rabbis but not from Comrades." On the question of Yiddish, Khrushchev asked Salsberg, "Shall we force (names prom[inent] Jews) to narrow themselves to write only in Yiddish?" Khrushchev now taunted: "You [are] saddled by [New York financier Bernard] Baruch and the Zionists ... saddle padded, not yet strapped, watch out." When Salsberg raised the "doctors' plot" affair, the prosecution of physicians, most of them Jewish, for allegedly conspiring to kill the Soviet leaders on orders from the American Jewish Joint Distribution Committee and Zionists, the response was: "Actually, more non-Jews than Jews were indicted in that unfortunate frameup, but it was perpetrated by Lavrenti Beria (now thoroughly discredited)." The accused doctors had been released and the whole issue buried. As for the suppression of the Anti-Fascist Committee, the new party line was that after the war it had become a "sort of aid society" to help Jews get jobs and accommodations, while its organ, the also abolished Yiddish newspaper *Einikeit*, was guilty of exaggerating Jewish contributions to postwar reconstruction. In any event, the paper was no longer needed because, it was asserted, most Jews read Russian now.[50]

Would the Soviets, Salsberg inquired, offer a public explanation, or an apology, for these terrible events?[51] The gist of the reply was: No! Why should they? Actions speak louder than words. The wrongs are being corrected. Beria's crimes had involved nationalities other than Jews, so why apologize only to Jews? Nor would the Soviets allow the revival of Yiddish newspapers, since there already was one issued in Birobidjan. They replied to the effect that Jews wanting to read it could subscribe, just as Ukrainians, Georgians, and Armenians throughout the USSR could access newspapers in their own languages from their respective homelands and republics. The pre-1948 policy of favouring the nationalities' cultural expression was different, the Soviets admitted, but it was argued that the context had changed. Jews shared Soviet values with their fellow citizens, it was claimed. Those who did not, or retained Yiddish as their language of reading choice, were described as anachronistic. To address Jewish cultural needs, the Soviets were prepared to stage some concerts, and a Yiddish almanac was to be published. But that was judged sufficient. To Salsberg's proposal that a democratically elected Jewish committee decide on their community's cultural needs, the Soviets replied that such a body was not helpful, because Jews were becoming Russians.

Upon his return to Canada with the rest of the delegation, Salsberg expressed his reservation with their report, which was, in his mind, not only uncritical but also inappropriately glowing with praise for the communist paradise. He was especially irked that Buck "expressed agreement with Suslove's [*sic*] explanation of [Soviet] policy towards Jews ... [Buck] agrees that CPSU will provide [cultural] opportunities as need is established."[52] Lengthy dissertations by party officials in Canada and the

Soviet Union followed on the evolution of communist ideology in different countries intended to direct the Canadians into line.

What Salsberg found especially worrisome were Khrushchev's statements about Jewish distinctiveness: Jews in the Romanian territories incorporated after the Second World War into the USSR chose to return to Romania rather than accept Soviet citizenship; Jews refused to sweep the streets in Czernovitz; Soviet Jews who went abroad as tourists tended not to return; and the proposed re-establishment of Jewish settlements in the Crimea destroyed by the Germans during the Second World War stalled on the supposed grounds that it would incite anti-Semitic activity. When Khrushchev made his snide remark about Jews and synagogues, Salsberg lost it. He could not believe his ears: "[Khrushchev's] approach to the problems of the Jewish people is an unforgivable violation of socialist democracy ... If Khrushchev's distrust of the Jewish people is justified then it is a terrible indictment not of the Soviet Jews, but of the Stalinist crimes and distortions of their nationalities policy in general and particularly as applied to the Jewish people."[53] Tim Buck, who also heard Khrushchev's remarks, was more blunt. In a private conversation with Morris Biderman, a prominent Toronto party member, he noted unambiguously, "Khrushchev is an antisemite."[54]

These painful realities, Salsberg concluded, needed immediate attention. Foremost was that despite Khrushchev's exposure of Stalin's numerous crimes, including the crushing of many nationalities' cultures, not just Jewish, the new Soviet regime was doing little to correct things.[55] A return to the policies of the twenties (and Leninist "first principles") of fostering, or at least allowing nationalities in the USSR to develop their own distinctive cultural personalities was needed. Salsberg pointed out that the policy was most severe on Jews because, unlike Georgians or Ukrainians, who enjoyed their culture and language in their own national territories, Jews had no viable territory outside of Birobidjan, which was failing and provided only "a dimly flickering cultural candle." His recent conversations in Moscow, Joe confided to *Vochenblatt*'s readers, left him convinced that "the Soviet party and the Soviet leaders have still not returned to the principled track [Leninism] in their nationalities policy."

Bourgeois democracy allowed such cultural diversity in Western Europe and North America, where a multi-language press existed, Salsberg argued. So why could not a similar situation prevail in a socialist state? The belief that socialism should allow and protect such "democratic" rights illustrates how idealistic – and naive – he remained about the nature of socialism in the Soviet Union, where the very word "democracy," if used at all, was an empty slogan and where, under Stalin, the pursuit of "socialism in one country" had destroyed the pursuit of proletarian internationalism. This ideological simplicity or self-delusion is incongruous, even given Salsberg's enduring faith in the possibilities of Soviet socialism. Yet, it is clear that his beliefs overcame whatever private doubts he may have had. Pointing to the Polish government's condemnation of anti-Semitism as "demoralizing to the ranks of the party's cadre," he argued that if the Polish regime – only ten years in power – was directly confronting anti-Semitism, surely the Soviets, after nearly forty years, could be expected to do no less. But such was not the case. Despite improvements since Stalin's death, the official attitude to Jewish culture continued to perpetuate the Stalinist outlook.

Meanwhile, in New York, Khrushchev's 1956 revelations and their aftermath destroyed the faith of long-time believers, like John Gates and many others, who were also dismayed by displays of old-style Russian imperialism in Hungary and Poland.[56] In Paris, comrades such as Haim Sloves were shattered, and furious debates and splits ensued among Yiddish-speaking communists.[57] Back in Canada, some steadfast Ukrainian communists also were offended at Soviet anti-Semitism.[58] The Jewish question amidst the continuing crisis of the nationalities issue was, in Salsberg's mind, at the very centre of the struggle for a return to communist first principles. He wrote: "The struggle for the full revival of all-sided Jewish cultural activity in the Soviet Union is part of the general struggle to return to socialist democratic norms in all spheres of Soviet life: and ... every step in the direction of democratization is at the same time contributing to the revival of Jewish cultural life."[59] Salsberg believed in the possibility of realizing "socialist democracy" in the Soviet Union because, under Lenin, and until Stalinism's repressive show trials in the 1930s, Jewish cultural and communal expression had thrived.

In his final *Vochenblatt* article, on 20 December 1956, Salsberg expressed his refusal to despair. The "serious [Stalinist] distortion of socialist theory and ethics ... cannot long continue," especially now that the international situation was becoming more stabilized, and because of the unstoppable process of "doing away with the distortions and evils of the Stalin period."[60] Moreover, because of the spread of socialism to other countries, in other words, because of its universalism, the necessary variety of approaches "will affect the approach to the Jewish question in the USSR." Besides, he added, the Soviet Union's Jews will not give up the struggle for "cultural reemergence," noting, prophetically,

that it "will have vital effects on the life of Jews everywhere." Nevertheless, he continued, the ideological and political struggle must be fought
by Jewish socialists within the socialist family, not allowing "ourselves to
become partners with the enemies of socialism, of those who use the
Soviet Jewish problem as an excuse for their anti-Sovietism." And the
collegial ideological struggle should be carried on internationally, so
that communists everywhere would pressure Soviet leaders to address
their nationalities policies "and especially the Jewish questions" more
sympathetically.

Salsberg made essentially the same case in a statement he presente-
ed to the party, but more emphatically than he did in *Vochenblatt*. And he
pulled no punches. The Canadians, he said, went to Moscow in the
spirit of the joint declaration of the communist parties of the Soviet
Union and Yugoslavia in June 1956, which proclaimed "cooperation ...
voluntariness ... [and] equality" in the "comradely exchange on con-
troversial questions," to ask about how the national question, and the
Jewish problem in the USSR, were being solved.[61] "A full answer has yet
to be found," he said, "for the burning question how it was possible to
steadily narrow down and finally to make a nightmare caricature of socialist justice in the Soviet Union" since the late 1930s. And while it was
encouraging to hear that steps were now being taken to return some
powers to the national republics and "to rectify the crimes and injustices
committed against the Jewish nationality [which] resulted in a complete
temporary extinction of every and all forms of Jewish cultural activity in
the Soviet Union," this was far from adequate and less than what flourished between 1917 and 1930. On this matter the Soviet government
should take an example from Poland, where the People's Democratic
Republic had encouraged and supported a democratically elected Jewish Social and Cultural Association to administer a wide range of Jewish
cultural activity.[62]

Salsberg's autumn 1956 *Vochenblatt* articles (published in both English and Yiddish versions) aroused intense interest among readers, many
responding with the same deep concerns. In fact, the articles were so
famous that New York's Yiddish daily, the left-centre *Forverts*, commented
on Salsberg's views, while the communist *Morgen Freiheit* reprinted the series.[63] Even the *New York Times* offered favourable response. Condensed
versions were published in Paris's *Naie Presse*, in the New York quarterly
Klorkeit, and in the Tel Aviv *Drachim Chadashot*.[64] Obviously, then, there
was international interest in the opinion of a first-hand observer of Salsberg's standing about the fate of Jews in the Soviet nirvana, and the

Canadian debate in *Vochenblatt* illustrates the depth of feeling among believers. Now galvanized, Salsberg tried to enlist support among British and United States communist activists, as he explained to Hyman Levy in London, to organize "pressure ... to literally compel the Communist Party of the Soviet Union to adopt a change in policy and attitude to the Jewish question." "Objectively speaking," he continued, "the greatest contribution that can be made to silence the anti-socialist and anti-Soviet propagandists is the correction of errors, the wrong policies and the miscarriage of justice in the Soviet Union." Replies to his pleas were sympathetic but only rhetorical.

Vochenblatt editor Joshua Gershman, however, remained loyal to Moscow. In early January 1957 he wrote that "this mighty socialist nation is a land of contrasts" and that complete negativity would not do the Soviet Union justice.[65] Without glossing over "the grim crimes against the Jewish people committed ... during the Stalin regime [and] the fact that even since the 20th Congress very little has been done to make up for the injustices against Jewish communal life in the USSR," Gershman stressed that this was a nationalities issue, not just a Jewish question. And in any event, "the socialist flower, which blooms and glows despite the thorns and weeds, cannot be ignored, and must not." The fact is, he stressed, we Jewish communists did not "strongly demand of the Soviet leaders what happened to Jewish cultural institutions, cultural leaders and others since 1948." And it was "a crime" not to have spoken out. But, while Gershman gave his own perspective on these matters, he did not contradict Salsberg's essential message.

In fact, Gershman informed his readers that Yiddish culture, far from declining as more Soviet Jews were becoming Russified, was actually thriving. In a meeting with a sizeable group of Yiddish writers, Gershman learned that books in that language were not only selling very well, but in some cases were also getting translated. Over eight million copies of Kvitko's (one of the executed writers) works, for example, had been translated into thirty-four languages.[66]

As for alleged low attendance at Jewish artistic performances, the writers told Gershman that in Ukraine, White Russia, and Latvia there was strong interest, while down in Baku a drama group was forming up, folk songs were being collected, Yiddish books were selling out quickly, and Yiddish was well in use as a first language.[67] During these and other discussions, Gershman wrote, "I became even more convinced that the official argument that there was no natural desire among Jews for unique cultural expression was incorrect."[68]

In a meeting he had with the editors of *Pravda* (one of them a Jew), however, Gershman learned that "there is no natural desire for a Jewish theatre, Yiddish paper etc." Moreover, whatever little anti-Semitism remains was depicted as a carry-over from czarist days and the German occupation, and insinuations that the Soviet government was anti-Semitic was "a criminal distortion of the truth."[69]

While objecting to the fact that Salsberg's articles were being used by "the old, chronic enemies of the USSR ... to deepen and expand their deadly propaganda," Gershman nevertheless supported his revelations of the system's injustices. And he endorsed his demand for a democratic assembly for Soviet Jews to express their cultural aspirations. Finally he argued: "If the charges against the Jewish writers were false, if their liquidation is seen as a crime, then institutions like the Jewish publishing house, Jewish theatre, [a] Yiddish journal, etc., should be revived, because they were closed down not because there was no need for them but because of spurious charges against their leaders."

Some readers of Salsberg's and Gershman's *Vochenblatt* articles were unhappy with their drift. Labour activist Sam Walsh – also a recent visitor to the USSR – was puzzled. In a two-part contribution at the end of February, entitled "*Voohin Gaistu, Vochenblatt?*" ("Where are you going, *Vochenblatt?*"),[70] he challenged assertions that official documents which carried a designation of Jews as Jews were evidence of anti-Semitism: national identities were registered for all groups in the Soviet Union. In any event, Lenin's policy of fostering the nationalities was intended only for the more "backward ones." Thus, when the Soviet government insisted on diversity in groups like young musicians, it was not (as Salsberg had suggested) anti-Semitic to limit Jewish representation. Rather, it was an expression of "the policy towards training national cadres in the formerly backward republics and regions."[71] "Don't we do the same to foster some national unity in Canada?" Walsh asked. As for Russian Jews pining for Yiddish culture, this was poppycock. Moscow's Yiddish Art Theatre played to almost empty houses; instead, Jews flocked to the Bolshoi. They read classic and current Jewish writers, yes, but in Russian, not Yiddish. The journal *Emes*, Walsh had heard in Moscow, had fewer than 500 readers in the Soviet Union and only about 1000 subscribers abroad. So, "for the *Vochenblatt* to insist that cultural expression in ... Yiddish ... has been extinguished as a result of criminal, anti-Leninist, chauvinist acts of brutal police terror ... is very false and misleading."[72]

As for the closure of the Jewish Anti-Fascist Committee in 1948, all the other similar national committees established during the Second World

War to mobilize support for the Great Patriotic War had also been disbanded. Moreover, Walsh continued, it was "childish" to ask the Soviets to set up a Jewish congress of the sort Salsberg proposed; this carried the anti-revolutionary flavour of Bundism and Social-Democracy. What should be done? Walsh suggested ignoring Salsberg's complaints because "the Jews of the Soviet Union march onward and upward, alongside all their Soviet brothers, to the conquest of all obstacles, relics of backwardness and mistakes, in triumph and brotherhood to communism." "Does *Vochenblatt*," Walsh ended, "no longer address itself to the interests of the [Jewish] working people?" Or "has it begun with socialism ... and ended with nationalism ...?"

Walsh's attack was too much for Salsberg's long-time friend Morris Biderman, whose reply in *Vochenblatt* was entitled "*Vu Bistu Farkrochen, Sam Walsh*" (literally, "Sam Walsh, where did you drag yourself to?" Or, perhaps, "You are really off track"!) "I have rarely read anything containing so many quarter and half truths, such twisting and distortion of facts and history, taking the written word and drawing false, distorted conclusions," Biderman wrote.[73] He thought it nonsense for Walsh to say that Jews had assimilated to Russian culture. Some of them drifted away, but certain "administrative - moral" pressures for Russification were exerted on Jews and other nationalities, causing "much suffering and tragedy." Demands that the USSR "return to the national policy" of Lenin was not anti-socialist; nor was it Bundist, as Walsh alleged. He was just "throw[ing] sand in people's eyes." Incontrovertible evidence existed that large numbers of Jews wanted a Jewish theatre, newspapers, and a writers' committee. What a paradox, Biderman continued, that the government offered Jews the publication of a prayer book and the establishment of a yeshiva, but declared that Yiddish newspapers and books written by Jewish workers and revolutionaries were an impossibility!

Letters from a number of readers, including one from the noted Montreal Yiddish poet Sholem Shtern, essentially supported Salsberg, Gershman, and Biderman.[74] However, Gershman decided to terminate this lively debate with a lengthy and blistering attack on Sam Walsh, whose "letter certainly did not contribute to ... the socialist solution to the ageslong, painful Jewish questions ... His theories are alien to Marxists who want to win the Jewish people for socialism."[75]

Salsberg also responded, but not in *Vochenblatt*. With his growing body of supporters, he chose to fight it out in the party and in the UJPO, whose Toronto executive advanced the date of its 1956 annual conference to 8–9 December to highlight what it called "the Tragic Events and crimes committed in the Soviet Union."[76] He decided to address the conference and mobilize support for a full-fledged attack on the Soviet Union's record of crimes and anti-Semitism. At a secret emergency meeting in October 1956 attended by over two thousand party members, he rejected Tim Buck's appeal for party unity and praised recent anti-Soviet demonstrations in Poland as "a very good thing for the Polish people and for socialism in general" and described the Hungarian revolt as "the product of serious evils and errors in the Soviet system" to loud applause.[77] Such painful experiences "profoundly shocked ... the members of our organization," S. Shek announced in a report indicating that Salsberg's protests had gone unanswered by the communist hierarchy. As a result, UJPO members were dissatisfied with the organization's tradition of "follow[ing] the political line of the Labor-Progressive Party" because "this influenced the organization and stood in the way of the broadest development of our cultural and educational work." A conference manifesto put it this way:

> For many years we accepted uncritically all developments in the Soviet Union. This was wrong. There were members who questioned the sudden disappearance of Jewish writers and cultural institutions. Their questioning was rejected and dismissed without justification. Developments and events in the Soviet Union, shall be examined and our attitude to them determined on the basis of full, free discussion in the organization.[78]

Finally ready to break away, UJPO would soon sever its ties with the communists, create a fully democratic atmosphere in its ranks, and become an independent organization devoted solely to the advancement of Jewish culture in Canada, with a "positive attitude" to the State of Israel. Moreover, UJPO's previous financial support for *Vochenblatt* would be ended and members not obliged to contribute. Ended was slavish adherence to the party line, restraint on protests against Moscow's anti-Semitism, and isolation from the Jewish mainstream: "The UJPO will work unstintingly in the interests of its members, their families, and the Jewish community as a whole."[79] Salsberg and his UJPO supporters were now effectively out of the party.

It is not entirely clear, however, whether Salsberg jumped or was pushed. In November he was ousted from the national executive committee (technically, he failed to be re-elected) because of "sharp differences of opinion."[80] He then offered to resign as Metro party leader, a post he had reluctantly accepted after returning from Moscow in September.

Toronto communists were experiencing major turmoil and serious an-
tagonisms since Salsberg had gone public in *Vochenblatt*. Equally disruptive were his outspoken demands at party meetings "for a realignment of
socialist forces in Canada, for a new Party of Canadian Marxism." For this
initiative he was assailed for his "right opportunist tendency" to undermine the essentials of Marxist-Leninism. The air at party conclaves was
blue with accusations and what he called "petty bickering and manoue-
verings." He wanted out of this "place d'armes for factionalism" and resigned. After acrimonious debate, his resignation was formally "rejected"
by the Metro committee. But he was now, in reality, out of the communist
movement. A journey that had begun in 1926 was nearly finished.

Finally willing to admit the obvious and, more important, what he had
known for years, Salsberg stated that the USSR's Jewish question was a
symptom of even more fundamental problems; the Jewish issue provided
a window on the failings of the communist movement and the crisis within
its ranks. Canadians, he said at the CPC plenum, had been so subservient
to the CPSU that "this crippled our ability to think independently." The
LPP, therefore, must refocus and realistically address Canadian issues,
within the Canadian context; it must escape its current political isolation by seeking a new approach to the CCF – breaking with his previous
antipathy to this party – and the trade union movement.[81] Within such
an alignment of socialist forces, only a democratic and independent political party "based on Scientific socialism" could appropriately address
Canadian issues and chart a path to socialism. But "the LPP, with its long
history of subservience to the CPSU, its dogmatism, its sectarianism, its
isolation from the masses and the distrust with which it is regarded cannot be transformed into such a party." The Jewish question had broken
Salsberg's faith. In a speech he gave at the January 1957 meeting of the
Metro committee of the LPP that followed a similar oration delivered at
its December 1956 plenum advocating "a Socialist Realignment in Canada," he wrote that the party "violated our moral integrity ... Enough. I
do not offer amendments because main line is wrong."[82]

"Enough," yes, but Salsberg was not content to just up and quit. Experienced communicator that he was, he wanted his position to be known
widely and influentially in communist circles everywhere. He wrote letters to comrades in Britain, Israel, and the United States stressing to
one correspondent the need for "more organized pressure ... to literally compel a change in [Soviet] policy and attitude towards the Jewish
question ... What is necessary now is an organized public campaign by
all those who have always been loyal to the Soviet Union," followed by a

specific proposal for change that he would publish soon in *Vochenblatt*.[83] He thought that the changes he had in mind were only possible if "a number of prominent people in and around our movement [would] stimulate it, head it, and pursue it to a logical conclusion." He received in return letters of sympathy and support.[84]

His combativeness now aroused, Salsberg went on the attack. With four others, he set up a new organization, a mysterious formation called the Forum for Socialist Education, according to a report by the United States Federal Bureau of Investigation (FBI), "to exchange information and get together once in a while."[85] He also refused the party's appeals for a reconciliation and described the CPC as a "straightjacket." Communist officials were deeply concerned about the widespread disaffection Salsberg's resignation and frequent speaking engagements were causing, especially in Hamilton and Montreal, where the Jewish groups were in serious disarray. Brushing aside an offer that the party was "willing to get along with him and reach some agreement, like the one that the Soviet Party has reached with [Yugoslavia's Marshal] Tito," Salsberg told officials that he would speak out whenever and wherever he chose.

The *Vochenblatt*'s editorial and UJPO's support for Salsberg's critique caused deep concern in the Labor-Progressive Party, especially when, at its sixth convention in April 1957, his supporters attempted to get the party's backing for pressuring the Soviet Union on the Jewish issue.[86] Labelling these moves "revisionist attempts to liquidate our party or turn it into an appendage of social-reformism," the party's National Executive Committee (in May 1958) condemned those behind this "right wing attack" on communist principles. The NEC castigated these crypto-Zionists and nationalists who had abandoned Marxism, quitting the party and even seeking readmission to the Canadian Jewish Congress, that bastion of the bourgeoisie (which, as everyone knew, was headed by Montreal whisky tycoon Samuel Bronfman). The NEC wanted nothing to do with those advocating support for the CCF and raising money for social-democratic causes in Israel. The executive condemned *Vochenblatt* and the "deviationist" leadership of UJPO for their "serious errors" (which should be "criticized in a comradely fashion") because "efforts to ascribe anti-Semitism to the Soviet Union's policy [towards its Jewish minority], no matter how cunningly concealed, are slanders against socialism and the Soviet Union, and are attempts to create fertile soil for anti-Marxist revisionism in Canada."

Finally, communists "should resist all policies and actions which kowtow to the Jewish bourgeoisie or to Right social democracy."[87]

Subsequent party documents kept up this attack, even naming Salsberg and his close associate, Sam Lipshitz, as leading the attempts to win over the UJPO for their "revisionism" against the Soviet Union by "[incorrectly] present[ing] the Soviet Jews as an oppressed nationality suffering discrimination and anti-Semitism." Party stalwarts also condemned Salsberg's and Lipshitz's enthusiastic support for the British-French "imperialist" attack on Egypt in 1956, presumably because of Israel's involvement.[88]

Salsberg's protest had such a powerful effect on the Party that Tim Buck devoted part of his report to the National Executive Committee meeting (31August–2 September) to the "right-wing confusion" amongst Jewish members, and the need for clarity "on the national question as a whole" and the Jewish question in particular.[89] And in a lengthy statement to members, Buck made a pointed attack on the "recurring sickness [of] revisionism, ... the current of opportunism which reflects the pressure of bourgeois ideas within the Marxist movement." Revisionism encouraged the illusion that the "irreconcilable conflict between Marxism and bourgeois ideology" can be eliminated and that "capitalism can grow into socialism by a purely evolutionary process of social reform."[90]

This, of course, was heresy, long recognized since the times of Marx and Engels, who faced down enemies who disguised themselves as Marxists. Buck stressed that the party had always "repudiated the opportunist line." And it must do so again, on the Canadian field of ideological battle. Salsberg, in particular, had shown his true colours when he failed to critique the deviationist Gui Caron (a Montreal comrade who had run for the LPP in Saint-Louis riding in the 1948 Quebec provincial election campaign), who had publicly declared that "Marxism failed to explain reality." Salsberg, moreover, had blatantly informed a newspaper – a capitalist one yet – that he saw promise in the CCF and that he would like to lead a movement of "individuals who have lost faith in Communism."[91] Buck's diatribe against Salsberg went on for many pages in the August–September 1957 issue of *Marxist Review*, which also contained other attacks on "revisionism" by party ideologues and reprinted an editorial from *Pravda* on the necessity for unity in the party.

The major purpose of Buck's assault, of course, was to counter a serious challenge from one of the party's best-known figures and undermine his credibility. In this he had little success. Many non-Jewish as well as Jewish party members were shaken not just by the Khrushchev revelations of "Stalin's crimes," but also by the Soviet invasion of Hungary in October 1956. Among most Jewish communists the contest between their beloved

Yosele Salsberg and Tim Buck was a non-starter, accusations of deviationism, opportunism, and other ideological impurities be damned. Joe
was one of them, a Yiddish-speaking brother tried and true, a friend to
all, loved by the masses of working-class Toronto Jews, communist and
non-communist alike. He had now spoken out for the oppressed of his
people – a little late, perhaps, but clearly and unequivocally – and most
of them were with him.

Joe's departure left some observers sceptical, however. Bill Walsh refused to quit, though urged to do so by Salsberg, replying to his former
mentor, "What do you have to replace the Party with?"[92] A few years later,
Maurice Spector, once the party's leading intellectual and a major figure in Canadian communism's formative years until he was expelled for
Trotskyism in 1928, commented acidly and accurately:

> Salsberg ... could have broken with the Comintern over many issues involv-
> ing such serious things as the Nazi-Soviet Pact, the purging of six million
> kulaks, the pick-ax assassination of Leon Trotsky ... He chose, for reasons
> that he will clear with his own conscience, to remain with the Communist
> Party until a time he went to Russia and discovered that ... Yiddish writers
> had been liquidated and purged by the Stalin terror. So he broke with Rus-
> sia because of the persecution of Yiddish. I ... and others have broken over
> other issues. Everyone chooses his own moment.[93]

Joshua Gershman, one of the few leading Canadian Jewish communists who stayed on in the party, was also unsympathetic: "Salsberg was
already aligned with people not only in Canada but in other countries
as well ... [They met] in Paris. They had grand illusions ... He [had]
the great idea that he will become one of the leaders of an international
movement against Moscow domination."[94]

Are these observations fair? How should the historian assess Salsberg's
behaviour on both the suppression of Jewish culture in the Soviet Union
and his support for the party, which denied it and removed him from
its senior councils? He was, above all other aspects of his identity, a loyal
communist, a Stalinist really, who, despite mounting personal angst
which he expressed to close friends, chose to believe what the Soviets
told him and to accept Canadian party discipline – until the autumn of
1956.[95] Where, outside of the party, could he find a political home suit-
able for his continuing Jewish pursuit of the socialist project? He was
no closer to the CCF in 1957 than he had been twenty years earlier. He
was on the outs with the Canadian Jewish Congress, which he publicly

condemned in 1954 for its refusal to protest against the rearmament of Germany and what he called the "revolting stand of [Jewish Liberal MPs] [Leon] Crestohl and [David] Croll who voted in parliament for arming the Germans."[96] Since the UJPO had been expelled from the Congress, Salsberg could hardly find refuge in this august assembly (which called itself "the parliament of Canadian Jewry"), or in the Toronto Jewish community councils that were dominated by the haute bourgeoisie which had opposed him since the 1930s. Dispirited by the loss of his riding in the bitter provincial election of 1955 and increasingly concerned about the declining health of his wife, Dora, he clung – naively? certainly; dishonestly? probably – to the cause which had guided him for nearly thirty years, hoping – with declining enthusiasm, to be sure – that he could make a difference to the Soviet policy towards Jews. This was a kind of political schizophrenia, possibly, but then which politician is without similar tensions? However, in Bryan Palmer's view, the long delay in Salsberg's repudiation of Stalinism "seals [his] fate because ... he finds it difficult to negotiate alternatives; he is robbed of his capacity to ... stay within the official communist order."[97]

It is, incidentally, noteworthy that neither Salsberg nor any of his Jewish cohorts protested against the suppression of other nationalities in the USSR. In none of Salsberg's representations to Soviet bigwigs, the CPC, or in his writings is there any mention of the cultural repression of other groups besides Jews. Soviet nationalities policy became an issue for them, it seems, only when it affected Jews. Should not these good communists have cried out that Stalin's policies towards all nationalities were undermining "true" communism? By focusing on their own complaint within the family, they were revealing themselves as nationalists, chauvinists even, under the umbrella of socialism, a position not dissimilar from that of the much-reviled Bundists and Zionists. This was, in fact, what the Soviets alleged. Jewish critics apparently wanted to enjoy both socialism and *Yiddishkeit*. But as noted above, their secular Jewishness was their first identity; it was the essence of their being; it was in their very souls. In the final analysis, their answer to the question "For whom do I toil?" was in the response that Salsberg and many of his Jewish colleagues announced in 1956 when, at long last, they realized they could not have both – and they made their choice. After struggling within himself and the party for some months, Salsberg – along with three others, including his dear friend Morris Biderman – resigned on 16 May 1957, stating that "historic changes in the world and in Canada demand new thinking and new alignments for progress and for a democratic Socialist future," and that "it is now crystal clear that the LPP cannot and will not perform this task."[98] Salsberg appeared on television to make the same announcement. Appeals to reconsider, comment, and criticism followed, but he was out of the party.

Salsberg's involvement in the movement had arisen from his transforming engagement with Jewish socialism, the search for Jewish emancipation within Marxism, as well as a commitment to the concept, in historian Peter Campbell's words, of "revolutionary transformation brought on by the general strike"[99] and the concept of "working class self-emancipation." His ardent trade-union activity throughout his membership in the party testified that Salsberg was clearly wedded to the CPC's focus on "electoral activity," but was not necessarily supportive of "the mainstream's resistance to rank-and-file activism that might damage the party's growth." Indeed, Salsberg's communist career demonstrates that he did not see these paths as inconsistent. He pursued simultaneously all four: Jewish emancipation, electoral activity, party growth, and rank-and-file labour activism, while eschewing deep involvement in ideological disputation. That was because Salsberg was essentially a man of the street, the Jewish street, seeking practical solutions to real problems. And he pursued his goals within socialist/Marxist ideological contexts that were inconsistent with improving labour conditions and social welfare.

While evidence of his ideological leanings are slim, there is nothing in his writings or speeches that is identifiable as specifically Leninist, "Trotskyist," or Stalinist. He was simply a loyal party man, obviously, and as such clearly adhered to the Comintern and Josef Stalin. Through thick and thin, he remained loyal – until 1956 – and as such he accepted what was done in the name of the party, including the Soviet Union's purges in the 1930s, the murderous collectivization in Ukraine, the suppression of ethnic cultural distinctiveness, and the postwar anti-Semitic campaigns. And in the Ontario legislature he once sang the praises of Stalin, who was later exposed as one of history's worst murderers. Why? He was not stupid, naive, blind, or uninformed. He was, like many prominent historical figures, a flawed man. Though brilliant in his own way, Salsberg, like so many others in the movement, was prepared to accept the imperfections, even evidence of the Stalinist atrocities, because he believed in the achievability of the ultimate goal of social justice through communism and he saw no viable alternative. While others fell away, Salsberg remained steadfast until he snapped in 1956, not long after being defeated politically and rendered irrelevant in labour issues. Downcast in his personal life – Dora was ill – and worried about rising anti-Semitism in Eastern Europe, he could no longer continue. But he left the party with his reputation unsullied among some of his closest former comrades. His WUL collaborator Tom Ewen wrote at the height of this contretemps that while Salsberg was "not all we could wish for in a strictly inner-family sense ... [he was, nevertheless, one of] the most devoted fighters for the people this or any other country ever had."[100]

Chapter Six

Still Counselling Otherwise

Never a full-fledged Leninist, or a compliant member of the Communist Party of Canada, Joe Salsberg had nevertheless been loyal to the cause – in his own way. Unlike most of his comrades, he was not "Moscow trained … literally nor figuratively, i.e., shaped by Moscow's agents, in a party that was not a cipher of the Kremlin."[1] Though "a fine, practical trade unionist but not a great Leninist," according to some, however, he suffered from "theoretical shallowness." He was immensely likeable – even loveable – to the many who called him Yosele, and one journalist observed that "he was that rare bird: a Communist with a sense of humour." Even the RCMP, which kept a very close watch on Salsberg, and likely maintained a thick file on him for decades, regarded him as "a humane, genteel, and intelligent Communist."

Nevertheless, Salsberg had knuckled under to party discipline in the late twenties and remained ideologically "a good boy" thereafter, never publicly voicing dissent from the Comintern line until 1956. He accepted the Hitler-Stalin pact apparently without dissent (though numerous other comrades – many of them Jews – bolted over this travesty), just as he had stayed quiet during the 1930s over the horrors of the Ukrainian famine, growing evidence of Soviet brutality towards suspected dissidents, and the show trials. Even mounting anti-Semitism during the 1930s in the workers' paradise, as noted above, got not a public peep of indignation out of Salsberg, though he claimed later to have complained to comrades about it.

Now out of the party, he was on his own in all respects. Financially, Salsberg no longer enjoyed whatever modest payments he had formerly received. Dora had a good position with Jewish Family and Child Services, but her salary would have been a modest one. So, exploiting his connections in the Jewish community, he decided to sell insurance ("Capitalism if necessary …"?), which he did successfully over many years, entirely from home, a modest apartment on Rusholme Road, northwest of the old downtown Jewish enclaves. He is said never to have made a call on a client; so well-known, respected, and loved was Salsberg that he did not have to; he simply stayed at home and answered his telephone, which rang often enough for him to earn a sound income as the proprietor of Model Insurance Agency.

His main concern, however, was Dora. In failing health, she was diagnosed with cancer and died on 20 March 1959,[2] leaving Joe heartbroken over the loss of his beloved companion. He was bitter over the failure of former political comrades to express any sympathy, considering him a traitor to the sacred cause and shunning him. He mourned Dora deeply and, though still only middle-aged, never remarried. Without children and cut off from many of his old comrades, he was lonely, unfulfilled, and bitter. He felt that he needed a platform from which to speak and write. He was, after all, not without a considerable ego. So, together with a few dozen of his former associates, Morris Biderman and Sam Lipshitz in particular, Salsberg formed the New Fraternal Jewish Association to meet and discuss current social and political issues. He wrote regularly for their monthly publication, *Fraternally Yours*, on many of these topics.

And he was coming home. Salsberg also gradually re-engaged with the mainstream organized Jewish community, notably the Canadian Jewish Congress. He also became a fixture in the *Canadian Jewish News*, the principal weekly serving eastern Canada, and wrote occasional articles for the *Globe and Mail*. His columns in the *CJN* from the early 1970s until the mid-1990s, many of them referring to a fictitious, wise interlocutor "Uncle Eliezer," were generally reminiscences and reflections on Jewish life and lore, with a heavy emphasis on his personal perspectives on political and social issues of the day. In this new phase, in reality the second half of his life, Salsberg became what he truly was, and perhaps wanted to be, a public Jewish conscience, a secular rabbi pursuing causes that would elevate the minds and spirits of Toronto Jews caught in what he saw as the downdraft of North American modernity.

While some elements in the Toronto Jewish community were sceptical of this new formation, thinking that "the habits of the [communist] past cannot be broken," Salsberg saw the New Fraternal Jewish Association as a fresh forum for socialist thought and debate, much more than just another social and cultural organization on the Toronto scene.[3] He intended it to be a spearhead for the advancement of Jewish secular culture in the community. "We are not like other fraternal organizations," he asserted in a January 1962 article. While recognizing that there were still certain "ideological" questions to be resolved within the group and that "the defense of secularism and its strengthening in the community must ... be a keynote in our work," he urged the organization to "turn outwardly ... [and] bring the benefits of our fine cultural work more and more to the community at large, in a public way."[4] This outreach, he explained in a Rosh Hashana (new year) message in 1963, was needed to counteract the "chilling middle class atmosphere [that] has enveloped ...wide areas of our communal life," especially the growth of "religious institutions, [which] attract young and middle-aged couples, many of whom are devoid of genuine religious faith or of religious practices."[5] Salsberg was certain that large numbers of Jews rejected the view that "a Jew is only he who adheres to the Judaic religion," instead believing that Jews are a nationality, a culture, a community, and it was the task of the NFJA to provide the "cohesion and instrumentalities for collective expression and action." "We could, were we to will it, stimulate discussions and certain actions which would lead to broader and more far-reaching attainments in the days ahead." Let NFJA members become missionaries "for a good cause, for a way of life which we consider worthy and essential."

Although witnessing and supporting what Harold Troper demonstrates were "the cascading events of the 1960s [which] profoundly altered Canadian Jewish self-definition, even as it dramatically remade the communal Jewish agenda," Salsberg's abiding concern was with the life within.[6] As important as the eclipse of overt anti-Semitism, "prestige pride" in Israel's 1967 military victory, and the campaign for Soviet Jewry were in this transformation, Salsberg strove to change Jews themselves by bringing them back to values that were at the core of their traditions. This was his mission now, his purpose in counselling otherwise. He would not have accepted Morton Weinfeld's prescription that "Jewish influence ... and Jewish philanthropy – rooted in both cultural traditions and social circumstances – is the foundation for the proliferation of communal organizations and thereby Jewish survival. The will to survive is not enough."[7] Salsberg would have countered that the will to survive was the vital element, the sine qua non, and if that will –the will to survive meaningfully – was not nourished, then the vast superstructure of communal organizations were but empty shells. And he would have looked askance at the assertion that the Canadian Jewish "people survives, and thrives" because thriving without the life of the mind was, to him, meaningless.

Salsberg reissued this challenge frequently, spurring his comrades to greater outreach in a community he saw was losing its way in materialism, "middle class conformism," and cultural ignorance; he saw Jewish life as "a tumultuous market place."[8] Unlike secular Jews in the past who were bound together by a Yiddish culture and socialist values, in the 1960s their children were without "ideological leadership" and "outside of all organized Jewish life," many of them completely "alienated from all Jewish interests."[9] He called for a "meeting of minds" which would lead to "unified efforts by all who accept the general thesis of secular Jewishness as a way of life." Jewish identity was in crisis and he urged his *chaverim* (friends) in NFJA and other secular organizations like the Workmen's Circle (*Arbeter Ring*) and the Labour Zionists (*Farband*) to unite to "display greater initiative and daring ... [to] make worthy contributions to responding collectively."[10] Salsberg, however, confronted the fact that even in the NFJA there was no agreement on first principles, a specific "ideological identity," even though its members had firmly rejected "everything our former affiliation [UJPO and the Communist Party of Canada] represented."[11] "Let those we have parted from ossify in the stagnant pool of deadly dogmatism," he ranted at one point.

But even his eloquent orations did little to move any secular forces towards the kind of activism he favoured. "Who will sound the alarm?" he pleaded in a November 1970 column, asserting that none of the secular organizations had so far shown the necessary leadership.[12] If not the Workmen's Circle or the Farband, then who? "Are there any other aspirants for this historic task? There is a crying need for greatness in thought, concepts and leadership." Gone now were the old ideological disputes between the opposing organizations on the Jewish left; they had to unite, this rapidly greying old guard, to combat the forces of decay, ignorance, mindless and superficial religiosity, and the abandonment of the socialist cultural values for which they had battled for so long.

Salsberg celebrated the signs of secular Jewish renewal, noting happily in December 1970 the formation of Jewish cultural groups on university campuses, and the establishment of a school in Toronto by the Secular Jewish Association, which announced that "it is becoming increasingly more difficult to maintain a non-religious Jewish identity in a community which is becoming ... more synagogue centred."[13] These developments, he exulted, are "symptomatic of the stirrings among our young people who seek a meaningful secular Jewish environment for themselves and all others who share their outlook."

There was always a strong note of the didactic in Salsberg's *FY* articles. He obviously assumed that here he was preaching – urging, cajoling almost – to old comrades, veterans of many ideological battles, and fellow travellers in the broad socialist movement. In his *CJN* contributions, however, Salsberg was more restrained and circumspect, though between the lines no less committed to his values, because his readership was the Jewish community at large. Here he sometimes was "Uncle Eliezer," his mythical other, really Joe himself, speaking to *Amcha*, the people, the Jewish street, where the religious and the secular, the affiliated and the unattached, people of all social and economic classes, and of all ages and with wide-ranging political views, congregated. In the *CJN*, therefore, Salsberg was generally indirect, and fatherly, addressing his public as "dear" or "esteemed" reader, or making other attempts at closeness.

Often, Salsberg wrote about "the good old days," mapping out a landscape of memory about the face of Jewish Toronto of yesteryear: the Lyric theatre at the corner of Dundas and Bay Streets; and the Standard Theatre (Dundas and Spadina); the transformation of Spadina as "a crucible for Jewish change"; hot summers of the 1930s; the "yummy food smells of Pesach time"; "when elections brought coal to the shtiblach [small prayer halls]"; and "the spirited Simchat Torah of yesteryear"; besides many others.[14] He wrote about its personalities, notably his contemporaries on the Left like Labour Zionists Rivke and Samuel Hurwich and fur workers union leader – and one-time opponent – Max Federman, and humble millinery worker Mendel Berger.[15] In his *CJN* columns he reminded readers of their modest economic and social origins only a generation beforehand. In one entry, on the eve of Passover 1975, entitled "Our Fathers once made clothes for all Canada," he told them that "above all trades and occupations [Jews] became clothing workers" in the sweatshops. "And so," he continued, "as the Haggadah would relate our ancestors groaned under the burden and yearned for relief and liberation. And thus there arose unions and strikes in the camps of our immigrant forefathers. And our fathers liked what they heard and they, even the lowly among them, became armed with courage and excelled in battle beyond expectation and succeeded in removing much that was bad and harmful and ... put in its place much that was good and beneficial."[16]

His heroes and heroines included community leaders Lipa Green, Henry Rosenberg, and Sam Kronick, among others.[17] He was telling his readers that, amidst struggle and poverty, immigrant life in the city was often sweet, lively, and interesting: "You might be an 'alrightnik' now, in other words, but your Yiddish-speaking parents' lives included hard labour, struggle and resistance, but also cultural enrichment, commitment and *menschlichkeit* that needs renewal in our days. Let me show you the way." He might well have been thinking of his mother, Sarah-Gitel, who had taken him and his baby sisters from Lagow, Poland, across Europe and the Atlantic Ocean to Quebec and on to Toronto in the summer of 1913, there with little material wherewithal to mother a huge family and establish a major charity for the Jewish poor.[18] He visited her often at the family home on Cecil Street where, after Abraham's death in 1951, Joe conducted the hugely attended family Passover Seder, skullcap on his head and fulsome in song. And he continued this tradition well after Sarah-Gitel died in March 1977.[19]

While concerned about the community's shortcomings, Salsberg celebrated the Canadian Jewish Congress, which "retains an unquestionable relevance to the far-flung Jewish community in the country."[20] The Congress is, he proclaimed, "the highest authority in Canadian Jewish life." Besides having an abiding interest in the general, sometimes divisive, issues before its triennial plenaries, Salsberg was especially active in its committee on Yiddish, which he headed for a number of years, attempting to ensure the survival of the "priceless gifts of this monumental treasure ... [the] national inheritance" of the Jewish people.[21] Though no longer the lingua franca of Toronto Jews, except for a few old-timers, Yiddish still held for Salsberg and other devotees a unique quality of connection with the secular past they were desperate to preserve.

Having been embraced by the Congress, Salsberg dutifully attended its conventions and reported on them to readers with enormous enthusiasm. In 1971 he decried moves he called "dragooning, stampeding and putschist tactics" to establish a Jewish Community Council, which would undermine, in his view, the supreme authority of the democratic, popularly elected Congress.[22] "The will of the people is unmistakably clear: to continue Congress's priority in Jewish life," he asserted. The sixteenth convention, he proclaimed, "clearly illustrated what the constituent bodies of Congress expect from the highest authority in Canadian Jewish life,"[23] praising the seriousness of the concern, dedication and determination evidenced by the active youth involvement and the "grass roots participation."

The council proposal resurfaced at the 1974 Congress plenary, essentially a move he believed was initiated by the city-based fund-raising bodies, the Allied Jewish Community Services in Montreal and the Welfare Fund in Toronto, to "determine policy for the community because of [their] control of the purse-strings."[24] This would "diminish ... Congress ... catastrophically to a mere public-relations position while putting Canadians under the influence and control of [a] new and undemocratic establishment ... [and] ... would also usher in a period of the most dangerous degree of alienation from the establishment-run community of our most sensitive and important sections." He was referring to the segment of Jewish youth that was "outside the community merry-go-round ... [who] ... search for meaningful values which they do not find."[25] Although fearing that the transformation was inevitable, he was opposed to the tax-collecting arms of the communities, the councils or federations which were elite-dominated, determining the priorities and policies of the democratically elected parliament of Canadian Jews, the Congress. When the marriage of the Jewish Welfare Fund of Toronto and the Toronto section of the Congress was finally accomplished in February 1976, Salsberg hoped that the democratic tradition would continue: "Uncle Eliezer says that the road to a successful marriage begins after and not before the wedding."[26]

On the eve of the May 1977 plenary, Salsberg advised his *CJN* readers of three crucial issues: the future of the Jewish community in Quebec, "culturally the most advanced portion of Canadian Jewry," the needs of Israel, and the challenges "com[ing] from Jews in the Soviet Union and Arab countries and the reemergence of anti-Semitic propaganda of the overt kind, or of the covert, the 'anti-Zionist' kind."[27] Besides the concentration of power in the hands of the few, he worried about the tendency to tinker with the structure of Congress that reflected "the alarming tendency to seek easy organizational solutions to problems that are social, spiritual and national in character."[28]

And what were these challenges? The first was the fact that "the vast majority of Jewish youth is totally uninvolved in Jewish life and its problems."[29] The same was true of Jewish academics, creative artists, and professionals of all kinds, while intermarriage, "an entire new phenomenon," had reached 40 per cent. Besides, there were the largely isolated and unaffiliated Jews – "the Israelis, Russians, and French-speaking recent immigrants," a growing presence in the 1970s. These realities are "somber indeed" and no amount of activity defending "Jewish rights" in Canada, fund-raising for Israel, and "tinkering with the organizational structure of Congress" would help in addressing these issues, which were central to Jewish survival. Salsberg returned to these topics repeatedly over the years,[30] always urging the constituent parts of Congress to make their opinions known in this important forum. "At the next plenary," he pleaded in June 1990, in perhaps his valediction on the subject, "let a hundred voices be heard!"

At the same time, Salsberg became an advocate for the preservation and strengthening of Yiddish, the vernacular of East European Jewish immigrants, now disappearing in the younger generation. Desperate to preserve this cultural treasure, he decried this trend, proclaiming that the language was "still very much alive throughout the world. It refuses to die."[31] On the inauguration of the first Yiddish credit courses at the University of Toronto, York University, and Seneca College in 1972, Salsberg was overjoyed by the presentation of the Yiddish drama group. "What blessing does one offer for such a delight?" Uncle Eliezer asked. He rejoiced, too, at the revival of Yiddish in Israel[32] and numerous other countries as a "conscious and dramatic binding together of the totality of our cultural heritage ... a necessary condition in the light for oneness of our peoplehood." He celebrated the Continuation of Montreal Yiddish literary tradition, when Chayim Leib Fuks in 1981 published in Yiddish his *100 Years of Yiddish and Hebrew Literature in Canada*, and labelled the Shtern, Sholem, and Zipper family, who were featured in the volume, "our first family of Jewish letters in this country."[33] Salsberg saw the revival of Yiddish as a major element of the secular Jewish culture he was championing, not in opposition to the spread of Hebrew in the community's schools, but as a window on the rich political and literary secular culture of the vanished world of East European Jewry in which Yiddish, not Hebrew, was the common vehicle of communication. He once included the complete Yiddish text of the old lullaby "Yankele" in a *CJN* column, inviting readers to find someone to help them with the translation, but "if you should fail, get in touch with me and we will see what can be done to help you."[34] This was not just nostalgia on his part – though how could he not be at least a little teary-eyed? – it was Salsberg's insistence that Judaism embraced more than just religious observances and the study of holy texts.

He wrote on many other issues, such as the 1961 trial in Jerusalem of Adolph Eichmann. The trial's main purpose, he thought, was "to present to mankind the gruesome record of the most inhuman, barbaric case of genocide in history and to help the Jews and the whole world draw appropriate lessons from this horrifying experience."[35] Pointing out that "ALL Jews were slated for destruction ... It would have been an offence against historic justice to have tried [Eichmann] elsewhere than in Israel and by other than Israeli judges," because Israel was acting on behalf of all Jews, pursuing "not merely anti-Jewish but anti-human and anti-Socialist ... acts ... in general whether they are directed against Jews, Russians, Ukrainians or Tadzhiks, who violated civil or criminal laws."[36] The trials of German death-camp murderers in Frankfurt in the spring of 1963 taught the same lesson: "Canadians as well as all other people of the world have to be told, and told again, what gruesome savagery Nazism had reached and what unbelievable, inhuman, monstrous crimes were committed against our people ... The key word is unbelievable."[37] "Let's recognize and admit that we all failed to believe." May it be a call to the Jewish leadership who are "guilty of blindness" to new evidence of anti-Semitism in Canada.

From the beginning of his new career in journalism, Salsberg made clear his reconversion to Zionism, and he strongly backed the fundraising efforts of the United Jewish Appeal and the lobbying by the Canada-Israel Committee. Israel was the focus of the vast majority of his essays, which included discussion on a wide range of issues including inter-Arab conflicts,[38] Israel's security situation, politics, and the fortunes of the left-wing parties.[39] The immediate aftermath of the 1967 Six Day War resulted in "a very significant strategic setback for the Soviet Union and its allied countries."[40] The Soviet Union's "universal political crusade against Israel" was morphing into outright anti-Semitism – its leaders using phrases like "the merchants of Tel Aviv" – that aroused "the anti-Semitic vermin that hid in [the Kremlin] woodwork ... [which] blossomed forth with malodorous noxious weeds." Blatantly anti-Jewish cartoons had appeared in the Soviet press, while terror tactics were directed against the Jewish communities there. However much he celebrated the emotions generated by the 1967 Israeli victory, Salsberg remained ambivalent about its long-term effects on Jewish consciousness and the sense of "oneness" between Israel and the Jews in the Diaspora.[41]

Every Israeli election was carefully analysed and political transformations assessed, Salsberg never hiding his preference for Labour, his apprehensions about Likud, and his views on the shortcomings of the Israeli electoral system.[42] Above all, he stressed the country's need and hopes for peace, which, despite impressive military victories, seemed to him almost unattainable because of Arab refusal to accept Israel's right to live. Not that Israel was occasionally without fault in its external relations, especially in its 1982 war in Lebanon, which he thought raised "profoundly troubling questions of a moral and political nature."[43]

Some of Israel's most serious problems, he frequently pointed out, were internal, including the attempts to restrict religious rights to only the Orthodox, a move that "would open a dangerous division between the communities."[44] Though he recognized the country's monumental achievements in absorbing massive immigration while defending itself against life-threatening attacks, he pointed to the decline in moral values, the loss of idealism, the cultural struggle, the growing religious militancy, and the polarization emerging in Israeli society, all of the challenges facing its younger generation.[45] He vented "a spiritual outcry of alarm" against the corruption showing up in Israel's public life in the mid-1970s when theft by two prominent leaders of the labour movement "distort moral and ethical values ... and gnaws at the very soul of our existence." ("And who can say," he added parenthetically, "that our own Canadian Jewish community is free of such elements ... that erupt as ugly sores on our national and social body from time to time.") Worse still, he thundered – as if up on his feet bashing Tories in the Ontario legislature – these "corroding and destructive trends ... are in conflict with every teaching, preaching and concept of what is Judaism, and what is Jewish ethics and values, of what is Yiddishkeit that deserves living and dying for." Notwithstanding these difficulties, Israel had increasingly important meaning for Diaspora Jews because of the energy, focus, and sense of broad purpose it gave to Jewish communities such as those in Canada.

Salsberg made several visits to Israel during these years and always enjoyed reflecting on the transformations he observed there. Although he was disturbed by some of them, he nevertheless hoped for better, in June 1975 stressing that "only kibbutzim can halt the erosion of social, moral and ethical values" there.[46] As a socialist with strong collectivist values he argued that only the "kibbutz movement ... possesses the moral authority to speak out against the harmful erosion process and to provide the militant leadership required to reverse the process and to reestablish the pioneering dedication to our highest standards of values." "The kibbutz movement," he continued, "that most authentic and most ethical of Israel's achievements, has the moral right to cry out with one voice: 'Let's halt the erosion! Let's return to basic principles!'" "If not they," he queried, "then who will?" He seldom returned to that topic in his journalistic career, perhaps recognizing that for Israel, as well as for the Diaspora, old values and the comradely democratic spirit had gone forever. In one of his last *Fraternally Yours* columns, however, he issued another summons to action: "We and all progressive Jewish elements everywhere

must strengthen, by every means, the heirs of 'pioneering Israel' to re-
tain and enlarge their influence – social and political – among the people of Israel."[47]

Oddly, for someone with Salsberg's background, he wrote only occasional pieces on Canadian politics. When he did comment, for example,
on elections, he had only vague suggestions to offer to the New Democratic Party in Ontario which – under Donald MacDonald and Stephen
Lewis – was struggling. In the wake of the fall 1963 general election, he
urged the NDP |leadership and rank and file to study some "objective
conditions" underlying the Tory victory, concluding airily, "I have some
thoughts on this matter but I can hardly begin to expand on them in this
article."[48] Commenting on the May 1964 meeting of EPIC (Exchange
for Political Ideas in Canada), made up mainly of NDP elements and
chaired by Members of Parliament Douglas Fisher (NDP) and Pauline
Jewett (Liberal), Salsberg was scathing: "Its ... conception and germi-
nation, is, as far as I am concerned, enveloped in a mystifying and im-
penetrable mist." The puffy and cliché-ridden document issued by the
two left him confused and apprehensive about the purposes of the new
formation: "Is Fisher the homing pigeon that seeks to bring the Liberal
birds into the NDP loft or is Miss Jewett to sound the siren song that
will lure the NDP ship to the hidden rocks that will shatter it? Or are
they envisaging an entirely new home that EPIC will sprout?"[49] Steam-
ing over the document's description of the struggle against poverty and
underdevelopment as mere "residual problems of the 1930s," Salsberg
expostulated: "Is the danger of war no longer existing? Is the world-wide,
truly epic struggle of the vast majority of mankind for a new, better and,
broadly speaking, socialist or collective national societies real, or is it
imaginary?" Verbally up on his feet, as if he were still in the Ontario legislature, he continued: "Is the current crisis in Canadian confederation
a fact or is it a figment of someone's imagination?" There was nothing
about these issues and the EPIC spokespersons seemed to be focused
instead on the "problems of 'abundance and boredom' ... I don't know
whether one is to laugh or cry over what is taking place."

Salsberg reflected occasionally on the national picture. In March 1970
he observed that while domestic conditions were generally satisfactory,
"there are many pains, aches and festering sores which are plaguing
the economic and social body of Canada,"[50] such as inflation, pockets
of unemployment in the Maritimes and Quebec, unmarketable wheat
surpluses in the West, poverty, "the plight of our Indian and Metis peoples," the need for a "democratic solution of the national question in

Quebec[,] the resolution of other regional grievances," and Canada's growing economic dependency on the United States. He stressed the need for an independent foreign policy that focused on international atomic disarmament. "There is nothing to stop Canada from becoming the leader of the potentially powerful bloc of middle powers whose fear of Armageddon is shared by all mankind and whose [hope for] just and lasting peace will receive the support of men and women everywhere." While Salsberg backed the New Democratic Party, he was not sanguine about its fortunes on the national or provincial scenes. Recognizing the central role of Ontario in national affairs, he wrote with concern about political events there.

In the aftermath of John Robarts's resignation from the leadership of the Ontario Conservatives in 1971, Salsberg sensed the continuation of that party's dominance, observing that the Liberals were stuck and "even the NDP has not, in my opinion, shown sufficient awareness of the new role which 'destiny' has placed on the shoulders of [its] leaders and spokesmen."[51] The national picture was clouded in a "voyage without charts," because no party (with the exception of Liberal Eric Kierans), not even the NDP, was addressing seriously enough "the key issue that will affect the destiny of the country – the issue of Canadian independence," the "gut issue" of foreign control that is "inseparable from such hard-nut problems as economic planning, employment, [the] value of the Canadian dollar, inflation, etc."[52] From the national prospect, he was pessimistic about the Mulroney government's advent in 1984, predicting a long list of negative changes to social and fiscal policies, including tax increases, reduction of social services, increases in military expenditures, alterations in oil and gas taxation, and the sell-off of government-owned corporations.[53]

Paradoxically, Salsberg wrote very little on labour issues, but his comments conveyed some of the passion of old battles, as, for example, in the spring 1976 national debate on wage and price controls, when he approved the Canadian Labour Congress's demand for its "rightful place as a major force in the policy-making process," although he regretted that "most of the leaders failed to expose the fallacies of leftist phrase-mongering."[54] Reflecting on the failure of labour unions to significantly affect the outcome of the May 1979 federal elections, Salsberg observed that, to impact electoral results, the union movement had to eschew selfish, narrow, sectional interests – such as opposition to wage controls – and, instead, represent themselves as defenders of the national interests. In fact, opposition to wage controls had resulted in massive labour rank-and-file desertion from the NDP, the party that union leadership officially supported: "Above everything, labour's program must be in full accord with the best interests of the nation ..., and it must be clearly seen by the people at large to be just that."[55]

Salsberg's main Canadian political concern was the government's responses to Jewish and Israeli issues. "I will not apologize for suggesting that there are some vital Jewish concerns that should find expression in the political arena where the election battles are fought," he stated on the eve of the federal general elections in October 1972.[56] He had only contempt for Canada's performance at the United Nations in October 1974, when it abstained on the vote to invite Palestine Liberation Organization chairman Yasser Arafat to address the General Assembly: "Ottawa speaks with forked tongue and votes with a withered hand."[57] Even worse was the same spinelessness of Canadian delegates at the July 1975 assembly of the International Labor Organization, who abstained on the vote giving the PLO official-observer status. "For me this policy is wrong, immoral, inexcusable and harmful to Israel." To journalist Dalton Camp's suggestion, written during a tour of the Middle East from Saudi Arabia that the Canadian government take a "second look" at its Middle East policy, Salsberg asked, "Who would benefit from such a look that Dalton is asking for?"[58] And he had condemned Joe Clark's "political opportunism" when he flip-flopped on his pre-election promise to move Canada's embassy in Israel from Tel Aviv to Jerusalem.[59] There was nothing wrong with lobbying "to ask our political leaders and their standard bearers in the ridings to publicly undertake to support Israel's struggle for peace by endorsing the proposal for direct negotiations between Israel and its neighbours." "It's kosher, it's Canadian and ... it is our duty to do it right now while the election campaign is on."[60]

Salsberg lost few opportunities to slam the Soviet Union and its satellites for anti-Semitic and anti-Israel activities in the Middle East, especially the recrudescence of anti-Semitism there. In April 1962 he exposed the Soviet Union's pettiness in its ban on the distribution and consumption of matza. "Let us not be surprised," he prophesied, "if the Matza, the symbol of slavery and liberation, will now that it has been banished by Soviet Authorities, emerge to greater symbolic heights for Soviet Jews than it ever had in the past." In March 1963 he slammed the USSR for "unmistakable expressions of Anti-Semitism, persecution and foul destructions of Jewish lives" during the recent rash of "economic crimes" trials there; one regional party newspaper even revived the ancient blood libel. "The execution of people for black-marketeering or for stealing social property reminds one of the ages long past," he mused, possibly referring to the horrors of the Soviet regime during the 1930s.[61] He persisted in his exposure of anti-Semitism in the USSR for many years,[62] whether it was Khrushchev's 1956 "too many Rosenbergs obsession," the book *Judaism without Embellishment* "adorned with the ugliest ... Hitlerite cartoons" (published in 1963 by the Ukrainian Republic Academy of Sciences), the reappearance of the blood libel, the anti-Zionism directed at Jews living within Soviet bloc countries, or attacks on the State of Israel. He also condemned the "unclean hands of the present Polish communist leadership [in 1968] which is lowering the final curtain on Jewish life in their country while the desecrated and plundered scene shows the last mourners departing."[63] And he sometimes could not resist taking a shot at CPC policy inconsistencies, such as the 1967 decision to allow the Yiddish party organ, *Vochenblatt*, to take a sharply different line on the 1967 Israeli-Arab war than that stated in the CPC's organ, *Canadian Tribune*. "Talk about political consistency," he mocked. "It's a cynical, double-faced, opportunistic game."[64] He levelled another blast at "Moscow's yesmen" in Canada, who applauded the Soviet Union's most repressive policies. "Lousy but loyal," ... he thundered at them in a powerful 1968 indictment of the crushing of dissent in Czechoslovakia.[65]

The Soviet Union's hostility to Israel rankled: "The clique that now controls the Soviet government ... and ... Moscow-dominated communists such as those in Canada and the USA ... utilizes the banner of Communism to completely misrepresent the facts of the Middle East crisis," representing feudal Arab states as progressive and democratic Israel as reactionary."[66] By June 1970 he was warning his readers of Soviet expansionism in the Middle East, which threatened the existence of Israel; he urged the Canadian government to take a pro-Israel stand.[67]

When the movement to advance national and human rights for Soviet Jewry grew in the early 1970s, Salsberg urged Canadians not to wait but "to accelerate the struggle" for the embattled three and a half million Jews in USSR, "who have begun to speak out bravely and with amazing resolution for their rights."[68] "What a thunderous condemnation of the 'national policy' of the Soviet Union this Zionist revival in Russia represents. What a demonstration of the Jewish national will to survive and continue is being revealed. And what tribute to the stimulating and inspirational role of Israel," Salsberg chortled.[69] This self-assertion "has resulted in another near-miracle in the ranks of world Jewry," inspiring "the most massive demonstrations of solidarity with their kinfolk in Russia." When Soviet Premier Alexei Kosygin visited Toronto in October

1971, Salsberg employed Sholem Aleichem's famous story *The Plot* to ridicule Kosygin's inconsistencies and non-sequiturs.[70] The massive Ottawa demonstration in October that year by Jews chanting "Let my people go" within earshot of Kosygin – and a displeased Prime Minister Pierre Trudeau – Salsberg hailed as "most impressive and effective."[71] This campaign put Canadians in debt to Soviet Jewry, because it "enrich[ed] national consciousness, strengthen[ed] ties of kinship, [giving] intangible gifts to the totality of Jewish life and ... continuity."[72] Even more, it was raising a generation of highly committed young Jews, many of them students. He viewed Moscow's campaign of anti-Zionism as interchangeable with anti-Semitism.[73]

The overarching concern Salsberg expressed throughout his journalistic career was the complacency that had overtaken Canadian Jewry. The community was, in his view, too compliant with prevailing materialism and too comfortable with its "benefits." There were too many "alrightniks" out there, people who did not care about the drift to, and avid pursuit of, comfortable, prevailing bourgeois values. This trend was prevalent mainly in a younger generation disengaged from the spirit of protest and reform of their parents' generation, the Yiddish-speaking socialists of various stripes who acted on the belief that "something must be done" to achieve a better world for the Jewish people and all mankind. Until his final columns in *Fraternally Yours*, Salsberg was "a one-note Charlie," exhorting his comrades, veterans of the UJPO and the Communist Party of Canada, to band together with progressive like-minded members of the Workmen's Circle and the Labour Zionists to lead in the reaffirmation of secular Jewish values and spirit in the community. In the *CJN* too, he declared war on "alrightnikism" and its corrosive non-values, always urging, begging almost, for a return to commitment.[74] Salsberg was disgusted by the huge fees demanded by Israel's military hero, Moshe Dayan, on his speaking tour of North America in the autumn of 1975 – further evidence of corruption in Jewish life – and by the alleged potty-mouthed performance by comedian Buddy Hackett at an Israel Bonds campaign event in Toronto in May 1975.[75] Such "vulgar and offensive shtick," he fumed, "did more harm than good." And he was equally scathing about Jews who baulked when asked to contribute to fund-raising campaigns and offered "transparent lies as excuses for ... evasions of duty and responsibility," labelling them "affluent shnorers [beggars], rip-off artists, smarkatches [smarties]."

Salsberg tried to inject some of his own enthusiasm and concern into his readers. "Don't forget your roots," he pleaded to the 'snowbirds' who annually flee Toronto for sunny southern climes ... And come back, hungry for action and eager for engagement in the good fight."[76] "Come on," he was saying, "follow me." He was begging them to listen to him, as if teaching them the passage from the Talmud: "The work is hard, the labourers are sluggish and the hour is late. But the reward is great – and the Master of the House is waiting!"[77] This was, in many respects, the Joe Salsberg of yore, still Yosele to his close friends who would gather to schmooze with him in his latest hangout, Stubby's at Bathurst and Lawrence – of the days he spent patrolling his beat on Spadina Avenue, along College Street, and through Kensington Market and neighbourhood byways. It was reminiscent of his days as a child worker in the clothing factories, an organizer in the garment workers' unions and in the Workers' Unity League, and as spokesman for human rights and progressive labour legislation in the Ontario legislature. Regarded as the "rebbe," the beloved teacher, he extended advice and encouragement to many of those he had known from the old days.[78] It harkened back to his powerful performance in the legislature on their behalf, and his attentiveness on Thursday afternoons in Abella's luncheonette at the corner of Spadina at Queen and in his crowded office to his constituents.

But he was not loved by all. Some Toronto Jews never forgave him his "sins," especially his support of Stalinism. In 1986 an attempt was made to bar Salsberg from the board of the Canadian Jewish Congress because of his communist past, a move that drew a sharp rebuke from Rabbi Irwin Schild, who described Salsberg as a *ba'al tshuva*, a repentant.[79] But in fact Salsberg never repented his past. On the seventieth anniversary of the October Revolution, he proclaimed it to have been a "tragic and lamentable failure" because it led not to democratic socialism, instead degenerating into a "dictatorship of one person."[80] "With the exception of Lenin," he wrote, "there has hardly been a single Soviet leader who was not, after his death or expulsion, accused of and proven to have been a brutal dictator, a violator of 'Socialist norm,' and executioner on a grand scale." This was "galling ... especially for some of us, who, blinded by the 'Socialist sun' were incapable of seeing the bitter consequences." This is as close as Salsberg ever came in print to admitting that he was wrong: he was confessing only to being hoodwinked for so long. But it was not an apology.

And why should it have been? In what was to be his final *Fraternally Yours* column, in January 1993, which he entitled "The World Didn't Evolve as I Planned It. – So?," he acknowledged that the communist experiment in the Soviet Union, Eastern Europe, and China had "totally failed." He admitted that he and many others "saw in the Soviet Union the global vanguard that was destined to lead the whole world to ... a new socially-just world family of nations."[81] But he refused to apologize for supporting communism and for the crimes of Stalinism: "Apologize for what we did then? No. From a historic perspective it is understandable." Turning a blind eye to the horrors of the Stalinist era while they were under way was "understandable," Salsberg was saying, "from a historic perspective" because, notwithstanding them, all was destined to turn out well for the cause of social justice for the "world family of nations." This was a refusal to acknowledge that the "god that failed" had perpetrated monstrous crimes and that he and other communists knew, or should have known, that they were taking place – and stayed silent. And at age ninety-one, when this column appeared, Salsberg continued to say nothing about that, instead proclaiming his continuing search for the ideal: "It would be inexcusable if as a result of that [Soviet] experience we were to turn our backs on the progressive social forces in our present state of history, and become delinquent bystanders in the inevitable struggle of the deprived majority in their striving for social justice." He had acted his entire life on the meaning of the words in Moses's valediction in Deuteronomy 16:20 ("*tzedek, tzedek tirdof*") justice, justice shalt thou follow![82] From his early studies of the Mishna portion (Ethics, 2:21) he understood, too, the mandate from Rabbi Tarfon: "You are not obliged to finish the work. But you are not free to desist from it!"

When, in April 1996, Salsberg composed his final will, two years before his death, he left the bulk of his estate to "charitable purposes of an educational nature," not an unworthy gesture for a man whose life was that of a committed educator in the causes he believed in, whether in the world communist movement, with all its flaws, or in the Canadian Jewish community, with all its shortcomings: "Something must be done," he was saying. "We cannot sit idly by." "Come, join me."

In retirement Salsberg had become a living source on the Left. He gave numerous interviews to journalists, scholars, and archivists wanting to document his huge fund of knowledge of Canadian labour history, his immense knowledge of Jewish Toronto's places and personalities – especially Spadina Avenue in the old days – as well as his recollections about his past and his twelve-year experience in the Ontario legislature.[83] He spoke to many groups large and small throughout Toronto Jewry, reminiscing, but never apologizing for his communist past. He was indeed an artefact, a living veteran of the communist experience in Canada, of the party's drive to organize industrial unions during the Depression.

He was a legend in his own time: the eloquent spokesman for humanitarian causes. Living for forty more years after quitting the Communist Party, though wearily admitting in 1986 that he was "not old enough to have adjusted comfortably to the current lifestyle that governs the life of more and more of us," he never regretted using his time and strength in the cause of bettering the material and social conditions of Canadians.[84] He reaffirmed this commitment at his ninetieth birthday celebration, when NFJA friends and family raised a substantial sum of money for Histadruth's medical facilities in Israel. He admitted failure: "The world that our kind of dreamers attempted to build now lies in ruins ... The 'new world' has yet to be won."[85] But, he proclaimed, "that 'new world' has to be helped to arrive ... [and] we, of the N.F.J.A will never shirk that task and duty."

Joe died at home on 8 February 1998 after a long decline, and was buried next to Dora in the NFJA section of Bathurst Lawn Memorial Park. At the funeral, Irving Abella, who at age five had observed long line-ups of people waiting to pour out their hearts to Joe and remembered how tenderly he treated each one of these petitioners, spoke to the large crowd of mourners. "Joe's legacy is profound," he said. "It is us. It is a vigorous, committed, confident Jewish community. It is the open, tolerant, humane, decent Canadian society for which Joe and his companions struggled so fearlessly. How lucky we were to have known him. How lucky we were to have had him with us for so long. [His] passion for social justice, for the oppressed and the dispossessed motivated him to the end of his life." For many Toronto Jews, Joe's memory lived on. Ten years after his death, a large crowd of them gathered to pay honour to him, remembering his good deeds, his *menschlichkeit* (loving kindness), and his commitment to, as he put it, "do the right thing."

Salsberg's shift from pragmatic goals, so prominent in his early career as labour organizer and politician, to more abstract and academic ones was exactly the same pursuit in a changed context. His broad purpose since boyhood exposure to the teachings of the Prophets and the humanist mandates of the Mishna and Talmud had been a striving, as he once stated in the legislature, for "a more humane point of view." As MPP for St Andrew, he regarded his bailiwick as a community and, as an activist in the Communist Party and labour organizer, he visualized that "a better world's in birth" and strove to bring it to realization. Even though he was now out of the party and ousted from politics, the question of "what is to be done?" still rankled. He could not leave it suspended in mid-air. He had to act. He was still the rebbe of Spadina, still its *shaliach tsibur* (people's delegate), and he had to reach out to and counsel them on what had to be done. The advancement of Yiddish – a cause especially dear to his heart – and Jewish secular culture would be the vehicles for the strengthening of their traditional values and identity. Amidst mindless materialism – upscale housing, expensive clothes and cars, foreign vacations, exotic cruises, and other hoity-toity lifestyle features – the search for the meaning of these timeless attributes was seriously in peril, and Salsberg saw it as his duty to call the community to account and to urgent action. He always returned to first principles, as he did when news broke of the arrival of a group of "boat people" in Nova Scotia in August 1987, reminding the Jewish community of the passages in Leviticus "The stranger that sojourneth with you shall be unto you as the homeborn among you and thou shalt love him as thyself; for ye were strangers in the land of Egypt."

Perhaps the best summation of his life in public affairs was stated by Salsberg himself many years earlier. When discussing *The God That Failed* on a CBC program (in May 1962) that also featured Arthur Koestler and Stephen Spender, two of the contributors to this book that exposed the evils of Soviet communism, Salsberg stated that while Stalin, "who was defined as the god of communism, proved to be a most disillusioning and disastrous failure[,] … the god which the Koestlers, the Spenders and I began to worship was one that encompassed the broad concepts of socialism, with its equalitarianism, its social and political democracy and universal brotherhood." "We cannot say," he continued, "that that god has failed, for he has yet to be reached."[86] That god of justice and righteousness was the core of the Messianic dream, of a world repaired, as Amos (5:25) demanded, if only the faithful would "let justice well up as waters; and righteousness as a mighty stream" or, as Isaiah (58:6) proclaimed, "to loose the fetters of wickedness, to undo the bonds of the yoke, and to let the oppressed go free."[87]

Salsberg, then, was like one moved by these mandates taught to him by his *tzedaka* (righteousness)-minded mother, Sarah-Gitel, and by Lagow and Toronto rabbis so long before. His life's journey was a striving in the belief that this commitment to "do the right thing" was necessary to achieve *tikkun olam*, the repairing of the world and – filtered through Marxist ideals of universal social justice, according to the Kabbalistic tradition revered by Hasidim like his deeply devout father, Abraham – the seeking out and gathering up of the scattered sacred sparks and, finally, bringing them home.

Notes

Preface: Spadina

1 Public Archives of Ontario (PAO), C56-7, David Troster Fonds, box 5, file "Spadina Treatment Originals," reprint from *Canadian Tribune*, 20 Sept. 1955.

2 Rosemary Donegan, *Spadina Avenue* (Toronto: Douglas & McIntyre, 1985), 7.

3 Ontario Jewish Archives (OJA), Salsberg Fonds, 98-12-5: interview, Sharyn S. Ezrin with Norman Penner, 24 June 1991 (transcript), 2.

4 Erna Paris, *Jews: An Account of Their Experience in Canada* (Toronto: Macmillan, 1980), 157.

Chapter One

1 Family background information was supplied by Thelma Pritzker, Itche Goldberg, and Sharyn Salsberg Ezrin during interviews in May and June 2003 and by Esther Tile in March 2004.

2 Antony Polonsky, *The Jews in Poland and Russia*, vol. 2, *1881 to 1914* (Portland, OR: Littman Library of Jewish Civilization, 2010), 90; Erasmus Piltz, *Poland: Her People, History, Industries, Finance, Science, Literature, Art, and Social Development* (London: Herbert Jenkins Ltd, 1909), 131, 260–2, 270–5. See also Ezra Mendelsohn, *The Jews of East Central Europe between the World Wars* (Bloomington: Indiana University Press, 1983), 15–23.

3 *Canadian Jewish News*, 10 Sept. 1981, quoted in *Kielce-Radom SIG Journal* 5, no. 3 (summer 2001), 8.

4 Shmuel Levin and Rachel Grossbaum Pasternak, "Lagow," ed. Jerry Tepperman, in *Pinkus Hakehillot, Polen*, vol. 7 (Jerusalem: Yad Vashem, 1999), 267–9; translated from the Hebrew by Seymour Baltan and Warren Blatt,

"Lagow," *Kielce-Radom SIG Journal* 5, no. 3 (summer 2001), n.p. Samuel Kassow, "Introduction," in *The Shtetl: New Evaluations*, ed. Steven T. Katz (New York: New York University Press, 2007), 1–28, 16. Polonsky, *Jews in Poland and Russia*, 2: 100. Marcin Wodzinski, *Haskalah and Hasidism in the Kingdom of Poland* (Portland, OR: Oxford University Press, 2005), 46. See also Gershon D. Hundert, *The Jews in a Private Polish Town: The Case of Opatow in the Eighteenth Century* (Baltimore: Johns Hopkins University Press, 1992), passim.

5 Polonsky, *Jews in Poland and Russia*, 2: 33–4.

6 Multicultural History Society of Ontario (MHSO), Tapes of interviews with J.B. Salsberg, 6146-SAL 1/19.

7 Polonsky, *Jews in Poland and Russia*, 2: 110; Jerome Hershman, "A Visit to Lagov. May 14, 1996," *Kielce-Radom SIG Journal* 5, no.3 (summer 2001), 19.

8 Polonsky, *Jews in Poland and Russia*, 2: 358–9; Shaul Stampfer, *Families, Rabbis and Education: Traditional Jewish Society in Nineteenth Century Eastern Europe* (Oxford: Littman Library of Jewish Civilization, 2010), 6, 23, 30, 154; Stephen Speisman, *Jews of Toronto: A History to 1937* (Toronto: McClelland & Stewart, 1979), 101, 104.

9 Margaret Bell, "Toronto's Melting Pot," *Canadian Magazine of Politics, Science, Art, and Literature* 41 (May–October 1913), 234–41.

10 Polonsky, *Jews in Poland and Russia*, 2: 275, 281; see also Glenn Dynner, "The Hasidic Conquest of Small-Town Central Poland, 1754–1818," in *Polin: Studies in Polish Jewry*, vol. 17, *The Shtetl: Myth and Reality*, ed. Antony Polonsky (Oxford: Littman Library of Jewish Civilization, 2004), 51–81.

11 Polonsky, *Jews in Poland and Russia*, 2: 275; J.B. Salsberg, "A 'Shif-karte' was what dreams were made of," *Canadian Jewish News*, 15 Jan. 1987; J.B. Salsberg, "It was shif-kantorn and shif-karten that did it," *CJN*, 8 Jan. 1987.

12 Speisman, *Jews of Toronto*, 101, 104.

13 See Ira Robinson, "'A Letter from the Sabbath Queen': Rabbi Yudel Rosenberg Addresses Montreal Jewry," in *An Everyday Miracle: Yiddish Culture in Montreal*, ed. Ira Robinson et al. (Montreal: Mosaic Press, Vehicule Press, 1990), 105; Leah Rosenberg, *The Errand Runner: Reflections of a Rabbi's Daughter* (Toronto: John Wiley and Sons, 1981), 41; J.B. Salsberg, "Bathurst St. shop sends me back to Chestnut St.," *CJN*, 11 Jan. 1990.

14 MHSO, Salsberg tapes, 1/19; Polonsky, *Jews in Poland and Russia*, 2: 295. See also Wodzinski, *Haskalah and Hasidism*, 114.

15 MHSO, Salsberg tapes, 1/19; OJA, Salsberg interview, Sept. 1985, #71.

16 MHSO, Salsberg tapes, 1/19.

17 Louis Rosenberg, *Canada's Jews: A Social and Economic Study of the Jews of Canada* (Montreal: Canadian Jewish Congress, 1939), 134.

18 Ibid., 308; J.M.S. Careless, *Toronto to 1918: An Illustrated History* (Toronto: James Lorimer and National Museums of Canada, 1984), 149.

19 For a superb pictorial and historical study of the Ward, see Robert F. Harney and Harold Troper, *Immigrants: A Portrait of the Urban Experience, 1890–1930* (Toronto: Van Nostrand Reinhold, 1975), 25, 36, 41. See also D. Hiebert, "Integrating Production and Consumption: Industry, Class, Ethnicity, and the Jews of Toronto," in *The Changing Social Geography of Canadian Cities*, ed. Larry S. Bourne and David F. Lei (Montreal: McGill-Queen's University Press, 1993), 199–213, 417–22.

20 See Stephen Speisman, "St. John's Shtetl: The Ward in 1911," in *Gathering Place: Peoples and Neighbourhoods of Toronto, 1834–1945*, ed. Robert F. Harney (Toronto: Multicultural History Society of Ontario, 1985), 107–20; and Careless, *Toronto to 1918*, 157–61.

21 Peter Oliver, *Unlikely Tory: The Life and Politics of Allan Grossman* (Toronto: Lester and Orpen Dennys, 1985), 11; quoted in Gerald Tulchinsky, *Branching Out: The Transformation of the Canadian Jewish Community* (Toronto: Stoddart, 1998), 19.

22 Michael Piva, *The Condition of the Working Class in Toronto – 1900–1921* (Ottawa: University of Ottawa Press, 1979), 6, 37, 43, 52, 77, 95–106.

23 Ian McKay, *Reasoning Otherwise: Leftists and the People's Enlightenment in Canada, 1890–1920* (Toronto: Between the Lines, 2008), 520.

24 Stephen Speisman, *The Jews of Toronto: A History to 1927* (Toronto: McClelland & Stewart, 1987), 111–16, 160, 187.

25 Ben Kayfetz, "The J.B. Salsberg Story – A Life of Care and Courage" (J.B. Salsberg, A Tribute. Wednesday, 13 November 1991. Sponsored by Canadian Kupat-Holim), n.p.; Daniel Soyer, "Class Conscious Workers as Immigrant Entrepreneurs: The Ambiguity of Class among Eastern Jewish Immigrants to the United States at the Turn of the Twentieth Century," *Labor History* 42, no. 1 (2001), 45–59.

26 Soyer, "Class Conscious Workers," 45–6.

27 See Deena Nathanson, "Peddling as a Threshold Occupation among Jewish Immigrants: The Jewish Peddlers of Toronto's Centre Avenue, Chestnut and Elizabeth Streets, 1890–1899" (University of Toronto, Department of History, 2000S essay, August 1988); City of Toronto Archives. Abraham Salsberg was listed as a peddler in the Toronto directory as late as 1940; Harney and Troper, *Immigrants*, 40; Thelma Pritzker interviews.

28 The best memoir of a Jewish junkman is Ted Allan's short story "Lies My Father Told Me," in in Gerri Sinclair and Morris Wolfe, eds., *The Spice Box: An Anthology of Jewish Canadian Writing* (Toronto: Lester and Orpen Dennys, 1981), 82–7. I have used this account and the movie version of the same

title to supplement memories of my Zaideh (grandfather), David Stemeroff, a junkman in my hometown of Brantford, Ontario, who with a decrepit horse and ramshackle wagon plied the streets of our neighbourhood humbly collecting whatever cast-offs he thought marketable. He stored this stuff in a smelly old barn nearby where he also stabled his horse, which for all I know was named Nudnik. Brokers occasionally came and took away his junk, leaving behind a few dollars that kept Zaideh's family going, just. As a little boy, I sometimes accompanied him on his rounds, absolutely thrilled by the adventure, and intrigued by the books that people had thrown out.

29 Salsberg, "Bathurst St. shop."
30 Bell, "Melting Pot," 238; J.V. McAree, "The Jews in Canada" (1912) and *Canadian Jewish Times*, March 1913, quoted in A.J. Arnold, "Many Unskilled Became Peddlers," *CJN*, 21 Feb. 1975.
31 While a Toronto alderman in 1938, Salsberg represented the Hebrew Peddlers Union, which vigorously denied charges that they were stealing items from householders' garbage. Salsberg tried, unsuccessfully, to keep the City from more than tripling peddlers' licence fees. *Globe and Mail*, 29 Sept. 1938; *Toronto Star*, 1 Nov. 1938.
32 Rosenberg, *Errand Runner*, 38–9.
33 Kayfetz, "Salsberg Story."
34 Ruth Borchiver interview with J.B. Salsberg, no date.
35 J.B. Salsberg, "Victory over carols was J.B.'s triumph," *CJN*, 22 Dec.1972; "Court ruling ends battle I began 70 years ago," *CJN*, 13 Oct. 1988. MHSO, Salsberg tapes, 5/19.
36 MHSO, Salsberg tapes, 1/19.
37 Christina Bates, "Shop and Factory: The Ontario Millinery Trade in Transition, 1870–1930," in *Fashion: A Canadian Perspective*, ed. Alexandra Palmer (Toronto: University of Toronto Press, 2004), 125–9, 131.
38 Charles H. Green, *The Headwear Workers: A Century of Trade Unionism* (New York: United Hatters, Cap, and Millinery Workers International Union, 1944), 161ff.
39 Ibid., 161.
40 Yud M. Budish, *Geschichte Fun Die Kloth Hat, Kapp un Milineri Arbeiter. Tsum 25 Yorigen Yubileum Fun Die K.H. Un N.A., 1901–1925* (New York, 1925), 366–7.
41 MHSO, Salsberg tapes, 5/19.
42 Budish, *Geschichte*, 369.
43 Ibid.
44 QUA, Salsberg Fonds, List of books donated to Queen's University.
45 Eli Lederhendler, *Jewish Immigrants and American Capitalism, 1880–1920: From Caste to Class* (Cambridge: Cambridge University Press, 2009), 26–7.

46 Programme of "J.B. Remembered. Tuesday, October 28th, 2008. Bialik Hebrew Day School [Toronto]," 2. MHSO, Salsberg tapes, 5/19.

47 *Daily Prayer Book*, translated and annotated with an introduction by Philip Birnbaum (New York: Hebrew Publishing Co., 1949), 430.

48 MHSO, Salsberg tapes, 5/19. See Mitchell Cohen, *Class Struggle and the Jewish Nation: Selected Essays in Marxist Zionism*, ed. Ber Borochov (New Brunswick, NJ: Transaction Books, 1984).

49 Mark A. Raider, *The Emergence of American Zionism* (New York: NYU Press, 1998), 29.

50 Moshe Cohen, "The Early Years," in *Builders and Dreamers: Habonim Labor Zionist Youth in America*, ed. J.J. Goldberg and Elliot King (New York: Herzl Press, 1993), 31–40; Moshe Cohen, "In the Beginning," in *Arise and Build: The Story of American Habonim* (New York: Ichud Habonim Labor Zionist Youth, 1961), 3–4.

51 J.B. Salsberg, "Recalling the old days, J.B. remembers when life was idealistic and romantic," *CJN*, 30 May 1975.

52 OJA, J.B. Salsberg Fonds, 2004 5/28, Hamlin to J. Salsberg, May 1923; Central Youth committee of Poalei Zion to Youth Clubs, Salsberg, 14, 26 May, 4 June 1923.

53 OJA, Salsberg Fonds, 2004 5/28, Rose Crupsky to J. Salsberg, 30 May 1923; unknown to J. Salsberg, 3 Aug. 1923.

54 Karl Radek, "Foundation of the Two and a Half International," *The Communist International*, 1922, nos. 16–17, pp. 31–43. http://www.marxists.org/archive/radek/1922/ci/two-half.htm.

55 Stewart Smith, *Communists and Komsomolkas: My Years in the Communist Party of Canada* (Toronto: Lugus, 1993), 68; *The Worker*, 4 May 1929.

56 Ian Angus, *Canadian Bolsheviks: The Early Years of the Communist Party of Canada* (Montreal: Vanguard Publications, 1981), 48.

57 Ibid., 77–8.

58 Ian McKay, "Maurice Spector," paper delivered to the Canadian Historical Association, 2003.

59 Ian McKay, *Reasoning Otherwise: Leftists and the People's Enlihgtenment in Canada, 1890–1920* (Toronto: Between the Lines, 2008).

60 *Globe and Mail*, 10 May 1962.

61 Myer Rosen, "An Interview with J.B. Salsberg," *Migdal*, 20 Sept. 1976; Morris Biderman, "Eulogy at J.B. Salsberg Funeral, Feb. 1998."

62 *Canadian Jewish News*, 31 Oct. 2002.

63 Speisman, *Jews of Toronto*, 316.

64 McMaster University, Dora Wilensky, Initial registration form, 23 Sept. 1919; Alumni Affairs, transcript, 1924.

65 OJA, J.B. Salsberg Fonds, 98-2-2, *Shpyzcart fun dem Graduairungs Ovent fun Raze Brownshtein, Pinchas Matenko, Un Dvoireh Vilensky* (Toronto, 1924).

Chapter Two

1 Queen's University Archives (QUA), Salsberg Fonds, box 9, file: "Theses on the Question of Palestine. By the National Jewish Committee, Labour Progressive Party of Canada," [Dec. 1945].
2 Jonathan Frankel, "The Soviet Regime and Anti-Zionism: An Analysis," in *Essential Papers on Jews and the Left*, ed. Ezra Mendelsohn (New York: New York University Press, 1997), 442–3; *The Worker*, 4 May 1929.
3 John Holmes, "American Jewish Communism and Garment Unionism in the 1920s," *American Communist History* 6, no. 2 (2007), 171. Alan Wald, "Between Insularity and Internationalism: The Lost World of the Jewish Communist 'Cultural Workers' in America," in *Dark Times, Dire Decisions: Jews and Communism*, ed. Jonathan Frankel, Studies in Contemporary Jewry, vol. 20 (Oxford: Oxford University Press, 2004), 136.
4 Linda Kealey, "Women in the Canadian Socialist Movement, 1904–1914," in *Beyond the Vote: Canadian Women and Politics*, ed. Linda Kealey and Joan Sangster (Toronto: University of Toronto Press, 1989), 173.
5 On early socialism in Canada see Ian McKay, *Reasoning Otherwise: Leftists and the People's Enlightenment in Canada, 1890–1920* (Toronto: Between the Lines, 2008); Donald Avery, *"Dangerous Foreigners": European Immigrant Workers and Labour Radicalism in Canada 1896–1932* (Toronto: McClelland & Stewart, 1979), 80; William Rodney, *Soldiers of the International: A History of the Communist Party of Canada, 1919–1929* (Toronto: University of Toronto Press, 1968), 25. On Jewish socialists in Winnipeg, see Roz Usiskin, "'The Alien and the Bolshevik in Our Midst': The 1919 Winnipeg General Strike," *Jewish Life and Times* 5 (Winnipeg, 1987), 28–49.
6 Library and Archives of Canada (LAC), M.G. 26, Borden Papers, O.C. series, #559, Memo, 11 Dec. 1919.
7 Gregory S. Kealey and Reg Whitaker, eds., *R.C.M.P. Security Bulletins. The Early Years, 1919–1929* (St John's: Canadian Committee on Labour History, 1994), 47.
8 Kealey and Whitaker, *R.C.M.P. Security Bulletins, Early Years*, 61–2, 756–7.
9 Rodney, *Soldiers*, 29. See Joan Sangster, *Dreams of Equality: Women on the Canadian Left, 1920–1950* (Toronto: McClelland & Stewart, 1989), passim, and Louise Watson, *She Was Never Afraid: The Biography of Annie Buller* (Toronto: Progress Books, 1976).
10 Rodney, *Soldiers*, 28.

11 Bryan D. Palmer, *Working-Class Experience: Rethinking the History of Canadian Labour, 1800–1991* (Toronto: McClelland & Stewart, 1992), 227–8. Ian McKay has given me much information on his career in the movement. In his biography of James Cannon, Bryan Palmer carefully evaluates Spector's role in the tense debates within the North American communist movement in 1928. See Bryan D. Palmer, *James P. Cannon and the Origins of the American Revolutionary Left: Labor Radicalism and the Uneasy Formative Years of American Communism, 1890–1928* (Urbana and Chicago: University of Illinois Press, 2005), chap. 11, passim.

12 On Murphy see Irving M. Abella, *Nationalism, Communism and Canadian Labour: The CIO, the Communist Party, and the Canadian Congress of Labour 1935–1956* (Toronto: University of Toronto Press, 1973), passim, and Bryan Palmer, ed., *A Communist Life: Jack Scott and the Canadian Workers Movement, 1927–1985* (St John's: Committee on Canadian Labour History, 1988), 249–51. On Walsh see Cy Gonick, *A Very Red Life: The Story of Bill Walsh* (St John's: Canadian Committee on Labour History, 2001).

13 Ester Reiter, "Secular Yiddishkait: Left Politics, Culture, and Community," *Labour/Le Travail,* 49 (Spring 2002), 145.

14 Henry Srebrnik, *Jerusalem on the Amur: Birobidjan and the Canadian Jewish Communist Movement, 1924–1951* (Montreal: McGill-Queen's University Press, 2008), 14.

15 Kenneth B. Moss, *Jewish Renaissance in the Russian Revolution* (Cambridge, MA: Harvard University Press, 2009), 4, 8.

16 James Laxer, *Red Diaper Baby: A Boyhood in the Age of McCarthyism* (Toronto: Douglas & McIntyre, 2004), 121–32; Gerald Tulchinsky, "Ben Lappin's Reflections on May Day Celebrations in Toronto's Jewish Quarter," *Labour/Le Travail* 49 (Spring 2002), 217.

17 David Priestland, *The Red Flag: A History of Communism* (New York: Grove Press, 2009), 124.

18 *The Labor Herald,* September 1922, p. 7, quoted in Theodore Draper, *American Communism and Soviet Russia: The Formative Period* (New York: Viking, 1960), 71.

19 Draper, *American Communism,* 167, 363.

20 Jim Mochoruk, "'Pop & Co' versus Buck and the 'Lenin School Boys': Ukrainian Canadians and the Communist Party of Canada, 1921–1931," in *Re-imagining Ukrainian Canadians: History, Politics, and Identity,* ed. Rhonda L. Hinther and Jim Mochoruk (Toronto: University of Toronto Press, 2011), 335.

21 Palmer, *Working-Class Experience,* 228.

22 Avery, *"Dangerous Foreigners,"* 127; interview with Morris Biderman, 22 July 2002.

23 *Globe*, 27 May 1927; clipping in a collection kindly loaned to me by Bryan Palmer. Editorials in major urban newspapers entitled "The Communist Fester" and the "Communist Menace" appeared in the twenties.

24 My father, Harry Tulchinsky, an immigrant who worked as a cleaner in a Toronto sweatshop (in what is now euphemistically labelled the "Fashion District") during the mid-1920s, remembered such tense incidents at Jewish public events that, he said, had nothing to do with politics.

25 *Globe*, 9 May 1929; Minerva Davis, *The Wretched of the Earth and Me* (Toronto: Lugus, 1993), 130–6; interview with Jocko Thomas, n.d.

26 Florence Freedlander Cohen, "Every Friday," *Canadian Jewish Review*, 23 Aug. 1929. See also *The Worker*, 2 Feb. 1929, for an account of another such incident. General Draper's roughhouse red-baiting continued well into the 1930s. See John Manley, "'Starve, Be Damned!' Communists and Canada's Urban Unemployed, 1929–1939," *Canadian Historical Review* 79 (September 1998), 477. See also Stephen Endicott, *Raising the Workers' Flag: The Workers' United League of Canada, 1930–1936* (Toronto: University of Toronto Press, 2012), 73, 93.

27 William Beeching and Dr Phyllis Clarke, eds., *Yours in the Struggle: Reminiscences of Tim Buck* (Toronto: NC Press, 1977), 104–5, 107.

28 Palmer, *Working-Class Experience*, 228.

29 Lita Rose Betcherman, *The Little Band: The Clashes between the Communists and the Political and Legal Establishment in Canada, 1928–1932* (Ottawa: Deneau, n.d.), 11.

30 Randi Storch, *Red Chicago: American Communism at Its Grassroots, 1928–35* (Urbana: University of Illinois Press, 2007), 135; Holmes, "American Jewish Communism," 186.

31 MHSO, Salsberg tapes, 6/19.

32 LAC, MG 10-K3, Comintern (Communist International) Fonds, Archival Documents of the Comintern and Its Organizations, and the Communist Party of Canada and Its Organizations, 1920–1943. Microfilm reel #K-275. Tuesday, 29 May 1928, Minutes of the Political Committee (Pol Com) Needle Trades Conference.

33 MHSO, Salsberg tapes, 1/19; Mercedes Steedman, "The Promise: Communist Organizing in the Needle Trades, the Dressmakers' Campaign, 1928–1937," *Labour/Le Travail* 34 (Fall 1994), 53.

34 Stuart M. Jamieson, *Times of Trouble: Labour Unrest and Industrial Conflict in Canada, 1900–1960* (Ottawa: Information Canada, 1971). Institute of Industrial Relations, University of British Columbia, Studies of the Task Force on Labour Relations, no. 22, 225; Gerald Tulchinsky, *Branching Out: The*

Transformation of the Canadian Jewish Community (Toronto: Stoddart, 1998), 87–103; MHSO, Salsberg tapes, #6.

35 Betcherman, *The Little Band*, 10; B. Garncaska-Kadry, "Some Aspects of Life of the Jewish Proletariat in Poland during the Interwar Period," in *Polin: Studies in Polish Jewry*, vol. 8, *Jews in Independent Poland 1918–1939*, ed. Antony Polonsky, Ezra Mendelsohn, and Jerzy Tomascewsli (London: Littman Library of Jewish Civilization, 1994), 248.

36 Daniel Soyer, "Transnationalism and Mutual Influence: American and East European Jewries in the 1920s and 1930s," in *Rethinking European Jewish History*, ed. Jeremy Cohen and Moshe Rosman (London: Littman Library of Jewish Civilization, 2009), 201–2.

37 *The Worker*, 1 Sept. 1928. See also *The Canadian Unionist* 2, no. 2 (August 192)8; Andrée Lévesque, *Jeanne Corbin* (Montreal: McGill-Queen's University Press, 2006); Andrée Lévesque, *Virage à Gauche Interdit: Les communistes, les socialistes et leurs enemis au Québec 1929–1939* (Montreal: Boreal Express, 1984), 54–5.

38 Colin D. Grimson, "The Communist Party of Canada, 1922–1946," MA thesis (McGill University, 1966), 80.

39 *The Worker*, 29 Sept. 1929.

40 LAC, MG 10-K3, Comintern Fonds, microfilm reel #K-275, Minutes of the Political Committee (Pol Com) Needle Trades Conference, 29 May 1928.

41 Ibid., #K-276, Meeting of the National Trade Union Department of the CPC, 26 Dec. 1928.

42 Comments by anonymous reader of manuscript, 7 June 2011.

43 LAC, MG 10-K3, Comintern Fonds, microfilm reel #K313, Minutes of the National Trade Union Department, 7 Jan. 1929; *The Worker*, 19 Jan. 1929.

44 *The Worker*, 26 Jan. 1929.

45 Ibid., 16, 23 Feb. 1929.

46 Ibid., 30 Mar. 1929.

47 See Ruth Frager, "Reflections on Jewish Identity, Class Politics, and Gender Dynamism among Jewish Activists," in *Jewish Radicalism in Winnipeg, 1905–1960*, ed. Daniel Stone (Winnipeg: Jewish Heritage Centre of Western Canada, 2002), 90–7; Irving Abella, "Portrait of a Jewish Professional Revolutionary: The Recollections of Joshua Gershman," *Labour/Le Travail* 2 (1977), 192; LAC, RG 27, vol. 343, file 58, clipping, *Winnipeg Tribune*, 7 June 1929.

48 LAC, RG 27, vol. 343, file 71, clipping, *Toronto Worker*, 6 July 1929; W.M. MacIntosh to Department of Labour, 24 July 1929.

49 *The Worker*, 31 Aug. 1929.

50 Ibid., 18 May 1929. On Winnipeg's garment industrial scene, see Jodi Gies-
   brecht, "Accommodating Resistance: Unionization, Gender, and Ethnicity
   in Winnipeg's Garment Industry, 1929–1945," *Urban History Review* 39, no. 1
   (Fall 2010), 4–19.
51 *The Worker*, 25 May 1929.
52 Ibid.
53 LAC, MG 10-K3, Comintern Fonds, microfilm reel #K-277, Minutes of the
   Pol Com, 16 May 1929; 28 June 1929.
54 Ibid., 13 July 1929.
55 Ibid., 3 Oct. 1929.
56 Ibid., microfilm reel #K-313, Letter to A. Lozovsky, December 1929.
57 *The Worker*, 25 Oct. 1930.
58 "Industrial Union of Needle Trades Workers of Canada. Report of the Second National Convention, May 23, 24, 25, 1931. Toronto," 50 (typescript at
   the Department of Labour, Ottawa). See also Catherine Macleod, "Women
   in Production: The Toronto Dressmakers' Strike of 1931," in *Women at Work:
   Ontario, 1850–1930* (Toronto: Canadian Women's Educational Press, 1974),
   309–29.
59 LAC, RG 27, vol. 359, Strike 9, clipping, *Toronto Telegram*, 17 Jan. 1934, microfilm reel #T2970, pp. 000031–6.
60 LAC, RG 27, vol. 375, clipping, *Toronto Worker*, 6 Feb. 1936, microfilm reel
   #T2984; RG 146, file 93-A-00183, part 2, Yiddish Language, Summarized by
   MHA at R.C.M.P. Headquarters, News 665, 20-1-39, Der Kamf ("The Struggle") vol. 14, no. 735, Toronto, 27 January 1938.
61 Ruth Frager, *Sweatshop Strife: Class, Ethnicity, and Gender in the Jewish Labour
   Movement in Toronto, 1900–1939* (Toronto: University of Toronto Press,
   1992), 210.
62 Mercedes Steedman, *Angels of the Workplace: Women and the Construction of
   Gender Relations in the Canadian Clothing Industry, 1890–1940* (Toronto: Oxford University Press, 1997), 237.
63 Ibid., 152.
64 LAC, MG 10-K3, Comintern Fonds, Joseph B. Salsberg, 1935 statement. This
   document was revised in interesting ways in 1936 and 1938; Ian Angus, *Canadian Bolsheviks: The Early Years of the Communist Party of Canada* (Montreal:
   Vanguard Publications, 1981), 290; David Priestland, *The Red Flag: A History
   of Communism* (New York: Grove Press, 2009), 131.
65 Public Archives of Ontario (PAO), RG 4-32, Records of the Ministry of the
   Attorney General, Central Registry Files, file #3188, 1931, "Listing of Communist Party of Canada Records."
66 LAC, MG 10-K3, Comintern Fonds, microfilm reel # K-277, Minutes of the
   Pol Bureau, 14 Oct. 1929.

67 Naomi W. Cohen, *The Year after the Riots. American Responses to the Palestine Crisis of 1929–30* (Detroit: Wayne State University Press), 91.

68 LAC, MG 10-K3, Comintern Fonds, microfilm reel # K-277, Minutes of the Pol Bureau, 14 Oct. 1929.

69 Ibid., Minutes of Pol Com, 20 Oct. 1929.

70 Ibid., "Statement of the Pol Comm of the CP of C on the Expulsion of Salsberg. Oct/Nov 1929."

71 PAO, RG 4-32, Records of the Ministry of the Attorney General, Central Registry Files, #3188, 1931, "Listing of Communist Party of Canada Records."

72 Mark Zuehlke, *The Gallant Cause: Canadians in the Spanish Civil War 1936–1939* (Vancouver: Whitecap Books, 1996), 29.

73 Angus, *Canadian Bolsheviks*, 225–45.

74 See Palmer, *Cannon*, chap. 11, passim.

75 Angus, *Canadian Bolsheviks*, 241.

76 Ontario Jewish Archives (OJA), Salsberg Fonds, 2004, 5/28.

77 Report of the Sixth National Convention of the Communist Party of Canada, quoted in Melvin Pelt, "The Communist Party of Canada," MA thesis (University of Toronto, 1964), 34.

78 Betcherman, *The Little Band*, 56; OJA, Salsberg Papers, 2004, C5/28, "To the Polbureau," CPC, Toronto, 10 May 1930.

79 Stewart Smith, *Comrades and Komsomalkas: My Years in the Communist Party of Canada* (Toronto: Lugus Publications, 1993). See also Colin D. Grimson, "The Communist Party of Canada, 1922–1946," MA thesis (McGill University, 1966), 105–10.

80 Norman Penner, *Canadian Communism: The Stalin Years and Beyond* (Toronto: Methuen, 1988), 15, 88; Stephen F. Cohen, *Bukharin and the Bolshevik Revolution: A Political Biography* (New York: Vintage, 1975), 292–3.

81 Comments from anonymous reader of manuscript, 7 June 2011

82 Comintern Fonds, microfilm reel # K-279, Minutes of Pol Com, 17 June 1930.

83 Ibid.

84 Comintern, J.B. Salsberg, 1938 statement.

85 Ibid.

86 OJA, *Toronto Jewish Directory*, 1931.

87 MHSO, Salsberg tapes, 5/19.

88 Henry Srebrnik, "Red Star over Birobidjan: Canadian Jewish Communists and the 'Jewish Autonomous Region' in the Soviet Union," *Labour/Le Travail* 44 (Fall 1999), 129–47; and *Jerusalem on the Amur*.

89 Comintern, J.B. Salsberg, 1938 statement.

90 QUA, Salsberg Fonds, box 9, file 1, clipping, *Canadian Tribune*, 6 Feb. 1950.

Chapter Three

1 Bryan D. Palmer, *Rethinking the History of Canadian Labour, 1800–1991* (Toronto: McClelland & Stewart, 1992), 229.
2 Desmond Morton with Terry Copp, *Working People: An Illustrated History of the Canadian Labour Movement* (Ottawa: Deneau Publishers, 1980), 137; Craig Heron, *The Canadian Labour Movement: A Short History*, 2nd ed. (Toronto: Lorimer, 1996), 62; Judy Fudge and Eric Tucker, *Labour before the Law: The Regulation of Workers' Collective Action in Canada, 1900–1948* (Toronto: Oxford University Press, 2001), 164; James A. Pendergest, "Labour and Politics in Oshawa and District, 1928–1943," MA thesis (Queen's University, 1973), 44; Colin D. Grimson, "The Communist Party of Canada, 1922–1946," MA thesis (McGill University, 1966), 111; Harold A. Logan, *Trade Unions in Canada* (Toronto: Macmillan Company, 1948), 340; Stephen L. Endicott, *Bienfait: The Saskatchewan Miners' Struggle of '31* (Toronto: University of Toronto Press, 2002), 44; Irving M. Abella, *Nationalism, Communism, and Canadian Labour: The CIO, the Communist Party, and the Canadian Congress of Labour 1935–1956* (Toronto: University of Toronto Press, 1973), 3.
3 Heron, *Canadian Labour Movement*, 62.
4 Fudge and Tucker, *Labour before the Law*, 154.
5 Ibid., 164; Joshua Gershman, "A Faulty Book of Reminiscences," *Canadian Jewish Outlook*, Feb./Mar. 1978, 10.
6 David Frank, *J.B. McLachlan: A Biography* (Toronto: Lorimer, 1999), 507; Abella, *Nationalism*, 5; John Manley, "Canadian Communists, Revolutionary Unionism, and the 'Third Period': The Workers' Unity League, 1929–1935," *Journal of the Canadian Historical Association, 1994* (Ottawa, 1995), 167, 195.
7 John Manley, "Communism and the Canadian Working Class during the Great Depression: The Workers' Unity League, 1930–1936," PhD thesis (Dalhousie University, 1984), 304.
8 John Manley, "'Audacity, audacity, and still more audacity': Tim Buck, the Party, and the People, 1932–1939," *Labour/Le Travail* 49 (Spring 2002), 13; Bryan Palmer, ed., *A Communist Life: Jack Scott and the Canadian Workers Movement, 1927–1985* (St John's: Committee on Canadian Labour History, 1988), 42.
9 Palmer, *Jack Scott*, 25.
10 *Workers' Unity*, 2 Dec. 1931; Palmer, *Jack Scott*, 26; James D. Leach, "The Workers Unity League and the Stratford Furniture Workers," *Ontario History* 60, no. 2 (June 1968), 39–48; Tom Ewen, *The Forge Glows Red: From Blacksmith to Revolutionary* (Toronto: Progress Books, 1974), 159; Desmond Morton, "Aid to the Civil Power: The Stratford Strike of 1933," in Irving Abella, ed.,

On Strike: Six Key Labour Struggles in Canada, 1919–1949 (Toronto: James Lorimer, 1975), 79–91, 88; Manley, "Communism and the Canadian Working Class," 274–83, 296; Manley, "Canadian Communists," 181; Stephen Endicott, *Raising the Workers' Flag* (Toronto: University of Toronto Press, 2012), 210–17.

11 Ewen, *The Forge*, 157.

12 *The Worker*, 13 Oct. 1934; Library and Archives Canada (LAC), Comintern Fonds, microfilm reel # K-290, 1935.

13 *The Worker*, 13 Oct. 1934; LAC, RG 146, Canadian Security Intelligence Fonds, vol. 18, file 92-A-00086, Part 1, Executive Board Meeting of the Workers Unity League Held at ... Toronto, Tuesday, December 16th 1934.

14 *Toronto Star*, 26 Feb. 1934

15 Marcus Klee, "Between the Scylla and Charybdis of Anarchy and Despotism: State Capital and the Working Class in the Great Depression, Toronto, 1929–1940," PhD thesis (Queen's University, 1998), 310 –12.

16 Ibid.; *The Worker*, 28 Apr. 1934.

17 *The Worker*, 19 May 1934; *Toronto Star*, 7 May 1934.

18 *The Worker*, 21 July 1934.

19 Klee, "Scylla and Charybdis," 314.

20 *The Worker*, 1 Sept. 1934.

21 Ibid., 9 Feb. 1935; *Toronto Star*, 15 Mar. 1935.

22 Dorothy Livesay, *Right Hand Left Hand* (Erin, ON: Press Porcépic, 1977), 116. My Queen's colleague Peter Campbell supplied this reference.

23 *The Worker*, 29 Aug. 1935.

24 Ibid., 21 Dec. 1935.

25 Manley, "Canadian Communists," 188.

26 William Kaplan, *Everything That Floats: Pat Sullivan, Hal Banks and the Seamen's Unions of Canada* (Toronto: University of Toronto Press, 1987), 12–13.

27 See Marcus Rediker, *Between the Devil and the Deep Blue Sea: Merchant Seamen, Pirates, and the Anglo-American Maritime World 1700–1750.* (New York: Cambridge University Press, 1987), 205–53.

28 Kaplan, *Everything*, 14.

29 Ibid.,16.

30 LAC, Comintern Fonds, K-290, 1935, Letter from J.B. Salsberg in *Election Bulletin* (Saskatchewan).

31 Kaplan, *Everything*, 17.

32 J.A. (Pat) Sullivan, *Red Sails on the Great Lakes* (Toronto: Macmillan, 1955), 43, 44, 67; Jim Green, *Against the Tide: The Story of the Canadian Seamen's Union* (Toronto: Progress Books, 1986), 16, 38.

33 QUA, Salsberg Fonds, box 1, file 18, JBS to Dear Comrades, 28 Apr. 1938.
34 Tim Buck, *Thirty Years 1922–1952: The Story of the Communist Movement in Canada* (Toronto: Progress Books, 1952), 119.
35 Manley, "Communism and the Canadian Working Class," 340.
36 John Manley, "Opportunities Lost: Communists, Labour Unity, and the Birth of the CIO in Canada, 1935–9,' paper delivered at annual conference of the Canadian Historical Association, University of Western Ontario, 31 May 2005.
37 Endicott, *Raising the Workers' Flag*, 316.
38 *The Worker*, 23 Jan. 1935; David Frank and John Manley, "The Sad March to the Right: J.B. McLachlan's Resignation from the Communist Party of Canada, 1936," *Labour/Le Travail* (Fall 1992), 121; Manley, "'Audacity,'" 19.
39 Daniel Cornfield, *Becoming a Mighty Voice: Conflict and Change in the United Furniture Workers of America* (New York: Russell Sage Foundation, 1989), 75.
40 LAC, Comintern Fonds, K-290, 1935; MHSO, Salsberg tapes, 12/19.
41 Abella, *Nationalism*, 25.
42 Leo Roback, "Quebec Workers in the Twentieth Century," in *Lectures in Canadian and Working Class History*, ed. W.J.C. Cherwinski and Gregory S. Kealey (St John's: Committee on Canadian Labour History, 1985), 175.
43 David Frank, *J.B. McLachlan: A Biography. The Story of a Legendary Labour Leader and the Cape Breton Coal Miners* (Toronto: Lorimer, 1999), 507; Abella, *Nationalism*, 5, 25. Rick Stow's interview with Salsberg, 9 Aug. 1992, includes useful reminiscences on Salsberg's tactics.
44 See "Injunction Extended against Bassel Pickets," *Daily Clarion*, 8 May 1936; "Toronto's Example. Weekly Trade Union Review," ibid., 30 May 1936.
45 *Daily Clarion*, 18 June 1936; QUA, Salsberg Fonds, box 2, file 3, Lee letter from C Mc [identities unknown], Sault Ste Marie, to JBS, 3 Oct. 1938, and file 3 on union conditions at Algoma Steel.
46 *The Worker*, 12 Jan. 1935.
47 Ibid., 26 Jan. 1935.
48 *Daily Clarion*, 9 Feb. 1935.
49 Ibid., 20 June 1936.
50 Ibid., 8 Aug. 1936. See also ibid., 26 Sept. 3 Oct. 1936.
51 Marcus Klee, "Fighting the Sweatshop in Depression Ontario: Capital, Labour and the Industrial Standards Act," *Labour/Le Travail* 45 (Spring 2000), 30.
52 *Toronto Star*, 23 Sept. 1936. See also Margaret Gould, *I Visit the Soviets* (Toronto: Francis White, 1937).
53 See Irving Abella, "Oshawa 1937," in Irving Abella, ed., *On Strike: Six Key Labour Struggles in Canada 1919–1949* (Toronto: James Lorimer, 1975), 93–128;

The Worker, 20 May 1936; Abella, *Nationalism*, 8; Buck, *Thirty Years*, 48. The best comprehensive account of the strike and its political ramifications is in Jack Saywell's *"Just Call Me Mitch": The Life of Mitchell F. Hepburn* (Toronto: University of Toronto Press, 1991), 316–26; LAC, Salsberg tape #6090.

54 See John Manley, "Communists and Auto Workers: The Struggle for Industrial Unionism in the Canadian Automobile Industry, 1925–1936," *Labour/Le Travail* 17 (Spring 1986), 105–33, and James A. Pendergest, "The Attempt at Unionization in the Automobile Industry in Canada, 1928," *Ontario History* 70, no. 4 (Dec. 1978), 245–80, for the background to and context of the Oshawa strike.

55 Buck, *Thirty Years*, 48; Abella, "Oshawa 1937," 95; Doug Smith, *Cold Warrior: C.S. Jackson and the United Electrical Workers* (St John's: Canadian Committee on Labour History, 1997), 49; Lita-Rose Betcherman, *The Little Band: The Clashes between the Communists and the Canadian Establishment 1928–1932* (Ottawa: Deneau, n.d.), 59.

56 LAC, Salsberg tape #6090; Larry Zolf, "Rebbe of Spadina: A Beadle's Notes from the Rabbinical Court of the Great J.B. Salsberg," *Toronto Life* 25, no. 14 (Oct. 1991), 164.

57 See *Daily Clarion*, 16 Apr. 1937; Buck, *Thirty Years*, 48.

58 The first local of the United Automobile Workers of America (UAW), Manley makes clear, was chartered in December 1936 at Kelsey-Hayes Wheel in Windsor, Ontario. Manley, "Communists and Auto Workers," 105.

59 QUA, Salsberg Fonds, box 1, file 12, JBS to Joe Spence, 18 Nov. 1938.

60 Abella, "Oshawa 1937," 93.

61 *Daily Clarion*, 13 Feb. 1937.

62 Ibid., 25 Mar. 1937.

63 QUA, Salsberg Fonds, box 1, files 1–23; Smith, *Cold Warrior*, 43.

64 QUA, Salsberg Fonds, box 1, file 22, JBS report to NTUC, 20 Nov. 1937. See Len Scher, *The Un-Canadians: True Stories of the Blacklist Era* (Toronto: Lester Publishing, 1992), 109–10.

65 Palmer, *A Communist Life*, 42; QUA, Salsberg Fonds, box 1, file 2.

66 Ibid., file 23, JBS to Dear Comrades, 12 July 1938.

67 Ruth A. Frager, *Sweatshop Strife: Class, Ethnicity, and Gender in the Jewish Labour Movement of Toronto 1900–1939* (Toronto: University of Toronto Press, 1992), 202–5; QUA, Salsberg Fonds, box 1, file 20, JBS to J. Stachel, 5 July 1938.

68 QUA, Salsberg Fonds, box 1, file 18, JBS to "Dear Comrades," 28 Apr. 1938.

69 Ibid., file 15, National T.U.C. to All Districts and T.U. Committees, 29 July 1938.

70 Ibid., National T.U.C. to All Provincial Committees and T.U.C's, 6 Oct. 1938.

71 Logan, *Trade Unions*, 364–5.
72 Abella, *Nationalism*, 49–51; Morton with Copp, *Working People*, 169.
73 See Laurel S. MacDowell, *Renegade Lawyer: The Life of J.L Cohen* (Toronto: University of Toronto Press and Osgoode Society for Canadian Legal History, 2001).
74 Abella, *Nationalism*, 25, 51, 221.
75 Klee, "Scylla and Charybdis," 473.
76 Manley, "Workers' Unity League," 304.
77 Ian McKay to Gerald Tulchinsky, email, 16 May 2011.
78 Ontario Jewish Archives (OJA), Salsberg Papers, box 98-12-5, file 1952.
79 OJA, Salsberg Papers, box 98-12-5, file 1952.
80 Faith Johnston, *A Great Restlessness: The Life and Politics of Dorise Nielsen* (Winnipeg: University of Manitoba Press, 2006), 201.
81 OJA, Salsberg Fonds, box 98-12-5, file 1952.
82 OJA, Salsberg Fonds, 2000-11-4, interview with J.B. Salsberg by Carol Rosenthal, 13 Mar. 1990.
83 J.B. [Salsberg], *A Wartime Labor Policy. For United All-Out War Effort* (Toronto: Canadian Tribune Publishing, 1941); reprinted from *Canadian Tribune*, 6 Sept. 1941, 1.
84 Ibid., *Wartime*, 32; QUA, Salsberg Fonds, box 9, file 1, "The Trade Unions in the Struggle against the Economic Crisis and the Menace of War" (co-report of J.B. Salsberg to National Committee Meeting, 21–3 May 1947).
85 QUA, Salsberg Fonds, box 1, file 9, clippings, *Canadian Tribune*, 11, 18 Oct. and 1, 9 Nov. 1948; 22, 29 Feb. 1950.
86 Stephen A. Speisman, *Jews of Toronto, A History to 1937* (Toronto: McClelland & Stewart, 1979, 245–56. See also Alan Gordon, "Taking Root in the Patronage Garden: Jewish Businessmen in Toronto's Conservative Party, 1911–1921," *Ontario History* 88, no. 1 (1996), 34–46; Alan Gordon, "Patrons, Brokers and Community Integration: The Patronage Practises of Edmund Bristol, 1911–1921," MA thesis (Queen's University, 1993); Ezra Mendelsohn, *The Jews of East Central Europe between the World Wars* (Bloomington: Indiana University Press, 1983), 25; B. Garncaska-Kadry, "Some Aspects of the Life of the Jewish Proletariat in Interwar Poland," in *Polin: Studies in Polish Jewry*, vol. 8, *Jews in Independent Poland 1918–1939*, ed. Antony Polonsky, Ezra Mendelsohn, and Jerzy Tomaszewski (London: Littman Library of Jewish Civilization, 1994), 243.
87 1931 *Toronto Jewish Directory*, 236–300.
88 MHSO, Salsberg tapes, 13/19; *The Worker*, 20 Aug. 1935.
89 *The Worker*, 28 Dec. 1935; *Daily Clarion*, 9 July 1936.
90 MHSO, Salsberg tapes, 5/19.

91 OJA, John J. Glass Fonds, MG 6B, box 2, file 7, "The Battle of St. Andrew by Politicus." Communists pulled out all the stops including intimidation to get Salsberg elected, it was alleged here. Professor James Walker kindly supplied this reference. David Lewis, *The Good Fight: Political Memoirs 1909–1958* (Toronto: Macmillan, 1981), 107. See also Peter Campbell, *Rose Henderson: For the People* (Montreal: McGill-Queen's University Press, 2011), 333, where the author speculates that Lewis's "support for Salsberg may have had as much to do with wanting to help a fellow Jew in a still anti-Semitic society as it had to do with any ideological commitment to the Popular Front."

92 OJA, "The Battle of St. Andrew"; taped interview by Rosemary Donegan with J.B. Salsberg, 26 June 1984.

93 Norman Penner, *Canadian Communism: The Stalin Years and Beyond* (Toronto: Methuen, 1988), 151. See also Stefan Epp, "A Communist in the Council Chambers: Communist Municipal Politics, Ethnicity and the Career of William Kolisnyk," *Labour/Le Travail* 63 (Spring 2009), 79–104.

94 *Globe and Mail*, 15 Nov. 1937.

95 *Toronto Telegram*, 13 Nov., 3 Dec. 1937. Following the 1930 dominion election campaign in Toronto-Centre, the *Telegram* pointedly advised the victorious Factor to resign to "save himself and the Jews of Toronto from 'paying the price' for victory" after defeating T.L. (Tommy) Church. *The Worker*, 2 Aug. 1930.

96 Stephen Smith, "Counciling Otherwise: The Left Experiences of James Simpson and Stewart Smith in Toronto Municipal Politics, 1930–1946," History 816 graduate paper for Professor Ian McKay (Queen's University, May 2011), 36–7; Canadian Jewish Congress Charities Committee (CJCCC), Montreal, Joseph B. Salsberg file, newspaper clipping, *Canadian Jewish Chronicle*, 4 Mar. 1938.

97 *Toronto Star*, 27 Dec. 1938; *Globe and Mail*, 3 Jan. 1939.

98 Public Archives of Ontario (PAO), RG 6-15, Ontario Ministry of Finance, Interministerial and Intergovernmental Correspondence of the Treasury Department, 1935–1942, box 9, Attorney General, Ontario Provincial Police, Secret and Confidential, 19 June 1940, to Commissioner, "[Report on] Tom Brown, 22 Soho Street, Toronto – recently employed as a ledger-keeper in one of the Provincial savings Banks Branches in Toronto," in William Stringer, commissioner of police for Ontario, to Chester S. Walters, Ontario Controller of Finance, 20 June 1940.

99 *Toronto Star*, 13 June 1938; *Globe and Mail*, 13 June 1938.

100 Canadian Jewish Congress Charities Committee (CJCCC), Salsberg file, William J. Nursey to Chief Inspector of Detectives, secret and confidential:

"Re Communist Party Activities," 27 Sept. 1939. Nursey also, absurdly, describes Sidney Hillman, president of the Amalgamated Clothing Workers' Union of America and one of President Roosevelt's key New Deal advisers, as "a well known communist."

101 Smith, "Counciling Otherwise," 36; Gregory S. Kealey and Reg Whitaker, eds., with intro. by John Manley, *R.C.M.P. Security Bulletins: The Depression Years, Part V, 1938–1939* (St John's: Canadian Committee on Labour History, 1997), 374; LAC, RG 146, Canadian Security Intelligence Fonds, vol. 64, file 96-A-00111, part 2.

102 Kealey and Whitaker, *R.C.M.P. Security Bulletins: The Depression Years*, 412–13.

103 Gregory S. Kealey and Reginald Whitaker, eds., *R.C.M.P. Security Bulletins: The War Series, 1939–1941* (St John's: Canadian Committee on Labour History, 1989), 107.

104 *Daily Clarion*, 16 Sept. 1939; LAC, Comintern Fonds, microfilm reel #311, newspaper clipping, *The Advocate*, 22 Sept. 1939; Merrily Weisbord, *The Strangest Dream: Canadian Communists, the Spy Trials, and the Cold War* (Montreal: Vehicule Press, 1994), 98–9.

105 *Toronto Star*, 23 Dec. 1939.

106 Jack Lipinsky, *Imposing Their Will: An Organizational History of Jewish Toronto, 1933–1948* (Montreal: McGill-Queen's University Press, 2011), 193.

107 Kealey and Manley, *R.C.M.P. Security Bulletins: Depression Years*, 412; Kealey and Whitaker, *R.C.M.P. Security Bulletins: The War Series*, 109.

108 Tim Buck, *Yours in the Struggle: Reminiscences of Tim Buck*, ed. William Beeching and Dr Phyllis Clarke (Toronto: NG Press, 1977), 308–12; Ian McKay to Gerald Tulchinsky, email, 16 May 2011; Palmer, *A Communist Life*, 37.

109 LAC, MG 30, A94, Jacob Lawrence Cohen Fonds, 1923–1951, vol. 31, file 29172 (1942), Pierre Taschereau to J.L. Cohen, 25 July 1942; MacDowell, *Renegade Lawyer*, 188–9; PAO, Leith McMurray Records Relating to the Communist Party of Canada, F-2157-4, box 14, file CPC, 1942, The Dominion Government Must Remove the Communist Ban. Statement of the N.C.D.R. Conference, Toronto, August 16, 1942.

110 University of Toronto Archives, Kenny Collection, MS 179, box 43. Reprint of letter by John W. Bruce to Toronto Star, 13 July 1942; Reg Whitaker, "Official Repression of Communism during World War II," *Labour/Le Travail* 17 (Spring 1986), 135–66,149.

111 *Globe and Mail*, 2 Jan 1943.

112 Ibid., 5 Jan. 1943.

113 Ibid., 5 and 6 Apr., 29 May, and 20 July 1943.

114 Ibid., 15 June 1943.

115 Nathalie Babel, ed., *The Complete Works of Isaac Babel* (New York, 2002), 197–331.

116 Nora Levin, *The Jews in the Soviet Union since 1917: Paradox of Survival* (New York: New York University Press, 1988, 2 vols.), 1: 258ff.

117 Ibid., 260.

118 See Isaac Deutscher, *The Non-Jewish Jew and Other Essays* (New York: Hill and Wang, 1968), 25–41.

119 Bryan Palmer, "Leon Trotsky: Planet without a Visa," *Left History* 9 (Fall/Winter 2003), 79–92, 88.

120 Ibid., 90.

121 Levin, *Jews in Soviet Union*, 265.

122 Gregor Aronson, "The Jewish Question during the Stalin Era," in *Russian Jewry 1917–1967*, ed. Gregor Aronson et al. (New York: Thomas Yoseloff, 1969), 179. Benjamin Pinkus, ed., *The Soviet Government and the Jews 1948–1967* (London: Cambridge University Press / Hebrew University of Jerusalem – Institute of Contemporary Jewry and Israel Academy of Sciences and Humanities, 1984), 3.

123 David Shneer, *Yiddish and the Creation of Soviet Jewish Culture 1918–1930* (New York: Cambridge University Press, 2004), 219. See also Gennadi Kostrychenko, "The Genesis of the Establishment of Anti-Semitism in the USSR: The Black Years, 1948–1953," in *Revolution, Repression, and Revival: The Soviet Jewish Experience*, ed. Zvi Gitelman and Yaacov Ro'i (New York: Rowman and Littlefield, 2007), 181.

124 MHSO, Salsberg tapes, 14/19.

125 Henry Srebrnik, "Red Star over Birobidzhan: Canadian Jewish Communists and the 'Jewish Autonomous Regime' in the Soviet Union," *Labour/Le Travail* 44 (Fall 1999), 129–48.

126 OJA, Salsberg Fonds, box 98-12-5, interview by Sharyn Salsberg Ezrin with Al Hershkovitz, no date, 5.

127 See Ivo Banac, *The Diary of Georgi Dimitrov 1933–1949* (New Haven: Yale University Press 2003), 22; Tom Ewen, *The Forge Glows Red: From Blacksmith to Revolutionary* (Toronto: Progress Books, 1974), 202; OJA, Salsberg Fonds, 98-12-5, Tom Ewen to J.B., Aug. 1939.

128 Yale University, Annals of Communism project, Georgi Dimitrov diary, 29 July 1939 (translation): "Discussion with Canadian representative Salzberg (member of the Canadian CPPB). Draft a report for the Secretariat. Party representative to the ECCI luven."

129 *Vochenblatt*, 25 Oct. 1956; Ruth Borchiver interview with Joe Salsberg, n.d.

130 Walter D. Young, *The Anatomy of a Party: The National CCF 1932–1961* (Toronto: University of Toronto Press, 1969), 258.

131 I thank Todd McCallum of the Department of History, Dalhousie University for this insight.

132 See Annette Aronowicz, "Haim Sloves, the Jewish People, and a Jewish Communist's Allegiances," *Jewish Social Studies* 9 (Fall 2002), 95–142.
133 Buck, *Yours in the Struggle*, 389.
134 Kostrychenko, "Anti-Semitism in USSR," 180–1.
135 Henry F. Srebrnik, *Jerusalem on the Amur: Birobidzhan and the Canadian Jewish Communist Movement, 1924–1951* (Montreal: McGill-Queen's University Press, 2008), 152–3. See also Srebrnik, "'The Jews Do Not Want War!': American Jewish Communists Defend the Hitler-Stalin Pact, 1939–1941," *American Communist History* 8, no.1 (2009), 49–71.
136 Kealey and Whitaker, *R.C.M.P. Security Bulletins: The War Series*, 34; *Daily Clarion*, 16 Sept. 1939; *Canadian Tribune*, 13 Sept. 1941, 11 Apr., 23 May, 8 and 15 Aug. 1942.
137 David Lewis, *The Good Fight*, 236–7.

Chapter Four

1 *Ontario Hansard*, 21 Mar. 1952.
2 Ibid., 24 Mar. 1955.
3 Canadian Jewish Congress Charities Committee (CJCCC), Montreal, Joseph B. Salsberg file, newspaper clipping, *Canadian Jewish Chronicle*, 4 Mar. 1938, "Public Statement of the Zionist Organization of Toronto." *Globe and Mail*, 13 July 1943; *Toronto Star*, 9 Aug. 1943.
4 See Gad Horowitz, *Canadian Labour in Politics* (Toronto: University of Toronto Press, 1968), 103–13 and David Lewis, *The Good Fight: Political Memoirs, 1909–1958* (Toronto: Macmillan, 1981), 151.
5 Horowitz, *Canadian Labour in Politics*, 79–80.
6 CJCCC, Louis Rosenberg Papers, Collection Series, DA2, box 1, file 38, "Information and Comment. Committee on Social and Economic Studies of the Canadian Jewish Congress, No. 5, May 1947." 1: Comparative Occupational Distribution. Gainfully Occupied Jews, Classified by Manufacturing Group and Sex Engaged in Manufacturing Industries in the Four Largest Cities in Canada, 1931 and 1941.
7 Louis Rosenberg, *Canada's Jews: A Social and Economic Study of the Jews of Canada* (Montreal: Canadian Jewish Congress, 1939), 364–70.
8 Henry Srebrnik, *London Jews and British Communism 1935–1945* (London: Valentine, Mitchell, 1995), 19.
9 John C. Bagnall, "The Ontario Conservatives and the Development of Anti-Discrimination Policy: 1944 to 1962," PhD thesis (Queen's University, 1984), 192–5, 240; Peter Oliver, *Unlikely Tory: The Life and Politics of Allan Grossman* (Toronto: Lester and Orpen Denys, 1985).

10 Liora Santopinto to Gerald Tulchinsky, 18 Mar. 2011.
11 Ontario Jewish Archives (OJA), Ben G. Kayfetz Fonds, 2000-11-4, untitled manuscript of Rosenthal interview with J.B. Salsberg, 26.
12 Gerald L. Caplan, "The Failure of Canadian Socialism: The Ontario Experience, 1932–1945," *Canadian Historical Review* 44, no. 2 (June 1963), 93–121.
13 See John T. Saywell, *"Just Call Me Mitch": The Life of Mitchell F. Hepburn* (Toronto: University of Toronto Press, 1991), 512–29; Lewis, *The Good Fight*, 264–5.
14 Young, *Anatomy of a Party*, 268. Norman Penner, *Canadian Communism: The Stalin Years and Beyond* (Toronto: Methuen, 1988), 146.
15 Lewis, *The Good Fight*, 150.
16 See J.L. Granatstein, "Changing Alliances: Canada and the Soviet Union, 1939–1945," in *Canada and the Soviet Experiment: Essays on Canadian Encounters with Russia and the Soviet Union, 1900–1991*, ed. David Jay Bercuson and David Davies (Toronto: Centre for Russian and East European Studies, University of Toronto, 1994), 75–88.
17 Horowitz, *Canadian Labour*, 90ff.
18 Lewis, *The Good Fight*, 265–8.
19 PAO, RG 47, 27-1-53, Ontario Historical Study Series, Oral History, interview with E.B. Joliffe, no date.
20 Gerald Tulchinsky, *Canada's Jews: A People's Journey* (Toronto: University of Toronto Press, 2008), 283–327.
21 James W. St. G. Walker, *"Race," Rights and the Law in the Supreme Court of Canada: Historical Case Studies* (Toronto: Osgoode Society for Canadian Legal History and Wilfrid Laurier University Press, 1997), 182–3.
22 Lara Campbell, *Respectable Citizens; Gender, Family, and Unemployment in Ontario's Great Depression* (Toronto: University of Toronto Press, 2009), 180.
23 Stephen Speisman, "Antisemitism in Ontario: The Twentieth Century," in *Antisemitism in Canada, History and Interpretation*, ed. Alan Davies (Waterloo: Wilfrid Laurier University Press, 1992), 113–34, 121.
24 Carmela Patrias, *Jobs and Justice: Fighting Discrimination in Wartime Canada, 1939–1945* (Toronto: University of Toronto Press, 2012), 19–44.
25 *A Black Man's Toronto 1914–1980: The Reminiscences of Harry Gairey*, ed. with an intro. by Donna Hill (Toronto: Multicultural History Society of Ontario, 1981), 26–7. "An Appeal to the Negro People in Spadina Riding" (pamphlet, 1955).
26 Bromley L. Armstrong, *Bromley: Tireless Champion for Just Causes. Written with Sheldon Taylor* (Toronto: Vitabu Publishing, 2000), 76.
27 Cyril Rosenberg to Gerald Tulchinsky, in conversation, summer 1957.
28 *Ontario Hansard*, 13 Mar. 1951.

29 See Sammy Luftspring with Brian Swarbrick, *Call Me Sammy* (Toronto: Pren-
    tice-Hall, 1975).
30 See articles by Lillian Petroff, "Sojourner and Settler: The Macedonian Pres-
    ence in the City, 1903–1940," and Zoriana Yaworsky Sokolsky, "The Begin-
    nings of Ukrainian Settlement in Toronto," in *Gathering Place: Peoples and
    Neighbourhoods of Toronto, 1834-1945*, ed. Robert F. Harney (Toronto: Multi-
    cultural History Society of Ontario, 1985), 177–204, 279–302; and Walker,
    "Race," Rights and the Law, 196.
31 PAO, RG 3-17, box 458, file 247-G, "Salsberg, Mr. Joseph B. Labour Progres-
    sive Party," J.B. Salsberg to George A. Drew, 2 Feb. 1944; Patrias, *Jobs and
    Justice*, 50–67.
32 Bagnall, "Ontario Conservatives," 17–19.
33 PAO, RG 3-17, box 458, file 247-G. "Salsberg, Mr. Joseph B. Labour Progres-
    sive Party." George A. Drew to J.B. Salsberg, 3 Feb. 1944. The by-law did not
    pass.
34 Ibid., "Addendum," J.B. Salsberg to George A. Drew, 2 Feb. 1944; *Globe and
    Mail*, 14 Feb. 1944.
35 PAO, Salsberg, "Addendum."
36 Bagnall, "Ontario Conservatives," 28, 29.
37 PAO, RG 3-17, G.A. Drew, General correspondence, 1943–1948, box 434,
    file: Discrimination Bill #46, Petitions re.; *Statutes of Ontario* 1944, CI.
38 *Ontario Hansard*, 7 Mar. 1944.
39 Bagnall, "Ontario Conservatives," 37–43.
40 J.B. Salsberg, M.P.P., "About the Ontario Race Discrimination Act," *Jewish
    Journal*, 18 Oct. 1944. Clipping in QUA, Salsberg Fonds, box 9, file 2.
41 *The Canadian Negro* 3, no. 3 (May 1955). This reference was supplied by Pro-
    fessor Barrington Walker of the Department of History, Queen's University.
    Globe and Mail, 26 Sept. 1944.
42 *Ontario Hansard*, 21 Mar. 1945.
43 Ibid., 28 Mar. 1946.
44 PAO, RG3-17, G.A. Drew, General correspondence, 1943–1948, box 436,
    file: Fair Employment Practises Act. Address – Rabbi Feinberg; Bagnal, "On-
    tario Conservatives," 99, 162.
45 James W. St. G. Walker, "The Jewish Phase in the Movement for Racial
    Equality in Canada," *Canadian Ethnic Studies / Études ethniques au Canada* 34,
    no. 1 (2002), 12; Carmela Patrias and Ruth A. Frager, "'This Is Our Country,
    These Are Our Rights': Minorities and the Origins of Ontario's Human
    Rights Campaigns," *Canadian Historical Review* 82, no. 1 (2001), 24–7.
46 *Ontario Hansard*, 7 Mar., 6 Apr. 1944; *Canadian Tribune*, 18 Mar. 1944.
47 *Ontario Hansard*, 7 Mar. 1944.

48 Ibid., 6 Apr. 1944.

49 Ibid., 16 Mar. 1944.

50 Ibid., 3 Mar. 1944.

51 Ibid., 15, 27 Feb. 1945.

52 *Globe and Mail,* 10 Mar. 1950.

53 Ibid., 3 Mar. 1945.

54 See Herb Colling, *The Ford Strike in Windsor, 1945, Ninety-Nine Days* (Toronto: NC Press, 1995), 16–17, 69; David Moulton, "Ford Windsor 1945," in *On Strike: Six Key Labour Struggles in Canada 1919–1949,* ed. Irving M. Abella (Toronto: James Lorimer, 1975), 129–62; J.B. Salsberg, "A Five-Point Program for Labor," *National Affairs Monthly* 3, no. 9 (Nov. 1945), 299–300.

55 PAO, RG 49-63, clipping, *Sudbury Daily Star,* 20 Nov. 1945; *Toronto Daily Star,* 27 Nov. 1945.

56 *Ontario Hansard,* 16 Mar. 1945.

57 Reg Whitaker, "Official Repression of Communism during World War II," *Labour/Le Travail* 17 (Spring 1986), 142; *Ontario Hansard,* 28 Feb., 7 Mar. 1945.

58 Ibid., 14 Mar. 1945.

59 Ibid., 21 Mar. 1945.

60. Ibid., 20 Mar. 1946.

61 Ibid., 13 Mar. 1946.

62 See Frank K. Clarke, "'Keep Communism Out of Our Schools': Cold War Anti-Communism at the Toronto Board of Education, 1948–1951," *Labour/ Le Travail* 49 (Spring 2002), 93–119.

63 *Ontario Hansard,* 3 Mar. 1952.

64 Ibid., 3 Mar. 1952.

65 Ibid., 4 Mar. 1948.

66 Edwin Goodman, *Life of the Party: The Memoirs of Eddie Goodman* (Toronto: Key Porter, 1988), 42–4.

67 *Globe and Mail,* 25 May, 2 June 1948.

68 Reg Whitaker and Gary Marcuse, *Cold War Canada: The Making of a National Insecurity State 1945–1957* (Toronto: University of Toronto Press, 1994), 215.

69 Ibid., 291.

70 Quoted ibid., 468, from Oliver, *Unlikely Tory,* 71.

71 Joseph Schull, *Ontario since 1867* (Toronto: McClelland & Stewart, 1981), 334; Bagnall, "Ontario Conservatives," 197.

72 *Ontario Hansard,* 28 Mar. 1951.

73 Donald C. MacDonald, *The Happy Warrior: Political Memoirs* (Toronto: Dundurn Press, 1998), 299.

74 Roger Graham, *Old Man Ontario: Leslie M.* Frost (Toronto: University of Toronto Press, 1990), 189; Trent University Archives, Frost Papers, 77-024/68/9, J.B. Salsberg to Leslie Frost, 16 Jan. 1969; Leslie Frost to William Rodney, 4 Sept. 1968, box 75, folder 12.
75 Oliver, *Unlikely Tory*, 60–1.
76 *Ontario Hansard*, 2 Mar. 1950.
77 Ibid., 21 Feb. 1951.
78 Ibid., 4 Mar. 1952.
79 Ibid., 22 Mar. 1950.
80 Ibid., 27 Mar. 1950.
81 Ibid., 30 Mar. 1950.
82 Ibid., 31 Mar. 1950.
83 Ibid., 5 Apr. 1950.
84 Ibid., 28 Feb. 1951.
85 Ibid.
86 Ibid., 30 Mar. 1950.
87 Ibid., 3 Mar. 1950.
88 Ibid., 23 Feb. 1951.
89 Ibid., 27 Feb. 1951.
90 Ibid., 21 Feb. 1951.
91 Ibid., 22 Feb. 1951.
92 Ibid., 7 Apr. 1952.
93 Ibid., 5 Apr. 1954.
94 Ibid., 31 Mar. 1954.
95 Ibid., 4 Mar. 1952.
96 OJA, Ben Kayfetz Fonds, 2000-11/4, untitled manuscript, 9; Ben Kayfetz interview with Sam Lipshitz, 28 May 1991; *Globe and Mail*, 7 Mar. 1953.
97 *Ontario Hansard*, 6 Mar. 1953.
98 Ibid., 26 Feb. 1953.
99 Ibid., 16 Mar. 1953.
100 Ibid., 4 Apr. 1951; 1 Apr. 1953; 25 Feb. 1954.
101 *Globe and Mail*, 28 Mar. 1953.
102 *Ontario Hansard*, 27 Mar. 1951.
103 Ibid., 8 Apr. 1952.
104 Ibid., 24 Feb. 1953.
105 Ibid., 4 Mar. 1953.
106 Ibid., 13 Mar. 1951.
107 Ibid., 13 Mar. 1951; 28 Feb. 1955.
108 Ibid., 27 Feb. 1952; 21 Feb., 7 Mar. 1955.
109 Ibid., 27 Mar. 1951.

110 Ibid.
111 Ibid., 29 Mar. 1951.
112 Ibid., 3 Mar. 1952.
113 Ibid., 19 Mar. 1951.
114 Ibid., 15 Mar. 1951; 15 Mar. 1955.
115 Ibid., 15 Mar. 1951.
116 Ibid., 16 Mar. 1951.
117 Ibid., 21 Mar. 1951.
118 Ibid., 27 Mar. 1951.
119 Ibid., 2 Apr. 1951.
120 Ibid., 4 Apr. 1951.
121 Ibid., 30 Mar. 1955.
122 OJA, Salsberg Papers, box 5, clipping, *Toronto Star*, 10 June 1955; see Oliver, *Unlikely Tory*, 64–74; *Telegram*, 7 May 1955; York University Archives, Allan Grossman Papers, 1980-010/057(01), newspaper clipping, *Hush*, 11 June 1955.
123 *Hebraishe Zhurnal*, 20, 28 May; 1 June 1955.
124 Stephen Endicott to Gerald Tulchinsky, email 9 Dec. 2011; Louis Rosenberg, "Population Characteristics of the Jewish Population of Toronto" (Montreal: Bureau of Social and Economic Research, Canadian Jewish Congress, Jewish Community Series, no. 3, 1 February 1955), 2; *Globe and Mail*, 10 June 1955; OJA, Salsberg Papers, 98-12-5, box 5, Harry Gould to Joe, 10 June 1955.
125 *Globe and Mail*, 17 Feb. 1954.
126 See Tony Michels, *A Fire in Their Hearts: Yiddish Socialists in New York* (Cambridge: Harvard University Press, 2005).
127 *Globe and Mail*, 3 Mar. 1953.
128 Pirke Avoth, *Ethics*, 2:21.
129 *Ontario Hansard*, 8 Apr. 1952.
130 See R. Warren James, *The People's Senator: The Life and Times of David A. Croll* (Vancouver: Douglas & McIntyre, 1990); Oliver, *Unlikely Tory*, 74–5.

Chapter Five

1 Bryan Palmer to Gerald Tulchinsky, 6 July 2011, email.
2 See Shimon Redlich, *Propaganda and Nationalism in Wartime Russia: The Jewish Antifascist Committee in the USSR, 1941–1948* (Boulder, CO: East European Quarterly, 1982), 167–70; Gregor Aronson, "The Jewish Question during the Stalin Era," in *Russian Jewry 1917–1967*, ed. Gregor Aronson et al. (New York: Thomas Yoseloff, 1969), 191.

3 Queen's University Archives (QUA), Salsberg Fonds, box 9, file 6, clipping, *Vochenblatt*, 8 Jan. 1948. This article was also published in English in *New Voice: An Anglo-Jewish Monthly* 3, no. 1 (January 1948) and in *Jewish Echo* (Glasgow), 30 Jan. 1948. Franklyn Bialystok, *Delayed Impact: The Holocaust and the Canadian Jewish Community* (Montreal: McGill-Queen's University Press, 2000), 40, 53.

4 Canadian Jewish Congress Charities Committee, Montreal, CJC Series CA, box 29, file 300 (1947), J.B. Salsberg to Saul Hayes, 12 Dec. 1947. See also Irving Abella and Harold Troper, *None Is Too Many. Canada and the Jews of Europe 1933–1948* (Toronto: Lester and Orpen Dennys, 1982), 254 for a fuller account of Salsberg's impressions.

5 *Jewish Echo*, 30 Jan. 1948.

6 Gerald Tulchinsky, *Canada's Jews: A People's Journey* (Toronto: University of Toronto Press, 2008), 402; QUA, Salsberg Fonds, box 21, file 22, letters from Dora Wilensky to Joe Salsberg, Nov.–Dec. 1947.

7 QUA, Salsberg Fonds, box 9, file 15; MHSO tapes, #6090.

8 QUA, Salsberg Fonds, box 9, file 12.

9 PAO, Troster Papers, C-56-7, file J.B. Salsberg, newspaper clipping, *Toronto Telegram*, 1 May 1971.

10 Yad Vashem Archives, Jerusalem, taped witness statement of David Fefferman, Tel Aviv, February 1967. Translated from Polish by Dr Ewa Dutkiewicz.

11 J. Larry Black, "Soviet Tactics and Targets in Canada before and after the Gouzenko Defection," in *The Gouzenko Affair: Canada and the Beginnings of the Cold War Counter-Espionage*, ed. J.L. Black and Martin Rudner (Newcastle, ON: Penumbra Press, 2006), 110. Salsberg did not report extensively on this Palestine trip to *Vochenblatt* readers, though he did give public lectures about it. See Henry F. Srebrnik, *Jerusalem on the Amur: Birobidzhan and the Canadian Jewish Communist Movement, 1924–1951* (Montreal: McGill-Queen's University Press, 2008), 293 n. 65. My colleague Myron Momryk has information suggesting that Salsberg might have met David Mangel there. LAC, Salsberg tapes, #6090.

12 See Srebrnik, *Jerusalem on the Amur*, 293; QUA, Salsberg Fonds, box 9, file 6, poster: "… A grus fun shlacht-front iyn erets yisroel … Y.B. Zaltsberg her vet reden by a MASN FARZAMLUNG, … februar 8-tn, 1948. victori teater [Toronto]." *Vochenblatt*, 8 Feb. 1948; see also ibid, 20 May 1948.

13 QUA, Salsberg Fonds, box 9, file 9, clipping, *Canadian Tribune*, 14 Feb. 1948.

14 *New Voice: An Anglo-Jewish Monthly* 3, no. 2 (February 1948).

15 Nahma Sandrow, "The Night of the Murdered Poets," *Jewish Ideas Weekly*, 12–19 August 2011, 3.

16 Aronson, "The Jewish Question," 195, 197.

17 Iakov Etinger, "The Doctors' Plot: Stalin's Solution to the Jewish Question," in *Jews and Jewish Life in Russia and the Soviet Union*, ed. Yaacov Ro'i (London: Frank Cass 1995), 103–24, 114–15.

18 While living in Israel in 1952–3, I witnessed ardent members of the Moscow-oriented *Hashomer Hatzair* (the Young Guard) from Buenos Aires, New York, Johannesburg, and Toronto in tears, and heard of their anguished all-night meetings where they tried to reconcile their socialist idealism with this un-avoidable evidence of anti-Semitism in the communist-block countries.

19 *Vochenblatt*, 1 Nov. 1956.

20 Merrily Weisbord, *The Strangest Dream: Canadian Communists, the Spy Trials, and the Cold War* (Montreal: Vehicle Press, 1994), 98.

21 *Vochenblatt*, 1 Nov. 1956.

22 Larry Zolf, "The Rebbe of Spadina," *Toronto Life*, October 1991, 52, 156–67, 162–3. Bergelson's wife was not yet a widow. Although arrested in January 1949, he was executed in Lubyanka during the "Night of the Murdered Poets" on 12–13 August 1952.

23 Ibid., 166.

24 Ruth Borchiver interview with Joe Salsberg, no date.

25 Ontario Jewish Archives (OJA), interview with Sam Lipshitz, no date.

26 Sam Lipshitz, "Lessons of the Prague Trials," *National Affairs*, February 1953, 20–8, 24, 27.

27 University of Toronto, Thomas Fisher Rare Books Library, MS Coll. 179, Kenny Collection, box 9, "Main Report Delivered at Conference of National Jewish Committee of the Labor Progressive Party on January 14, 1950"; Norman Penner, *Canadian Communism: The Stalin Years and Beyond* (Toronto: Methuen, 1988), 242.

28 Library and Archives Canada (LAC) MG 28, IV, 4, Communist Party of Canada, Convention and Central Committee Series, Convention and Committee files, 1921–1937, vol. 12 (microfilm reel H-1584, 1956), "Decisions of the Meeting of the National Committee, May 17–21, 1956."

29 Kenny Collection, box 9, "Enlarged Meeting of the National Jewish Committee, held April 18th [1954]," 3, 4.

30 Ibid., "Memorandum on the Work of the Jewish National Subcommittee," 2.

31 *Vochenblatt*, 26 Feb. 1953.

32 Ibid., 8 Nov. 1956.

33 Shimon Redlich, *War, Holocaust and Stalinism: A Documented Study of the Jewish Anti-Fascist Committee in the USSR* (London: Harwood Academic Publishers, 1995), 464, "Document 181. The Resolution to Close the JAFC (November 20, 1948)."

34 *Vochenblatt*, 8 Nov. 1956.

35 Ibid.
36 Benjamin Pinkus, *The Jews of the Soviet Union: The History of a National Minority* (New York: Cambridge University Press, Soviet and East European Studies, 1988), 144ff.
37 Jonathan Brent and Vladimir P. Naumov, *Stalin's Last Crime: The Plot against the Jewish Doctors 1948–1953* (New York: HarperCollins, 2003), 330.
38 Joshua Rubenstein and Vladimir P. Naumov, *Stalin's Secret Pogrom: The Postwar Inquisition of the Jewish Anti-Fascist Committee* (New Haven: Yale University Press, Annals of Communism, 2001).
39 *Vochenblatt*, 9 November 1956.
40 Ibid., 18 Aug. 1955.
41 Kenny Collection, box 9, "Notes for Discussion on the Significance of the 20th Congress for the Jewish People of Canada," 3, 5.
42 *Vochenblatt*, 12 Apr. 1956.
43 See *Vochenblatt*, 22 July 1956, for the full text of the statement in which Salsberg was reinstated to the party's National Jewish Committee as well as to the national executive.
44 LAC, MG 28, IV, 4, vol. 12. "Decisions of the Meeting of the National Committee, May 17–21, 1956"; "Resolution of the National Committee, Labor-Progressive Party on the 20th Congress of the Communist Party of the U.S.S.R., May 21, 1956"; *Questions for Today: Documents and Commentary of the Communist Party of Canada, 1952–1964* (Toronto: Progress Books, 1964), 11.
45 But see Morris Biderman, *A Life on the Jewish Left: An Immigrant's Experiences* (Toronto: Onward Publishing 2000), 136. The make-up of the delegation is a matter of some confusion. See Karen Levine, "The Labor-Progressive Party in Crisis: 1956–1957," unpublished research essay (York University, 7 March, 1977), 12, cited in Penner, *Canadian Communism*, 249.
46 *Vochenblatt*, 15 Nov. 1956.
47 Benjamin Pinkus, *The Soviet Government and the Jews, 1948–1967* (Cambridge, Eng., and New York: Cambridge University Press, 1988), 54–8.
48 QUA, Salsberg Fonds, box 19, file 14. Salsberg gave a somewhat different version of the conversation at this meeting to Bill Walsh. See Cy Gonick, *A Very Red Life: The Story of Bill Walsh* (St John's: Canadian Committee on Labour History, 2001), 212.
49 *Vochenblatt*, 22 Nov. 1956.
50 The Soviets were actually right on this point. See Mordechai Altshuler, *Soviet Jewry since the Second World War: Population and Social Structure*, Studies in Population and Urban Demography no. 5 (New York: Greenwood Press, 1987), 183.
51 *Vochenblatt*, 22 Nov. 1956.

52　QUA, Salsberg Fonds, box 9, file 14.

53　Ibid.

54　OJA, Salsberg Fonds, interview, Sharyn Salsberg Ezrin with Morris Bider-man, 24 June 1991, 6.

55　*Vochenblatt*, 13 Dec. 1956.

56　David A. Shannon, *The Decline of American Communism: A History of the Com-munist Party of the United States since 1945* (New York: Harcourt Brace, Com-munism in American Life, 1959), 309–10; see also John Gates, *The Story of an American Communist* (New York: Thomas Nelson and Sons, 1958), 168 and passim.

57　See Annette Aronowicz, "Haim Sloves, the Jewish People, and a Jewish Com-munist's Allegiances," *Jewish Social Studies* 9 (Fall 2002), passim; Maurice Szafran, *Les Juifs dans la politique française de 1945 à nos jours* (Paris: Flammar-ion, 1990), iiiff., and Jonathan Boyarin, *Polish Jews in Paris: The Ethnography of Memory* (Bloomington: Indiana University Press, 1991), 73, 75.

58　John Kolasky, *The Shattered Illusion: The History of Ukrainian Pro-Communist Organizations in Canada* (Toronto: PMA Books, 1979), 150.

59　*Vochenblatt*, 20 Dec. 1956.

60　Ibid.

61　Communist Party of Canada, "Draft Statement on LLP Delegation to Soviet Union." Submitted by J.B. Salsberg, October–November 1956.

62　Ibid. See also "Revision to Draft Statement by J.B.S."

63　Irving Howe and Lewis Coser, *The American Communist Party: A Critical His-tory* (New York: Praeger, 1962), 498.

64　OJA, Salsberg Fonds, box 5, "Mein Shlichos in Moskve," *Klorkeit* B (1957); "Shlichoti l'Moskva," *Drachim Chadashot* (1957). QUA, Salsberg Fonds, box 9, file 15, Salsberg to Hyman Levy, 15 Feb. 1957; another version appeared in the Paris publication *Undzer Eynikeit* (Notre Unité), February 1960, no. 12, 5–6, entitled "Shem Zich Nisht Mitt Dien Pine," (Don't Be Ashamed of Your Anguish).

65　*Vochenblatt*, 10 Jan. 1957.

66　Ibid., 17 Jan. 1957.

67　Ibid.

68　*Vochenblatt*, 31 Jan. 1957.

69　Ibid., 7 Feb. 1957.

70　"Voohin Gaistu, Vochenblatt?" *Vochenblatt*, 21 and 28 Feb. 1957.

71　Ibid., 21 and 28 Feb. 1957.

72　Ibid., 28 Feb. 1957.

73　Ibid., 14 Mar. 1957.

74　Ibid., 4 Apr. 1957.

75 Ibid., 18 Apr. 1957.
76 OJA, Salsberg Fonds, box 5, "Report to the Conference, December 8th and 9th [1956], by S. Shek, Secretary," 1.
77 *Toronto Star*, 25 Oct. 1956.
78 "Report to Conference," 1.
79 OJA, Salsberg Fonds, box 5, "Statement of Aims and Purposes of the United Jewish People's Order."
80 Ibid., Salsberg to Chairman and Members of Metropolitan Committee of LPP, Toronto, Ont., 2 Jan. 1957.
81 Ibid., "Position of Comrade J.B. Salsberg as Expressed at the Last Plenum …"
82 Ibid.; QUA, Salsberg Fonds, box 9, file 5, clipping "For a Socialist Realignment in Canada," *National Affairs Monthly*, February 1957, 3–4.
83 QUA, Salsberg Fonds, box 9, file 15, JBS to Hyman Levy, 15 Feb., 4 May 1957.
84 Ibid., Levy to JBS, 29 Mar., 1 June 1957; Morris Schappes to JBS, 23 May 1957; Hannoch Brosza to JBS, 14 June 1957.
85 United States, Federal Bureau of Investigation, Freedom of Information/ Privacy Acts Release, Subject Joseph Baruch Salsberg, August 2003.
86 Kenny Collection, box 9, National Executive Committee, Labor-Progressive Party, "Party Policy in the Jewish Field," 9 May 1958, typescript.
87 Ibid.
88 Ibid., "For NC Meeting, Aug. 30 – Sept. 1, 1958. On the Struggle for Marxism-Leninism among Jewish Canadians," 3.
89 *Marxist Review* 15, no. 157 (Oct.–Nov. 1957), 13.
90 Ibid., 6, no. 156 (Aug.–Sept. 1957), 18.
91 Ibid., 20.
92 Gonick, *A Very Red Life*, 13.
93 Extract from 'Whither the Party,' CBC *Horizon* documentary on the Communist Party of Canada, 1964. I am grateful to Ian McKay for this reference.
94 Irving Abella, "Joshua Gershman," *Labour/Le Travail* (1977), 210.
95 OJA, Salsberg Fonds, Hershkovitz interview, n.d.
96 *Vochenblatt*, 23 June 1955.
97 Bryan Palmer to Gerald Tulchinsky, 6 July 2011, email.
98 *Vochenblatt*, 23 May 1957.
99 Peter Campbell, *Canadian Marxists and the Search for a Third Way* (Montreal: McGill-Queen's University Press, 1999), 6.
100 University of British Columbia Special Collections, Lil Greene Papers, Tom Ewen to Lil Greene (Toronto), 8 June 1955; cited in Stephen Endicott, *Raising the Workers' Flag* (Toronto: University of Toronto Press, 2012), 351.

Chapter Six

1 Ian McKay to Gerald Tulchinsky, email, 16 May 2011; *Toronto Star*, 7 Apr. 1959; Len Scher, *The Un-Canadians: True Stories of the Blacklist Era* (Toronto: Lester Publishing, 1992), 125.
2 *Toronto Star*, 9 Apr. 1959.
3 *CJN*, 25 Mar. 1960.
4 *FY*, Jan. 1962, 6.
5 Ibid., Sept. 1963, 3.
6 Harold Troper, *The Defining Decade: Identity, Politics, and the Canadian Jewish Community in the 1960s* (Toronto: University of Toronto Press, 2010), ix, 296.
7 Morton Weinfeld, *Like Everyone Else ... But Different: The Paradoxical Success of Canadian Jews* (Montreal: McClelland & Stewart, 2001), 352.
8 *FY*, Apr. 1973, 3; Nov. 1978, 8; Apr. 1980, 10; Apr. 1972, 9.
9 Ibid., Apr. 1966, 5.
10 Ibid., Sept. 1964, 6.
11 Ibid., Nov. 1969, 8.
12 Ibid., Nov. 1970, 10–11.
13 Ibid., Dec. 1970, 2.
14 *CJN*, 8 Oct. 1971; 11 Jan. 1990; 30 May 1975; 13 Apr. 1973; 4, 11 Feb. 1972; 23 July 1987; 13 Dec. 1984; 10 Nov. 1972; 25 Jan. 1979.
15 Ibid., 23 Apr. 1976; 14 July 1972; 13 Dec. 1984; 23 May 1975; 5 Feb. 1981; 17 Nov. 1988; 13 Sept. 1990; 31 Oct. 1975.
16 *CJN*, 4 Apr. 1975.
17 Ibid., 31 Jan. 1977; 29 Oct. 1976; 3 Nov. 1972; 21, 28 Nov. 1985.
18 Ibid., 1 Apr. 1977.
19 Ibid.
20 *FY*, Jan. 1972, 8.
21 Ibid., July–Aug. 1982, 6.
22 *CJN*, 24 Sept. 1971.
23 *FY*, Jan. 1972, 8.
24 Ibid., June 1974, 2; *CJN*, 14 June 1974.
25 *CJN*, 6 Feb. 1976.
26 Ibid., 6 Feb. 1976.
27 Ibid., 6 May 1977.
28 Ibid., 10 May 1979.
29 Ibid., 17 May 1979.
30 Ibid., 2 May 1985; 13 Apr., 18, 25 May 1989; 28 June 1990.
31 Ibid., 23 Feb. 1973.
32 Ibid., 10 Sept. 1976.

33 Ibid., 21, 27 Aug. 1981.

34 *CJN*, 20 Jan. 1983.

35 *FY*, June 1961, 4.

36 Ibid., Mar. 1963, 5.

37 Ibid., Mar. 1964, 8.

38 Ibid., Oct. 1961, 3; *CJN*, 18 Apr. 1975

39 *FY*, May 1965, 4; Nov. 1965, 2; May 1966, 2.

40 Ibid., Sept. 1967, 4.

41 Ibid., Oct. 1967, 5. ·

42 *CJN*, 17 Dec. 1976.

43 *FY*, Nov. 1982, 4.

44 Ibid., Sept. 1984, 4.

45 Ibid., Jan. 1984, 4; Mar.–Apr. 1984, 4; May–June 1984, 4; *CJN*, 19 Nov. 1976.

46 *CJN*, 20 June 1975.

47 *FY*, Mar.–Apr. 1991, 3.

48 Ibid., Oct. 1963, 4.

49 Ibid., June 1964, 4.

50 Ibid., Mar. 1970, 4; *Globe and Mail*, 28 Sept. 1957.

51 *FY*, Jan. 1971, 3.

52 Ibid., Oct. 1972, 2.

53 Ibid., Nov. 1984, 3–4.

54 Ibid., Apr. 1976, 6; June 1976, 3.

55 Ibid., June 1979, 5.

56 *CJN*, 27 Oct. 1972.

57 Ibid., 4 July 1975.

58 Ibid., 7 May 1976.

59 Ibid., 8 Nov. 1979.

60 Ibid., 27 Oct. 1972.

61 *Globe and Mail*, 25 Apr. 1962; *FY*, Mar. 1963, 5; Sept. 1964, 4; Mar. 1968, 4;
    Sept. 1968, 4.

62 *CJN*, 12 Aug. 1977; 4 Oct. 1979.

63 *FY*, Sept. 1968, 5.

64 Ibid., Sept. 1967, 5.

65 Ibid., Oct. 1968, 6-7.

66 Ibid., Sept. 1969.

67 Ibid., June 1970, 2–3.

68 Ibid., Feb. 1971, 4; Mar. 1971, 2.

69 Ibid., Sept.–Oct. 1971, 2.

70 *CJN*, 21 Oct. 1971.

71 *FY*, Nov. 1971, 2.

72　*CJN*, 29 Sept. 1972.

73　*FY*, July–Aug. 1983, 6–7.

74　*CJN*, 10 Jan., 21 Feb. 1975.

75　Ibid., 9, 16 May, 10 Oct. 1975; 9 Mar. 1973.

76　*FY*, Sept.–Oct. 1995, 11.

77　Saul Raskin, *Pirke Aboth in Etchings* (New York: 1940), 34.

78　Larry Zolf, "The Rebbe of Spadina," *Toronto Life*, Oct. 1991, 52, 156–67.

79　*FY*, July–Aug. 1986, 9.

80　Ibid., Nov.–Dec. 1987, 3.

81　Ibid., Jan. 1993.

82　*The Holy Scriptures According to the Masoretic Text*, vol. 1, *Genesis to Kings* (Philadelphia: Jewish Publication Society of America, 1955), 463.

83　Zolf, "Rebbe," passim.

84　*FY*, Sept.–Oct. 1995, 11.

85　Ibid., Jan.–Feb. 1992, 5; Irving Abella to Gerald Tulchinsky, email, July 2011.

86　Queen's University Archives (QUA), Salsberg Fonds, "Text of Remarks by J.B. Salsberg on CBC Program: 'The God That Failed,'" Wednesday, 9 May 1962.

87　*Holy Scriptures*, vol. 2, *Isaiah to II Chronicles* (Philadelphia: Jewish Publication Society, 1969), 1089, 1454.

Index